ADVANCE PRAISE FOR
Augmented Intelligence

"Daniel Araya's book could not be more timely. Devoid of any utopian or dystopian hype, it provides a level-headed, deep, and critical examination of many of the most cutting-edge questions of our time, as ever 'smarter' machines continue to automate many human activities and decisions. From machines' roles in labor and learning to the importance of unique human sensing capabilities and of our physical embodiment of intelligence, and from issues of social justice and human values to the imperative of appropriate governance, Daniel Araya and his contributors have created an important primer, if not in fact a roadmap, for further exploration and policy-making that has yet to find its match among AI books. *Augmented Intelligence: Smart Systems and the Future of Work and Learning* leans forward to convert these questions into higher value, more focused hypotheses on the potential of intelligence augmentation: the emergence of collective intelligence and more people-centric co-creativity at work; promises and perils of brain emulation and cognitive prosthetics that drive cultural and political shifts; and redefinitions of what it means to be human and to live in societies that will have ever more differentiation of intelligence among us. A potent compendium for anyone concerned with large scale transformations in our world."
—*Olaf J. Groth, CEO at Cambrian.ai, Professor at HULT International Business School, and Visiting Scholar at University of California, Berkeley*

"As science fiction becomes fact, Araya's collection on augmented intelligence provides readers with an excellent survey of this evolving landscape. Technology has altered human life for centuries, but the current Computational Revolution is changing they way our species thinks—literally and figuratively—about everything. How will human and machine fusion remake our world? These essays explore this important question from fresh, sober, and inspiring perspectives."
—*Peter Marber, Center for Global Affairs at New York University, and author of* Brave New Math: Information, Globalization, and New Economic Thinking in the 21st Century

Augmented Intelligence

Colin Lankshear and Michele Knobel
General Editors

Vol. 81

The New Literacies and Digital Epistemologies series
is part of the Peter Lang Education list.
Every volume is peer reviewed and meets
the highest quality standards for content and production.

PETER LANG
New York • Bern • Berlin
Brussels • Vienna • Oxford • Warsaw

Augmented Intelligence

Smart Systems and the Future of Work and Learning

Edited by Daniel Araya

PETER LANG
New York • Bern • Berlin
Brussels • Vienna • Oxford • Warsaw

Library of Congress Cataloging-in-Publication Data

Names: Araya, Daniel, editor.
Title: Augmented intelligence: smart systems and the future of
work and learning / edited by Daniel Araya.
Description: New York: Peter Lang, 2018.
Series: New literacies and digital epistemologies; vol. 81 | ISSN 1523-9543
Includes bibliographical references and index.
Identifiers: LCCN 2017021048 | ISBN 978-1-4331-3334-3 (hardback: alk. paper)
ISBN 978-1-4331-3333-6 (paperback: alk. paper)
ISBN 978-1-4331-4543-8 (ebook pdf)
ISBN 978-1-4331-4544-5 (epub) | ISBN 978-1-4331-4545-2 (mobi)
Subjects: LCSH: Human-computer interaction. | Artificial intelligence.
Classification: LCC QA76.9.H85 A7887 | DDC 006.3—dc23
LC record available at https://lccn.loc.gov/2017021048
DOI 10.3726/b11342

Bibliographic information published by **Die Deutsche Nationalbibliothek**.
Die Deutsche Nationalbibliothek lists this publication in the "Deutsche
Nationalbibliografie"; detailed bibliographic data are available
on the Internet at http://dnb.d-nb.de/.

© 2018 Peter Lang Publishing, Inc., New York
29 Broadway, 18th floor, New York, NY 10006
www.peterlang.com

All rights reserved.
Reprint or reproduction, even partially, in all forms such as microfilm,
xerography, microfiche, microcard, and offset strictly prohibited.

Table of Contents

List of Figures vii
List of Tables ix
Foreword xi
    Ann Pendleton-Jullian and John Seely Brown

Introduction 1
    Daniel Araya
Chapter One: Augmented Intelligence and Society 10
    Colin G. Harrison
Chapter Two: The Future of Digital Cognitive Systems: Tool, Assistant,
    Collaborator, Coach, Mediator 40
    Jim Spohrer and M. Abul Kalam Siddike
Chapter Three: Augmented Intelligence: Work and Class in the Age of
    Machine Intelligence 62
    Daniel Araya and Kevin Stolarick
Chapter Four: This Is Your Brain on Code: Embodied Intelligence
    Augmentation and the Evolution of Conflict 95
    Rodrigo Nieto-Gómez

Chapter Five: Intelligence Augmentation: Uploading Brain into Computer: Who First? 112
Yana B. Feygin, Kelly Morris, and Roman V. Yampolskiy

Chapter Six: The Intersection of the Human Senses and Exponential Technologies: Exploring Relevant Trends and the Future of the Senses 129
Jovan D. Rebolledo-Mendez

Chapter Seven: Augmented Intelligence Continues to Be Embodied Intelligence 145
Stan Ruecker and Susan Liepert

Chapter Eight: Augmenting the Posthuman: The Return of Humanist Discourse in Posthumanist Environments 158
Alix Rübsaam

Chapter Nine: What Augmented Intelligence? Power and Control in the Era of Open Networked Learning 173
Rita Kop

Chapter Ten: Augmented Intelligence with Human–Machine Integrity: Future-Oriented Hybrid Governance Integrating Holistic Analytics, True Cost Economics, and Open Source Everything Engineering (OSEE) 186
Robert David Steele

Chapter Eleven: For Pleasure or Productivity: Divergent Paths in Intelligence Augmentation 212
James D. Miller

Chapter Twelve: Building Human Character in a World of Augmented Intelligence 225
Darlene Damm

About the Contributors 237
Index 243

Figures

Figure 1.1:	Maslow proposes a hierarchy of human aspirations and motivations	28
Figure 2.1:	TACC hierarchy (tools, assistant, collaborators, and coach)	44
Figure 2.2:	Timeframe to impact industries	46
Figure 2.3:	Dedication to Douglas C. Engelbart	61
Figure 3.1:	Total employment	66
Figure 3.2:	Employed per 1 million	67
Figure 3.3:	Average wage (2014 $) A	67
Figure 3.4:	Wage % of national average A	68
Figure 3.5:	Average of regional share of employment	68
Figure 3.6:	Share of employment in region with highest share	69
Figure 3.7:	Total employment in region with highest employment	69
Figure 3.8:	Interacting with computers (2014) A	75
Figure 3.9:	Interacting with computers (2014) B	76
Figure 3.10:	Interacting with computers C	77
Figure 3.11:	Credit analysts A	78
Figure 3.12:	Statisticians A	79
Figure 3.13:	Graphic designers	79
Figure 3.14:	Degree of automation (1–5)	80

FIGURES

Figure 3.15:	Thinking creatively (2014) A	82
Figure 3.16:	Thinking creatively (2014) B	83
Figure 3.17:	Thinking creatively (2014) C	83
Figure 3.18:	Thinking creatively (2014) D	84
Figure 3.19:	Thinking creatively (2014) E	84
Figure 3.20:	Thinking creatively (2014) F	85
Figure 3.21:	Thinking creatively (2014) G	85
Figure 3.22:	Thinking creatively (2014) H	86
Figure 3.23:	Thinking creatively (2014) I	86
Figure 3.24:	Thinking creatively (2014) J	87
Figure 3.25:	Thinking creatively (2014) K	88
Figure 3.26:	Credit analysis B	88
Figure 3.27:	Statisticians B	89
Figure 3.28:	Graphic designers	89
Figure 3.29:	Average wage (2014 $) B	90
Figure 3.30:	Wage % of national average B	90
Figure 6.1:	Behavior of patent submissions per year	137
Figure 6.2:	Plotting of number of publications in journals based on Google Scholar from 2000 to 2015 (a), and projection of to 2045 with regression model (b)	138
Figure 6.3:	From survey to exponential technologies practitioners	139
Figure 6.4:	Difference of expectation of usage of different human senses by 2045, compared with usage in 2016	140
Figure 6.5:	Expectation of importance of exponential technologies by 2045	141
Figure 6.6:	Expectation of exponential technology usage frequency in interaction with human senses	142
Figure 7.1:	Anatomy of female reproductive system, contemporary	147
Figure 7.2:	Anatomy of female reproductive system, late 1400s	148
Figure 7.3:	The Aeolian Harp provided an image for how sympathetic vibrations worked in people	151
Figure 10.1:	Whole earth analytic model	191
Figure 10.2:	Full-spectrum human intelligence (HUMINT)	196
Figure 10.3:	World brain concept	201
Figure 10.4:	Earth intelligence concept	202
Figure 10.5:	Local to global information-sharing concept	203
Figure 10.6:	Computer-assisted tools for human intelligence	206

Tables

Table 1.1:	Prioritized general skills for 2015 and 2020	32
Table 2.1:	Top skills in 2020	45
Table 2.2:	Cognitive mediators as tool, assistant, collaborator, and coach	55
Table 3.1:	Defining the occupations in O*Net	70
Table 3.2:	Descriptions of O*Net data occupation content model	71
Table 3.3:	"Level" of work activity	73
Table 3.4:	"Level" of work activity in 2002	74
Table 10.1:	Eight information "tribes"	190
Table 10.2:	Operational analytic model in three dimensions	192
Table 10.3:	Open source everything engineering (OSEE) baseline	194
Table 10.4:	UN sustainable development goals	195
Table 10.5:	Preconditions of revolution	198
Table 10.6:	Integrated local to global education, intelligence, and research	205
Table 10.7:	True cost economics at point of sale	207

Foreword

ANN PENDLETON-JULLIAN AND JOHN SEELY BROWN

> The ever-accelerating progress of technology ... gives the appearance of approaching some essential singularity in the history of the race beyond which human affairs, as we know them, could not continue.
> —Von Neumann, 1958

> Within thirty years, we will have the technological means to create superhuman intelligence. Shortly after, the human era will be ended ... I think it's fair to call this event a singularity. It is a point where our models must be discarded and a new reality rules. As we move closer and closer to this point, it will loom vaster and vaster over human affairs till the notion becomes a commonplace. Yet when it finally happens it may still be a great surprise and a greater unknown.
> —Vernor Vinge, 1993

In his introduction to this paradoxically long overdue and prescient collection of essays, Daniel Araya frames the driving question, "what is the trajectory of human-machine symbiosis?" This is an important question and one that needs to be deeply considered. In 2005, Ray Kurtzweil wrote *The Singularity Is Near*, more than a decade after the concept of the Singularity was popularized by the mathematician/computer scientist/science fiction writer Vernor Vinge. But these ideas trace back even further, to the late 1950s when John Von Neumann introduced the concept of a technological singularity. So this book is long overdue in the sense that the topics it addresses are necessary to make sense of the world that is emerging around us. But it is also prescient in that it brings together diverse questions that are textured and sophisticated into a single intellectual space so that we, the reader, can see them like cards laid out on a table and productively move among them, rearranging themes to wrestle with the larger question Araya asks.

There are really big questions in this book:

- If powerful new technologies reinvent societies themselves, solving old problems while also creating new ones, how do we balance costs and benefits when the new technology in play augments and challenges one of the key characteristics that has historically defined us—our intelligence?
- How do we think about prosthetically motivated brain–computer interfaces that are used to enhance the human design in a more permanent way? How will these interfaces affect issues of social equality, justice and conflict, self-identity and community membership?
- How do we debate and negotiate bioconservatist versus transhumanist perspectives?
- If, as some believe, the final destination of the intelligence augmentation (IA) process is the complete merger of biological brains and computers, allowing for integration and mutual enhancement, then how do we think about super intelligence—pragmatically and ethically?
- How to think about the increasingly porous boundary between the human and nonhuman in a way that avoids the dominant human/nonhuman divide—the sociocultural bias that underpins the rejection of technological augmentation?

And then there are rather big questions about the future of social systems:

- In an era in which emerging technologies greatly enhance learning, what would it take to create a holistic vision for augmenting the human operating system in all of its diversities?
- What is the effect of embodied augmentation technologies on social conflict when the commodification of augmented cognitive ability has criminal value?
- Going far beyond the conventional meme of "smart cities," that overlays new smart connectivity on old industrial-era legacy artifacts, how might we think about augmented human intelligence that enables future-oriented hybrid man/machine governance that would lead to a prosperous world at peace?

- How will future IA correct or perhaps worsen human maladaptations? How will it play out to enhance productivity or invite and enable blissful disengagement?
- What new social skills will humans need to develop as we transition into a world of smart, fast networks where the tension between individual and society may only increase? And where experiences of time and space may disappear?

There are big questions about the future of work and learning:

- How will radical new forms of human–computer symbiosis affect the cities we might build, the kinds of medicine we might practice, and the kinds of education we might enable?
- How will networked cognitive collaborators embedded in smart service systems transform all occupations?
- What is the trajectory of work and learning in the 21st century when the work of skilled labor—the white-collar professionals, the "knowledge workers"—is augmented, and possibly even displaced, by technology?

And about the future of economic paradigms and design:

- What role will new technologies that enable computers and AI to understand users' feelings, and even engagement levels, play in future economic paradigms?
- If intelligence is an emergent property of having a body, as many believe, what are the implications for design in a future of bodily and sensory augmentation?

And these are just the beginning.

None of these are easy questions! And as individuals and groups debate them, we will see increasingly polarizing perspectives. These polarizing perspectives tend to align with a growing asymmetry around technological prowess and power; those that have the technological knowhow and capacity to understand, work with, and adapt to exponentially changing technological circumstances as the "machines" (although machine now is more metaphor than description) become pervasively integrated into what we do and who we are. Coupled to this is an asymmetry of power; we increasingly see power intensely concentrated in the hands of those that control the gateways to platforms, to artificial intelligence (AI), and to global networks (the Googles, Amazons, and Facebooks). Optimism, desire—sometimes even overt delirium—and skepticism often coupled to fear unfold across these asymmetries. In science fiction we see this playing out as technologically enabled utopias and technologically dominant dystopias.

Even if we remove the extreme emotions from the equation, we are still facing a radically unique moment of transition in which everything we do and everything we are is called into question. Alvin and Heidi Toffler introduced the concept of the Third Wave of society. From agricultural to industrial to information, each wave washes over us, assimilating older societies and cultures. We would like to suggest that a fourth wave is upon us. Indeed, AI/IA or human–machine symbiosis is about more than just how we interface with the world and construct societies around that, it is about redefining who and what "we" are.

With biotechno design bringing us even cheaper nanoscale computers, with intelligent technologies that understand and work autonomously with the data they collect and do so in concert with each other, with form and function of technologies becoming more and more anthropomorphic, with the mingling and mating of what were separate scientific fields through powerful technologies bringing us whole new sectors like biomechatronics, and with increasing disruption from all this,[1] it is clear that we need to find a way to make sense of and see our way through this new wave to transform what might be a cataclysmic tsunami into a powerful new wave to ride.

But how? Framing the questions and beginning to wrestle with them in a single forum, as this book does, is a strong step in that direction.

Another difficulty we face is that coupled to the asymmetries of technological prowess and power is the tendency for the technological "haves"—those with the capacity to understand, work with, and adapt to exponentially changing technological circumstances—to be technologically sophisticated to the detriment of their involvement with the aspects of life and work we tend to associate with humanism. Another asymmetry/divide. Moreover, when difficult questions are asked, they are usually asked in isolation. Questions are often examined in what would be called a reductionist mode—if you were an engineer, or as a result of academic silos—if you were a humanist. And popular culture, which is becoming increasingly influential, only intersects with these questions through mediated channels that rarely look deeply at issues.

It's a quandary when what we need now is a holistic framework for working forward toward a desired end, not a runaway default future full of unintended and unanticipated consequences of monumental proportion.

In 1999, at the very end of the 20th century, the director-producer Steven Spielberg did something very interesting when he convened a three-day "think tank summit" that brought together a cross-section of technologists, scientists, architects, planners, futurists, cognitive scientists, social scientists, philosophers, and artists that were working at the far edge of their fields on things not yet viable but potentially plausible several decades out. His goal was to "world build" Washington DC in 2050 under a series of premises about emergent technologies and trends, and a prompting "what-if" question coming from Philip K. Dick's short story Minority Report. Spielberg and his production designer, Alex McDowell, wanted to prototype the future by bringing together the most advanced thinking, trends, and inventions on the horizon to intersect with each other—world building together a not-yet-viable but future-possible world that was vastly constructed, highly textured, and coherent across many domains. In Minority Report, questions about technology intersect with questions about the ethics of security practices; questions about infrastructure intersect with questions about lifestyle and environmental duress; questions about individual rights bump up against new marketing technologies, and on and on.

What particularly distinguishes Spielberg's neo noir film is its dense detail of what life in a future Washington DC might be like. The movie, while futuristic, seems credible because of the rich detail that can be attributed to the vision and domain knowledge of the movie's expert collaborators. And it provides dense detail of what life in a future world might be like if one plays it out across a multitude of domains that have to converse with each other to create a coherent world space. Coherence is the key. No domain is separate from other domains. Philosophers and futurists had to debate with technologists and scientists. Humanists began to talk like scientists, embracing the possibilities as well as the problems, and technologists began to talk like philosophers, thinking about issues of identity and ethics.

The value in the summit was that Spielberg brought together scientists and humanists with futurists to talk to each other from their own areas of extreme expertise. He did not turn to the screenwriters first. He was out to build a vast, rich, and coherent world space as a speculative prototype and not merely tell another story. The value in using (what is referred to as) "world building" to prototype a future is that the domain experts were not there to speak abstractly. They were collectively imagining what the future might look like if they played out the questions that arose when their normally separate concerns intersected to create a world space.

In world building, one is making a whole range of viable and not so viable possibilities actually tangible enough that we are willing to consider them. And those possibilities are looked at holistically, not separately, across a vast and inclusive epistemological terrain.

There are different purposes for world building in cinema, literature, and games. One might aim to create an intensified experience—frightening, delightful, fantastic, or humorous; or to immerse us in an historical period; or critique the present. World building can help us play out hopes and fears. But it can also be used to prototype a future: playing out trends to see where they might go; interrogating conflicts and paradoxes; but also to imagine, or hypothesize, a future based upon an idea or desired outcome—to imagine an ideal state, an ideal response, or a better world, and then build the world around it in the world building space so that one can build toward it in reality.

The value of this for real-world situations and problems is just this: to imagine a desired future state, with texture, detail, and coherence, and then build toward it, as opposed to trying to solve for present problems—the kind that, in fact, cannot really be solved—in a fractured way.

Instead of choosing sides from among future unknowns, and instead of assuming things will play out in a specific way—that history is predetermined—we are in a moment in which it would be advantageous and important to wrestle with these questions in a space that helps us imagine both the worst future world we could make and the best, in order to non-naively work toward productive thinking and actions that shape the emerging futures at the scale of individuals, communities, corporations, nations, …

Complex questions like "what is the trajectory of human–machine symbiosis?" require thinking forward as well as interrogating the present. Imagining what a better future state could be and then working toward it. There is a phrase we love—"tyranny of the possible"[2]—which suggests that answers to questions and solutions to problems get limited when we are thinking only within the constraints of what we currently accept as reality. The "tyranny of the possible," when it looks forward, only sees trends of today playing out. It is stuck in only what is known. But if you think about it, the future—in any domain, any piece of it—is an unknown. More importantly, it is an unknown that we are constructing, whether consciously or not, with every decision or action we take, small or large. It will be only a default construction if we wrestle in real time with problems and opportunities constrained by both the tyranny of the possible and the tyranny of time.

Instead, can we rigorously take on these questions in a nonfiction world building space[3] where multiple trajectories of interrogation around the very big driving question of human–machine symbiosis are forced to converse with each other—where issues considered to be exclusive to the domains of humanism, or the irrepressible advances and interests in the domains of the sciences and technology, are holistically wrestled with?

In 1938, nuclear fission was discovered. In 1945, von Neumann (back to von Neumann) and others built the first weaponized "machines" of nuclear fission, a technological innovation that has transformed the geopolitical world. In 1969 we had the first interconnected digital networking system (ARPANET), in 1975, the first personal computer kits, and in 1991 the World Wide Web became publicly available. But it took the introduction, in 1997, and escalation of social media in the early 2000s to begin another process of radical transformation on a global societal scale. With both of these (and arguably there are others in the biological sciences), the genie has been let out of the bottle. And if you know genies, they are by nature tricksters with both good and bad up their sleeves. In both of these radical technological advances, we see moments in which there is a turning point, or an event horizon, where the system can no longer go back to where it was. When the computer program AlphaGo beat Lee Sedol, eighteen-time world Go champion, in March 2016, we hit another event horizon. It was a paradigm shift in AI because instead of programming, the computer had to create a computer version of a neural network that operated completely differently.

How we choose to take on the hard questions in a manner that shapes our future is now the immanent question. This is not for everyone, certainly not for the weak of heart or imagination. This book is an extraordinary contribution in the way it sets the stage by framing and wrestling with diverse questions in a single forum: questions from what it will mean to be human in a world of extreme human–machine collaboration, or human–machine symbiosis even, to what will work look like, or what will a world postwork look like.

Now is the time to interrogate and speculate holistically and with intellectual rigor while technology and science continue their irrepressible advance. The two together, so that interrogation and speculation inform advances, and advances contribute new questions and possibilities, in all domains and endeavors and at all scales.

Notes

1. From our colleagues Parag and Ayesha Khanna's work, especially their seminal piece "The Future is Now" in *Foreign Policy Journal*, September/October 2011.
2. From Stephen Duncombe, Professor of Media and Culture at NYU.
3. For more on world building, see Ann Pendleton-Jullian and John Seely Brown, Chapter 13 "World Building," in *Design unbound. Designing for emergence in a white water world*. Cambridge, MA: MIT Press, 2018.

Introduction

DANIEL ARAYA

Where the Agricultural Revolution harnessed domesticated animals for pastoral farming, and the Industrial Revolution tailored machines for factory production, so today the Computational Revolution is leveraging computers to augment human intelligence. Much as Douglas Engelbart (1962) first proposed, computer technologies are becoming critical to both expanding human capabilities and bootstrapping cognitive performance. This transcension of earlier stages of tool-mediated practice foreshadows a momentous transformation within postindustrial societies (Engeström, 1987; Vygotsky, 1978). As Engelbart (1962) writes,

> By "augmenting human intellect" we mean increasing the capability of a man to approach a complex problem situation, to gain comprehension to suit his particular needs, and to derive solutions to problems. Increased capability in this respect is taken to mean a mixture of the following: more-rapid comprehension, better comprehension, the possibility of gaining a useful degree of comprehension in a situation that previously was too complex, speedier solutions, better solutions, and the possibility of finding solutions to problems that before seemed insoluble.

Many now argue that the promise of exascale computing and accelerating technological innovation may represent a new threshold in human history. Machine learning, for example, has dramatically improved medical diagnosis, speech recognition, and data analytics. In truth, Homo sapiens have long been dependent on the affordances that cognitive tools provide (Gibson, 1977). From the abacus to advanced mathematics to the Internet, cognitive tools have enabled radical leaps in the amplification of human intelligence. What is perhaps most surprising about the advance of computational technology, however, is its expanding reach. As computers evolve from programmed calculation to dynamic learning, so the capacities of humans and machines are developing in concert. This human-machine symbiosis portends dramatic improvements in the kinds of cities we might build, the kinds of medicine we might practice, and the kinds of education we might provide.

Augmenting Human Intelligence

For researchers in intelligence augmentation (IA), "smart" technologies are seen as the key to evolving human cognitive capacities. Alongside efforts to develop artificial intelligence (AI), IA researchers seek to link human beings with the "bionic" enhancements that connect the brain with computational tools (Licklider, 1960). The key insight of IA research is the recognition that human intelligence and machine intelligence are complementary rather than adversarial. Scholars interested in amplifying human cognitive capabilities through IA tend to be skeptical of the view that human intelligence can be fully modeled by computers. Building on sociocultural theory and theories on extended cognition (Rowlands, 2010; Vygotsky, 1978), IA researchers make the argument that human intelligence is not reducible to algorithmic modeling but can be extended through the use of computational resources.

Perhaps the key distinction between AI and IA is that the latter is focused on research in computer systems as a supplement to human intelligence. Overlapping studies in human-computer interaction (HCI), IA focuses on the interactive relationship between humans and smart systems. Situated at the intersection of computer science, behavioral sciences, and design, it includes studies into the ways in which human beings leverage technological artifacts and systems. Human cognitive capacities are seen as extending beyond the body to include aspects of the external environment in which organisms are embedded. This includes brain-computer interfaces that augment the visual cortex and sensory cortex to enhance human cognition as well as control over material devices and objects. Research in this area includes the design of the graphical user interface (GUI), the evolution of handheld devices, experiments in virtual and augmented reality, and the ongoing evolution of search algorithms.[1]

Augmenting Work and Learning

Where AI researchers focus on machines that can match and exceed human capabilities, IA researchers aim to use computational tools to enhance human-machine symbiosis. Licklider (1960), for example, envisions a future where machine cognition transcends the limits of human cognition, as a basic stage of human evolution. But what is the long-term trajectory of human-machine symbiosis? Notwithstanding the fact that many optimists believe that a coming technological "singularity" will transform postindustrial societies for the better, more critical voices worry that a purely technological focus may threaten to destabilize postmodern societies. Given the combined power of digitization, exponential technological change and recombinant innovation, technology may soon be capable of replacing large segments of the labor force altogether. Indeed, a study by the Oxford Martin School suggests that nearly half of all occupations in the United States could be displaced through technological automation over the next two decades (Frey & Osborne, 2013).

To be sure, some researchers suggest that the accelerating speed of technological innovation is becoming a daunting challenge. In their book, *The Second Machine Age*, Massachusetts Institute of Technology researchers Brynjolfsson and McAfee (2014) highlight the dramatic evolution of technology and describe the magnitude of its impact on human society. Moving beyond the industrial revolution or "the first machine age," they argue that information and communication technologies (ICTs) will soon begin displacing human labor across multiple sectors of the global labor force.

Beyond routine tasks, computers are becoming increasingly adept at higher cognitive functions including language processing, data analysis, and computer control systems.

In contrast to the perception that it is only low-skilled labor that is most vulnerable to automation, theories on technological unemployment now argue just the opposite. According to *Moravec's paradox*, for example, it is in fact *knowledge-based* labor that is most vulnerable to computerization (Moravec, 1988). The reason for this is quite simple. Cognitive work that is based on precise, well-understood procedures is now easily codified and performed by machines, even as some factory automation remains specialized and expensive (Brynjolfsson & McAfee, 2014).

What is obvious is that underemployment has become a serious problem. In the United States, 25 million households (the bottom fifth of the income ladder) now earn $18,000 or less annually (Kenworthy, 2014). In fact, adjusting for inflation, wages in the United States have not increased since the mid-1970s. Recent data from the U.S. Bureau of Labor Statistics (2013) indicate that civilian labor-force participation has been declining since 2009. The truth is that advances in technological innovation are introducing massive changes across the global political and economic landscape.

The Future of Augmented Intelligence

Embedded within a unique history of social and technological transformation, IA is emerging as a foundational pillar in the digital transformation of postindustrial societies. Arguably, it is reshaping discussions on the nature of human intelligence and the future course of human evolution. This has significant implications for work and learning. As the Organization for Economic Cooperation and Development (OECD, 1996) suggests, economic activities are now closely linked to education and technological discovery. Innovation-driven economies are said to be dependent upon smooth flows of knowledge (both tacit and codified), and investments in "adoption capability" (or the knowledge embodied in skilled labor as "human capital").

Notwithstanding the fact that returns on investments in education have been substantial to U.S. economic growth over the past century (Goldin & Katz, 2008), new data points to significant social challenges ahead. The obvious question today is what should be the public policy response to accelerating technologies? Where OECD (2013) countries have emphasized the need for promoting competitive proficiencies overlapping advanced skills in literacy, numeracy, and problem-solving, one wonders whether this kind of skills-based training will be sufficient to overcome the challenges of technological disruption.

The hard reality is that disruptive computational technologies are forcing postindustrial societies into a complex "phase transition" that points to radical transformation within established systems of work and learning (Barabási, 2002; Siemens, 2005). Moving beyond the logics of mass industrial society and a world of iterative cultural change, Fordist-era systems of work and learning are now becoming obsolete. This suggests the need to redesign systems of work and learning to meet the demands of a computational knowledge economy (Wolfram, 2010).

This edited collection brings together researchers and experts across disciplines to explore this new world. It seeks to investigate both the impact of IA on postindustrial societies and the long-term consequences of disruptive technologies in reshaping work and learning. As these thinkers suggest, we are on the cusp of a sea change in our capacities to augment human intelligence, but many questions remain to be answered: What is the future of work in a computational knowledge economy? Will IA help us in transforming a waning industrial society? Or does it portend something more ominous?

Organization of this Book

In Chapter 1, Colin Harrison considers the impact of technology on the evolution of human society. "Where the Industrial Revolution opened the way to immense new sources of physical energy, the Age of Information", he argues, "has cracked open the door to the generation, integration, and analysis of vast amounts of information." As he explains, even as technology solves problems, it introduces new unforeseen problems as well. Examining the ways in which IA is changing postindustrial societies, Harrison considers how IA redefines work, expands the scope of knowledge and information, and transforms learning. Most importantly, he reflects on the ways in which IA reframes our collective intelligence while providing a basis for a highly creative future.

In Chapter 2, Jim Spohrer and Abul Kalam Siddike build on Harrison's broad analysis of the impact of IA. Looking specifically at "cognitive assistants" in the context of smart service systems, they explore the future of technologies that augment both cognitive and social intelligence. In their view, IA represents a watershed moment in which new technologies will inevitably boost the expert capacities of innovators. Empowered by evolving IA technologies, "T-shaped" professionals will be highly proficient at people-centered system redesign thinking, and the science of value co-creation and capability co-elevation (service science). Most importantly, Spohrer and Siddike consider the policy changes needed to ease the shift away from task-centered design and toward people-centered design in order to properly leverage cognitive technologies.

Daniel Araya and Kevin Stolarick explore the basic realities of technology's impact on the workplace in Chapter 3. Is technology enabling newer and more creative forms of labor or is it simply subsuming human labor entirely? Analyzing empirical data from the U.S. Occupational Information Network (O*Net), they explore employment characteristics nationally and across metro regions for three common occupations. Based on this data, they suggest that the digitization of labor is likely to further increase the demand for creative skills. Nonetheless, not all creative work is equally valued. To be sure, class-based occupational structures are significantly impacting the value and remuneration of creative work.

In Chapter 4, Rodrigo Nieto-Gomez looks at the implications of augmented intelligence for driving new stages of human conflict. Much as Steve Jobs once suggested, technology augments human cognitive capacities just as machines augment our physical capabilities—like a bicycle for the mind. Building on this metaphor, Nieto-Gomez explores the impact of embodied intelligence augmentation for the next generation of force multiplication. Looking at two case studies, he reflects on the implications for augmented intelligence in transforming the nature of conflict. As he concludes, embodied augmented intelligence is a kind of cognitive prosthetic that is beginning to drive profound political and cultural shifts, moving postindustrial societies ever closer to a transhumanist future.

Yana B. Feygin, Kelly Morris, and Roman V. Yampolskiy make the case for viewing brain emulation as the key to augmenting human intelligence in Chapter 5. They explore the practical challenges associated with IA in the context of "whole brain emulation" or "uploading." As they suggest, the implications for digitally reconstructing the brain at a level of detail sufficient to understanding and emulating its working design are profound. Indeed, in their view, the advance of IA through brain emulation opens the door to serious questions about humanity's long-term safety.

Expanding the discussion on the physicality of augmented intelligence, Jovan D. Rebolledo-Mendez examines trends at the intersection of human sense perception and exponential technologies in Chapter 6. Exploring the ways in which technologies facilitate a path for our senses to adapt and evolve, he considers the implications of technology for augmenting the senses. Differentiating between traditional and non-traditional senses, he examines the empirical research regarding trends in the discussion on sense augmentation.

In Chapter 7, Stan Ruecker and Susan Liepert consider a range of recent experiments in bodily augmentation and their relationship to intelligence in the broad sense of the word. In their view, the early 20th century model of intelligence as a brain supported by the body is now being replaced by a model that views intelligence as embodied and interdependent with its environment. They explore the historical trajectory of embodied intelligence and consider its implications for IA design in the future.

In Chapter 8, Alix Rübsaam builds on the ideas of Rueker and Liebert by arguing for a posthumanist interpretation of IA. As she suggests, artificial intelligence could represent both the pinnacle of human intelligence and the convergence of human and technological evolution. Responding to growing anxiety about the threat of technology, she makes the case for situating augmented intelligence within a broader critical posthumanist discourse. As she concludes, becoming posthuman is not "a biological, evolutionary, or historical rupture, but a shift in perception with regard to how we think about what it means to be human."

Much as Rübsaam, Rueker, and Liebert, Rita Kop argues against reductionist views of human intelligence in Chapter 9. As she points out, intelligence does not exclusively entail a cognitive ability narrowly based on language and mathematical ability, but something much more. It is for this reason that the design of technologies used to augment human intelligence remains complicated. She highlights some of the many emergent challenges and opportunities for working with algorithms and machine learning technologies for augmenting intelligence in networked learning environments. As she concludes, there is a particular value in including social scientists in the work of designing and developing tools for IA.

In Chapter 10, Robert Steele strongly criticizes what he regards as unsubstantiated claims within the Artificial Intelligence (AI) community. As he observes, the potential of machine intelligence is both severely over-stated and misses the fundamentally important role that humans have played—and continue to play—in the evolution of technology. In his view, the true cost of computing as practiced today includes the cost of failing to empower humans to learn, connect, and decide together at every level of scale from local to the global. In response to this, he outlines the need for human-centric IA that builds on a "World Brain" conceptualization in which Applied Collective (Human) Intelligence comprises 80% of the whole, while augmented (machine) intelligence provides only 20%.

James Miller considers the consequences of the current trajectory of IA in Chapter 11. Just as technology has increased the variation of physical ability between human beings, he predicts that IA will differentiate human intellectual and financial capabilities as well. Building out from a simple scenario in which cheap and effective "productivity-enhancers" become broadly available in the market, he considers the implications of IA on human social development. As he suggests, over the long run, "evolution will have just as much influence on human IA as it does on the size and shape of finches' beaks."

Finally, in Chapter 12, Darlene Damm explores the impact of technological innovation on accelerating social change. Like Miller, she sees technology as increasingly driving the evolution of postindustrial societies. As she observes, human beings have evolved from using giant computers in the workplace to augmentation devices such as wearables, implantable chips, earpieces, and goggles in a relatively short time. Given the accelerating pace of these technologies, she ponders their impact on society and on human character? Looking at the implications of augmented intelligence for the future development of human character, she recommends strategies that leaders and educators can implement as IA becomes more predominant in our lives.

Conclusion

Since its inception some sixty years ago, artificial intelligence has evolved from an arcane academic field into a powerful driver of social and economic change. Given the capacity of this technology to shape the future direction of work and learning, it stands to reason that planning for the future requires thoughtful debate. What is the long-term impact of IA and related disruptive technologies on the future of human evolution? How will human and machine symbiosis remake postindustrial societies?

What we do know is that the human species has been especially good at leveraging tools to amplify its mental and physical capabilities. Indeed, as Engelbart (1962) first observed, computational technologies represent the expansion of human intelligence in new and unexplored ways. Notwithstanding the fact that computational technologies have the capacity to displace human labor and learning across industries, technology is also enabling the human species to extend its cognitive capacities in ways that we simply do not yet fully comprehend. Together, the scholars and experts within this edited collection have sought to better understand the challenges we now face in order to provide some partial answers to these questions. This book is an attempt to help stimulate this debate in new and underexplored ways.

Note

1. Consider, for example, that the search algorithm underlying Google emerged from HCI research at Stanford University.

References

Barabási, A. L. (2002). *Linked: The new science of networks*. Cambridge, MA: Perseus Publishing.

Brynjolfsson, E., & McAfee, A. (2014). *The second machines age: Work, progress, and prosperity in a time of brilliant technologies*. New York, NY: W. W. Norton & Company.

Engelbart, D. (1962). Augmenting human intellect: A conceptual framework. Retrieved from http://www.dougengelbart.org/pubs/augment-3906.html

Engeström, Y. (1987). *Learning by expanding: An activity-theoretical approach to developmental research*. Helsinki: Orienta-Konsultit Oy.

Frey, C. B., & Osborne, M. A. (2013). The future of employment: How susceptible are jobs to computerisation? Retrieved from http://www.futuretech.ox.ac.uk/sites/futuretech.ox.ac.uk/files/The_Future_of_Employment_OMS_Working_Paper_1.pdf

Gibson, J. J. (1977). The theory of affordances. In R. Shaw & J. Bransford (Eds.), *Perceiving, acting, and knowing: Toward an ecological psychology* (pp. 67–82). Hillsdale, NJ: Lawrence Erlbaum.

Goldin, C., & Katz, L. F. (2008). *The race between education and technology*. Cambridge, MA: Harvard University Press.

Kenworthy, L. (2014). America's social democratic future: The arc of policy is long but bends toward justice. *Foreign Affairs, 93*(1), 86–100.

Licklider, J. C. R. (1960). Man-computer symbiosis. IRE Transactions of Human Factors in Electronics HFE-1, 1, 4–11. Retrieved from http://groups.csail.mit.edu/medg/people/psz/Licklider.html

OECD. (1996). *The knowledge-based economy.* Paris: OECD. Moravec, H. (1988). *Mind children: The future of robot and human intelligence.* Cambridge, MA: Harvard.

Rowlands, M. (2010). *The new science of the mind: From extended mind to embodied phenomenology,* Cambridge, MA: MIT Press.

Siemens, G. (2005). Connectivism: A learning theory for the digital age. *International Journal of Instructional Technology and Distance Learning, 2*(1), 3–10.

U.S. Bureau of Labor Statistics. (2013). *Occupational employment projections to 2022.* Retrieved from http://www.bls.gov/opub/mlr/2013/article/occupational-employment-projections-to-2022.htm

Vygotsky, L. S. (1978). *Mind in society: The development of higher psychological processes.* Cambridge, MA: Harvard University Press.

Wolfram, C. (2010). Moving to the computational knowledge economy. Retrieved from http://river-valley.zeeba.tv/moving-to-the-computational-knowledge-economy/.

CHAPTER ONE

Augmented Intelligence and Society

COLIN G. HARRISON

Introduction

For the purposes of this chapter, I consider augmented intelligence to mean: *the delegation of cognitive tasks normally performed by an individual human being, the delegator, to an external system of intelligence, the delegate, that is capable of taking instruction from the delegator, of performing the specified task, and of returning the result to the delegator.*

This is not intended as a formal definition, but rather a rough bounding of scope, leaving a number of factors, such as "intelligence," undefined. In describing the delegate as "a system," I consider it to be a black box, whose operation might or might not depend on information technologies (ITs). It could equally well be John Searle's Chinese Room (John Searle, n.d.), Amazon's Mechanical Turk (n.d.), or a blend of such approaches, but most likely involves some form of IT.

Societies develop technologies to solve problems that they face. Technologies then return the favor by creating new problems. Coal and other fossil fuels brought abundant energy for mining, manufacturing, and transportation, but produced dangerous pollution and climate change. Electricity brought the gift of abundant light and many other uses, but introduced new risks of electrocution and fire. Artificial fertilizers dramatically increased crop yields and enabled food production (if not distribution) to keep up with explosive population growth, but runoff from fields polluted water supplies. Cars gave us the liberty of personal transportation, but then created traffic jams, pollution, injuries, fatalities, and seriously impaired the quality of life of many cities. Science-based medicine has eradicated diseases that formerly took millions of lives, but led to the evolution of disease strains that are resistant to known treatments. ITs gave us instantaneous access to knowledge, but exposed us to new forms of fraud and loss of privacy. Successful technologies such as these also create societal dependencies that make the ever-broader application of the technologies largely inevitable, compelling human beings to maintain and develop their operation, and thereby preventing us from rolling back their use. In 1980, when machines were rapidly displacing farm workers, U.S. President Jimmy Carter's agriculture secretary, Robert Bergland, declared that the federal government would no longer finance research that could lead to the "replacing of an adequate and willing workforce with machines" (Porter, 2016). King Canute could not have expressed it better.

The technologies leading to augmented intelligence have emerged over several decades, but have developed greatly in the last ten or fifteen years as IT gave birth to the connected world in which we now live. The development of "personal intelligent agents"—today's "bots"—began in the early 1990s (Harrison & Caglayan, 1997). Already, augmented intelligence has solved or has begun to solve important societal problems: How to manage supply and demand for electricity at the scale of countries and subcontinents. How to optimize the use of seed, fertilizer, and increasingly scarce water to sustain food production in the face of climate change. How to manage the flow of people and vehicles through cities despite bad weather, breakdowns, and disruptions. How to detect, to treat, and to respond to global epidemics. How to predict demand for consumer goods and to manage global supply chains to satisfy those demands.

Beyond these applications to the problems of large organizations, as individuals we may also expect to acquire an entourage of helper bots with speech or visual user interfaces that can answer our questions, regulate our local environment, take care of our shopping, and get us to our destinations on time. Today's GPS navigation systems are a good example. These too are examples of augmented intelligence, tapping into the Cloud for server power and deep reservoirs of information about us as individuals and our place in the world.

But what new problems is augmented intelligence creating for us? This is the question to be addressed, though not fully answered, in this chapter. This is not about the technology itself. Nor is it about philosophical speculation on the meaning of artificial intelligence (Kurzweil, 2006). Rather it is about the ways in which practical augmented intelligence is changing us already as individuals and communities. The excluded topics are fascinating, provocative, touching the boundaries of human understanding and what it means to be human (Thomas, 2016). But augmented intelligence is already sufficiently real and practical so that we can consider this leading question with little or no speculation.

So how does augmented intelligence do such things? For the purposes of this chapter I consider augmented intelligence systems to provide the following capabilities.

Task Definition

The query systems and spreadsheets that have provided access to databases for several decades have given way to framing problems through dialogues and visualization to specify the desired outcome, although skillful searching remains a powerful tool. Augmented intelligence may also proactively suggest interventions based on its assessment of what the delegator appears to be trying to do.

Information Capture and Acquisition

This takes many forms: Data are captured from real and virtual sensors, which will expand rapidly as the Internet of Things (n.d.) expands. Real sensors are thermostats, toll systems, satellites, and so forth. Virtual sensors are, for example, people who leave trails of data as they live their lives. Data are acquired formally by licensing access to databases such as weather reports, stock exchange transactions, marketing reports, and so forth. Data are acquired informally by trawling the Web and retrieving relevant data.

Integration of Information

Data and information are scattered across multiple languages, formats, and structures. Bringing together, for example, all of the world's news stories on the European refugee crisis in a single language and a single format is one powerful example of integration. Even within the information and knowledge of a single profession—medicine is a good example—there are many semantic and technical challenges in achieving such integration. By virtue of the larger datasets that the augmented intelligence system can acquire, integrate, and structure, it should be able to produce a response that is better than could be achieved by the delegator alone in the sense that it is more accurate, has a higher probability of occurring, or has the minimum likelihood of negative side effects.

Semantic Structuring

Computers manipulate symbols and are making rapid progress in learning how those symbols relate to one another, but they have no concept of what those symbols mean in the real world (John Searle, n.d.). For this purpose, augmented intelligence systems still need to be trained by human beings. This involves human analysis of a substantial training set to identifying semantic examples. With sufficient examples the system can find similar patterns in the larger datasets it is required to manage. In the sense that the computer has now been given semantic knowledge of a particular dataset, we may say that it "understands" that information and can relate it to its interactions with the delegators, although that semantic meaning may represent only the views of its trainers.

Modeling and Analysis

Delegators are often seeking predictions: forecasts of the weather, the rise or fall of a stock price, the probability of a certain event, the best next move in a game or other strategy, the best treatment for a patient. Or the delegator may be contemplating some action, for example, selecting a certain therapy among a group of possibilities, and is seeking validation. There are many approaches to fulfilling that need. Some are purely statistical, based on correlations extracted by the system from its databases: "the last ten times that this situation occurred, the result was that." Others are based on exhaustive search of a rule-based system: "from that starting point, the best possible outcome or the only possible outcome is this." Still others are based on models in which the evolution from a present state is constrained by physical laws such as gravity or thermodynamics together with, for example, the physical infrastructure of a complex industrial plant. Much modeling simulates the behaviors of groups of people through populations of software agents. These entities generally model the behaviors of *Homo economicus* (Parkes & Wellman, 2015) in seeking to achieve some goal, possibly in competition with other agents. In addition to the ability to acquire and deal with vastly more information than humans, such models often structure that information into spaces with far higher dimensions, looking for multifactor dependencies or interactions that a human mind could not envisage.

Learning

Learning is the key attribute that distinguishes augmented intelligence from Big Data analysis. In learning, the system can compare its results (taxonomy, prediction, strategy, and so forth) against some ideal or real-world outcome. That is, an e-commerce system could model consumers' buying behaviors in a certain period based on historical data, compare the result to observed behaviors, and make adaptations based on discrepancies. This is why very large datasets are required for augmented intelligence as they provide greater opportunities for learning. Where the system being modeled has strict, well-defined rules, for example, a game, different versions of the augmented intelligence's learning algorithm can compete against one another over extremely large iterations and refine their strategies.

Explanation

In addition to providing a response to the delegator's needs, the augmented intelligence system must be able to explain how it reached that conclusion. This is essential if the delegator is to have confidence in the conclusion. The system may be able to point to facts or documents that support its conclusions, but it may also need to explain the outcome of high-dimensional analysis to a nontechnical delegator.

Action

In many cases the augmented intelligence system is acting in an open loop in which it receives tasks from the delegator and returns information or proposed actions, but the actual decision to act is taken by the delegator. However, in a world that moves ever more quickly and must cope with ever greater complexity, the latency of a closed-loop system or the complexity of the actions involved may require them to be taken by the system itself. Examples of these include the aerodynamic control systems of fighter aircraft, high-speed stock trading, management of city traffic, or the control of a large industrial plant. Such systems demand extremely high levels of trust and may employ "circuit-breakers" to suspend actions if the delegator or others determine that the actions are harmful or too risky.

Having now briefly introduced what augmented intelligence systems are and how they work, the rest of this article consists of sections on areas of application for augmented intelligence, on a few of the issues that may arise from these, and a conclusion that considers how we might prepare for the societal impacts it may produce.

Collective Intelligence

This section situates augmented intelligence in a framework based on our historical experiences of physical and cognitive collaboration. It takes as given that these systems can perform cognitive processes such as capturing, managing, and manipulating information in ways that have practical value to individuals and groups of human beings. It frames augmented intelligence in terms of our development of ways to externalize, to encode, to preserve, and to communicate information and knowledge and how this has shaped the development of our civilizations. It introduces collective intelligence (Collective Intelligence, n.d.) and the radius of cognition as concepts that emerge from applying augmented intelligence.

The notion of augmenting one's own capabilities by delegation is not new. Bilateral or multilateral delegation is the basis of all collaboration. Since prehistory we have augmented our physical strength, our ranges of sensing and acting, our skills, and our knowledge by leveraging the physical power of systems such as water, wind, and fire and the cognitive power of other members of *Homo sapiens* as well as those of other species. Many other species also display collaboration and social organization to lesser degrees. Hence the concept of augmenting the individual is older even than that of *Homo sapiens*, but its dominance in human society makes it a defining characteristic of our species.

As a species, we are unique in the degree to which we exploit the concept that information and knowledge can be externalized, can be represented and communicated via audible and visual symbols, and can be interpreted by others. To some degree other species engage in this progress, but the author is not aware of any species that exploits this concept to the degree of even the cave dwellers who painted meaningful scenes many millennia ago (Cave Painting, n.d.). The concept of externalizing information and knowledge—that what is going on in my mind could be transferred to another's mind and vice versa—is the basis of the Theory of Mind (n.d.) that plays a central role in theories of awareness and consciousness. Equally important is the concept that what goes on in my mind can be preserved by encoding it in physical symbols such as cave paintings, marks on clay tablets (Linear B, n.d.), or infinitesimally small pits on a plastic disk. From these breakthrough points of departure, it is a comparatively short distance to semantics, writing, geometry, documents, books, libraries, structured knowledge, and information retrieval, not to mention other, equally valid, representations such as painting, music, and dance. We have long lived in civilizations based on these flows of information. From a very early age we become aware that vast amounts of knowledge exist outside our own heads and that this external knowledge has strong influences over our lives. These examples of augmentation prior to the Age of Information (Perez, 2003) are similar to the concept of collective intelligence (Collective Intelligence, n.d.).

In this sense the notion of augmented intelligence is far from new, although IT enormously amplifies what has gone before. So this article frames augmented intelligence in terms of these existing effects of collective intelligence on our lives as individuals and communities. These include the following.

Ranges of Awareness and Action

The delegation of capturing, storing, and interpreting information expands the space and time over which we can communicate and act. A single, unaided human being can see human-scale events at most a few kilometers away and often only a few tens of meters and can hear at most a few hundred meters and often only a few meters. In the time domain, she or he sees only dimly back to early childhood memories and forward even less. Let us call these distances in sensory and semantic space and time the radius of cognition. The ability to send out scouts and guards and to post watchmen in towers spatially expands this radius of cognition, even without technology. Such delegation also expands the radius of cognition in the time domain, allowing historical events to be retrieved from archives and impending events, such as the movement of a prey or an army, to be anticipated. Thus collective intelligence expands the radius of cognition. The uncontacted tribes of Papua New Guinea (Diamond, 2013) perceive the extent of the world to be not more than perhaps 20 km. In developed societies young children already understand that the world is far bigger, even if they have never seen it directly. Thus collective intelligence expands our perception of the universe and changes our conception of our role in it.

Societal Scale

One person can coordinate the activities of a handful of people by means of gestures and speech, provided they are nearby. This is the scale of a family. Through the repetition of such communications such coordination may be extended to the scale of a clan, a few tens of people. With icons and other visual documents, such as totems and shrines, one can govern tribes of up to some two hundred people (Diamond, 2013). Beyond this scale some form of written expression seems to be necessary, which is a difficult but important step in the development of collective intelligence. Not only does it require technology (pigments, styli, clay, papyrus, and so forth), but it requires agreement on a set of symbols and on the relatively expensive training of scribes. Evidently this form of collective intelligence was sufficient to develop ancient empires in the Middle East, China, and Central America. The invention of alphabets, allowing the composition of very large numbers of words from a limited set of symbols, has occurred only a small number of times, but enormously expanded the scale of control, for example, of the Greek and Roman empires.

Cultural Identity

The expression of information involves encoding mental concepts into symbols, whether verbal, pictorial, or written. How information is expressed is itself a defining characteristic of a society and proficiency in one or more such methods is an important qualification for membership in a given society. Language includes and excludes people and is closely associated with political geography. Even today in developed societies, dialects and nuances of accent, inflection, vocabulary, and grammar define local communities. The author's mother, in the north of England in the 1950s, could localize people from her city within a couple of miles just based on hearing them speak. A society's expertise in developing and applying language is a powerful weapon in cultural expansion, enabling it to capture the minds of its neighbors and even its enemies, and to leave an imprint on a colonized region long after the colonists have departed.

Trust

Delegation and collaboration, particularly on matters where expertise is required and the outcome is important, depend on the establishment of confidence and trust, or generally the ability to rely on another person or a document as a source of information, cognition, or action. By confidence I mean the delegator's belief that the information returned by the delegate is accurate and dependable and supports the delegator's objectives. The delegator may establish means to verify the responses of the delegate, such as by confirming information already known to the delegator, or by employing two or more delegates. By trust I mean the delegator's belief that the delegate, over multiple transactions or long periods, is supportive of the delegator. Trust may be attributed to individuals and groups, both contemporary and historical, and also to documents, such as religious books, political constitutions, scientific publications, or government records. Trust is an essential component for societal cohesion and is an important outcome of collective intelligence in the development of public and private institutions.

Specialization

The ability to delegate tasks to others frees the individual to concentrate on topics that he or she finds more important. It also provides the opportunity to develop specialized expertise, for example, in hunting, gathering, domestication of animals, cultivation, construction of settlements, and eventually cities. Specialists need greater precision in their communications than the general public as they bring structure to their domains. Hence they create argots or professional languages, typically employing the semantics and syntax of their native tongue, but inventing neologisms or in some cases by imputing narrow meanings to common words. As with language in general, this serves not only the representation of specialized concepts, but also the definition of a subculture and the inclusion and exclusion of members and nonmembers. Specialists may acquire authority and eminence, particularly if they receive formal training and are then examined and certified by acknowledged authorities. When collaborating with the general public or engaging in transdisciplinary (Transdisciplinarity, n.d.) exchanges with other types of specialists, they must act as translators between their argot and the vernacular or among other argots. Anyone who has worked in a transdisciplinary team knows that this results in one of the greatest obstacles to human communication. Where two disciplines share or appear to share a common vocabulary or can even agree on definitions of words that are unique to a profession, they will almost invariably fail to communicate effectively, because they are using these same words to encode different mental constructs. Thus specialization adds value to society, but also separates its knowledge from everyday life.

Power

It should be evident from the above that knowledge and information confer power and status on individuals, communities, nations, and civilizations and can lead to various forms of wealth. Those who create or who are in possession of such assets may assert exclusive ownership and decline to share it. They may engage in legal or illegal methods intended to preserve its secrecy or to prevent its unauthorized use. As a result others, who could benefit from that knowledge or information, are obliged to act in partial ignorance. There may be situations where this is an ethically legitimate approach. For example, there are many examples of soldiers not being informed of known enemy activities in order to conceal a spy or other source of intelligence. But in most cases such secrecy is intended to preserve a competitive advantage. Those from whom the secret is kept may suffer a double disadvantage: not only do they not know the secret, but they may not know that the secret exists. Hence when we delegate to an information source that is unable to access complete information, we may receive responses that are accurate but incomplete.

Decision Making

Large societies require individuals and institutions to make complex decisions and this is supported by extending the radius of cognition and tapping into different expertise and experiences. This process, however, also poses a challenge to the decision makers—how to filter and assimilate larger volumes of information, how to decide which information sources to trust, how to deal with conflicting points of view. Great leaders—physicians, politicians, generals, chief executives—emerge based on their ability to develop and practice these skills. But in the last half century, even our most talented individuals have been overwhelmed by the dramatic expansion of the radius of cognition, the increased density of sources of information within it, and the frequency of complex decision-making. We begin to delegate not only the generation and communication of information to support decision-making, but also the decision-making itself.

As we approach these societal limits, collective intelligence has reached its limits and we need new tools such as augmented intelligence.

Augmented Intelligence

From the introduction it should be evident that augmented intelligence is a technology capable of extremely broad application, essentially any domain where value can be extracted from very large or diverse collections of information and where there is a need for decision-making in complex situations. Those criteria describe many personal, private, and public domains and more will emerge as the Internet of Things makes this an even more connected world. In this section we review some of the early adopters to consider the benefits and the problems they have encountered.

Government

The scale of government, especially national government, means that it has long been an early adopter of ITs for record keeping. In deep history we have the accounting tablets of Linear B (n.d.). In recent history we have Hollerith and the 1890 U.S. Census (Cortada, 2016), one of the trigger points leading to the Age of Information. Governments have many large-scale information problems including supporting operations (traffic, sanitation, public safety and emergency response, and so forth), economic development, fraud (taxes, health care, benefits, and so forth), urban planning, social services, and, not least, criminal and military intelligence.

With the exception of intelligence, governments have been slow compared to the private sector to go beyond record keeping and to adopt more analytical approaches and also to attempt the large-scale integration of their many sources of information. With some notable exceptions, government officials around the world are more likely to come from a Humanities background than from Science or Engineering and to think more in terms of case histories than deep analytics.

So it is perhaps not surprising that it was a businessman, Michael Bloomberg, who established the Mayor's Office of Data Analytics (MODA 1, n.d.) in New York City. However, it was a lawyer, Michael Flowers, who initially led MODA, pioneered the DataBridge (MODA 2, n.d.) as a citywide data sharing platform, and began treating municipal challenges as information problems. It appears that human misbehaviors are frequently correlated. For example, parking tickets and restaurant hygiene violations may both be associated with the same individual. Finding hygiene violations requires physical inspections, but information on parking tickets is easy to find. Hence parking tickets may become indicators for targeting hygiene inspections. MODA's analytic tools, applied across widely different sources, such as building inspections and property tax violations, helped in discovering patterns such as this and in then prioritizing limited enforcement resources. But despite MODA's successes, few cities have chosen to adopt augmented intelligence of this kind.

It is in national security that governments have made the greatest use of augmented intelligence to expand their radius of cognition to identify and track persons of interest (Persons of Interest, n.d.) such as potential terrorists and foreign enemies. Acknowledged information sources for this include telephone call detail records, air, land, and sea travel records, tracking of mobile telephones via base station connections and GPS, and vehicle tracking via toll payment systems, the interception of e-mails and text messages. Intelligence services have the challenges of identifying the activities and relationships of some hundreds of thousands of persons of interest and in particular of finding patterns of activity or signatures that may be indicators of an attack or other threatening activity. Some of these processes must also work in near real time, say hours or a few days.

While the use of computing systems has a long history in this field, beginning with the breaking of the German message codes in World War II, it has expanded dramatically since 9/11 and, although the U.S. budget for national security services is secret, it has been estimated in the region of $1 trillion (Smithberger, 2016) since the 9/11 attacks. This suggests that the U.S. government, at least, is highly convinced of the value of augmented intelligence and other nations are widely believed to make similar investments.

It has also been disclosed informally (Priest, 2016) that in the United States this money pays for the production of some 50,000 security reports under 1,500 titles, some published daily, others weekly, monthly, or annually. According to Priest, the result of this flood of analyses is that "A good deal of once valuable, expensively obtained information had been leached of its value, by virtue of the delay in getting it to the relevant people. If, that is, the relevant people even found it among mountains of pages and millions of kilobytes."

We see here that while augmented intelligence can find needles in extremely large haystacks, it is also capable of producing new haystacks of its own and powerful augmented intelligence can be undermined by low organizational intelligence. A related challenge for intelligence agencies is mutual distrust, even within the same country, which results in the fragmentation of "expensively obtained information." The effectiveness of augmented intelligence in this domain is difficult to assess. It is in the nature of security organizations that often they cannot divulge their successes or substantiate their claims. Even so, testimony before the U.S. Congress is less than convincing (Cohn & Kayyali, 2014). Augmented intelligence cannot overcome dysfunction in organizations and their processes.

Finance and Economics

Stock markets exist to allocate capital to the listed companies. As the projected yields of individual stocks fluctuate, money flows toward or away from them. In an efficient market (Efficient Market, n.d.), all participants should be equally informed, and, if they act rationally, the price of a stock should reflect that knowledge, and this should lead to low volatility in prices. In practice, markets are not efficient and this yields opportunities for augmented intelligence to identify information that has not yet been "priced in." The task for a stock trader therefore is to capture and interpret information across some hundreds or thousands of stocks as quickly and effectively as possible. Thus, each trader wants his or her own radius of cognition to be as large as possible and competing traders' Radii of Cognition to be as small as possible. As a result, stock trading was a pioneer of complex analysis over large datasets.

In the 1990s, the "quants" (Patterson, 2011) used mainframe computers to seek pairs of stocks with negatively correlated prices—meaning that the price of one always falls when the other's price rises and vice versa. Hence, money can be made simply by buying and selling them together. In the early 2000s, large traders were using supercomputers to find imbalances in trading prices where a stock market had not yet priced in some information and they were building data centers close to the stock market trading systems to shave microseconds off response times.

This is a domain where information literally is money and so we should not be surprised to see extreme applications of augmented intelligence. The rewards are potentially extremely large and there is no shortage of funds to invest in extremely high-performance systems and extremely talented analysts. Large amounts of financial information are available (Bloomberg, n.d.) and almost any other kind of real-world information may be added to the mix.

Whether this serves any purpose for the rest of society is debatable. Speculative trading is a form of gambling that may involve very high risks and rewards. In *Dark Pools*, Patterson (2013) points to the risks of instability in global markets that could arise from such methods and a small number of such events have occurred, but markets have been protected by "circuit-breakers" that suspend public trading until the anomaly is identified. On the positive side, as the main early adopter outside intelligence services, these augmented intelligence systems created a market both for technology and for analysts capable of exploiting the technology and thus opened the door to other areas of application.

E-Commerce

The advent of online shopping for consumers in the 1990s quickly led to recommendation systems and other techniques for generating suggested purchases. One of the very first recommendation systems, RINGO from the MIT Media Lab, actually predates online shopping by several years (Collaborative Filtering, n.d.). It used e-mail submission to generate a database of musical tastes and set an early pattern for recommendation systems based on the "people like you also liked this" algorithm. The emergence of broad-based merchandisers such as Amazon and Alibaba widened the opportunities for cross-selling and provided many more interactions with each customer. As the breadth of offerings and the numbers of clients grew (Amazon serves more than 65 million customers each month), large transaction datasets are accumulated and these provide ever better statistics for understanding each customer's interests and buying patterns.

The systems may also incorporate the effects of weather, the local or national economy, news events, and so forth, thus further expanding the radius of cognition. Walmart was a pioneer in studying the dependencies of sales on weather and so forth during the 1990s and integrating demand predictions with its supply-chain management system, but such in-store purchases do not always reveal the customer's identity or enable personalized recommendations. The online channel provides an almost global radius of cognition for these marketing organizations. The online channel also provides an instrument on which to conduct experiments with customer interfaces (A. Wiegend, personal communication), such as where the "shopping basket" should appear on the display to yield the maximum probability of the customer completing the purchase. This rich knowledge base serves for the development of learning algorithms to predict individual customers' purchases and hence aggregate demand by product. This is such a powerful approach that Alibaba and other Chinese retailers run annual competitions (Tianchi, n.d.) for the algorithm that most accurately predicts actual sales during the fourth quarter of the previous year based on buying data from earlier in that year. Winners get substantial prizes and Alibaba gets improved algorithms.

Another business model for this space came from Google, whose revenue is based on selling advertising opportunities using vast knowledge that was derived originally from its users' query streams. The advertising industry quickly developed systems that can in real time receive a placement offer from Google, decide whether to buy the opportunity, and then serve up the appropriate advertising content. As Google's own services have expanded to include Gmail, Drive, Maps, and many more, each of these services is developed to yield insights on users' interests—thereby further expanding the radius of cognition—that can be used to drive advertising opportunities. This approach has been extended from personal computers to mobile devices, the latter also providing high-resolution information on the user's geographic location. The breadth of information was also expanded through other data trails left by consumers including credit card transactions and mobile telephone connections, both of which provide geographic information.

Ironically, while these broad-based retailers appear to know their customers intimately, the sheer breath of products they offer means that they know little about these products beyond the manufacturers' specifications. When an Amazon customer has a question about a possible purchase, the question is referred to other customers who have already bought that product. Further it appears that no effort is made to learn from this stream of information other than by making it available for the puzzled customer to sort through. However, this leaves open niches for vendors who are willing to employ human intelligence to assist their customers and thus offer a different kind of value in the relationship.

The emergence of online retailing has thus created an immense, global network of systems for capturing, integrating, and analyzing or individual behaviors as consumers. These systems, which are no doubt expensive to develop and operate, earn their keep by enabling myriads of supply chains to accurately forecast demand and hence minimize costs. The scale of major retailers such as Alibaba, Amazon, and Walmart also enables them to put pressure on suppliers to accept the lowest price and some of these savings are passed on to consumers. Anyone who wishes to make use of online retailing is required to allow the merchant essentially free use of any information that this may generate, not only for its own benefit but also for sale to associates. While some of this information had been available previously, through credit card systems, travel reservations, and so forth, the volume, the level of detail, and timeliness of the contemporary systems are astonishing and of great concern to those who take privacy seriously.

Science

It is said that Sir Francis Bacon (n.d.), the 17th-century statesman and philosopher, was the last man to have learned all that was known about the world. Scientific inquiry, of which he was one of the inventors, has since fragmented knowledge into ever smaller niches contested by ever greater numbers of researchers. Even within these niches, the torrents of knowledge produced outstrip specialists' ability to find, read, and internalize it. The Worldwide Web (n.d.) was, in large part, invented to facilitate the global sharing of information among researchers in particle physics, but has had an even greater impact on research and practice in the highly fragmented areas of biology and medicine, as well as its more mundane uses.

Scientific method as developed by Bacon and others has made enormous advances by creating or imagining environments in which one particular interaction can be studied in isolation. This can produce compact, mathematical theories with universal validity, for example, Newton's Laws of Motion. But such isolated environments rarely occur in the real world and the search for compact, mathematical theories breaks down already at the Three Body Problem (n.d.). Having thoroughly explored these single-factor interactions, science is now increasingly applying complex systems methods (Complex Systems, n.d.) to domains where many factors are at play, not least biology, ethnography, and medicine, but also cities, climate, economics, and finance, among others. See, for example, the Global Systems Science and Policy program in Europe (Global Systems, n.d.). To understand such global or urban phenomena, we recognize the need for transdisciplinary studies (Transdisciplinarity, n.d.). For example, climate science requires us to combine information and understanding across studies of the atmosphere, oceans, vegetation, the sun, and many subareas within each of these. This is hard for humans, in part because of the sheer volume and varied types of information, but also because our individual understanding is heavily shaped by our professional or disciplinary cultures. Even when transdisciplinary teams can agree on vocabulary, they still do not think in the same ways. Augmented intelligence has the power to reintegrate such knowledge across immense Radii of Cognition by mapping taxonomies without the limitations of human memory or the biases of human cultures.

The results of such complex systems studies are no longer compact, universal theories expressed in the language of mathematics, but rather models representing the dynamics of many simultaneous interactions at various spatiotemporal scales that are specific to this planet. While systems methods enable us to deal with problems that would otherwise be intractable, we are no longer able to understand the results in the same way that we can understand, say, Newton's Laws of Motion. Thus, while augmented intelligence enables us to expand knowledge and understanding of the real world, it also detaches that understanding from human cognition.

Healthcare

In recent decades, medical science has vastly expanded our understanding of the human body and mind and their pathologies. In the 1980s, medicine was one of the very first domains of knowledge to begin the computerized classification of the vast numbers of journal and conference papers being published. The advent in the late 1980s of early digital medical records, although still only partially realized, and the complexity of coding medical procedures further added to the vast volume of information about clinical practice and the effectiveness of treatments. The fragmentation of medicine into ever more finely divided subspecialties has demonstrated the truth of John Ziman's observation (n.d.) that "A scientist is a person who knows more and more about less and less, until he knows everything about nothing." Even within narrow subspecialties, a practicing physician will struggle to keep up with the volume of material being published.

During the 1970s and 1980s, while working in radiology, the author was often told that "doctors practice on the basis of the last ten patients they have seen" with a given condition. Despite the torrents of journal articles, not all medical knowledge is published openly, as medical institutions may not reveal details of procedures that they consider to provide a competitive advantage. In particular, specialists are highly likely to be unaware of relevant results outside their own field or their own country. An augmented intelligence system that could integrate these vast bodies of knowledge and could then assess the most effective treatments and the conditions under which they would be indicated or contraindicated would have enormous humanitarian and commercial value.

The IBM Watson Health team (Watson 1, n.d.) took on this challenge in 2014 following their 2011 success in the Jeopardy! contest (Watson 2, n.d.). The contest had demonstrated Watson's ability to integrate and digest vast amounts of unstructured information and then to generate, in real time, specific questions from punning clues. However, the development of a clinical advisory system proved to be far more difficult (Lohr, 2016). The Jeopardy! contest, like the domains considered above, dealt in accepted facts and had one correct response. But, despite several decades of medical science, healthcare exposes the ambiguity of the human condition and of the practice of its most complex profession—there may or may not be one correct answer for a specific patient—and early progress was difficult.

From the small number of examples given earlier, it is evident that augmented intelligence is a technology capable of extremely broad application, essentially any domain where value can be extracted from very large or diverse collections of data and there is a need for decision-making in complex situations. The early-adopter examples given earlier are characterized by organizations that are large and well-financed, which is typical of the introduction of new technologies. But they are also organizations that generate or have access to the large volumes of information that make augmented intelligence effective.

IT offers both powerful means to collect and to centralize information and to enable top-down control as well as offering the means to disseminate information and to distribute action and bottom-up control. Both approaches can be broadly beneficial. While these early adopters demonstrate how augmented intelligence can foster the former approach, we should imagine eventually the emergence of immense numbers of applications that demonstrate the latter, down to the level of individuals. The tension between centralized and distributed use of augmented intelligence is one of a number of societal issues to be explored in the following section.

Societal Impacts

Having now considered some of the roles of augmented intelligence in our past, framed what augmented intelligence could mean in our present and near future, and reviewed some existing examples of augmented intelligence, we have some understanding of the problems this technology may address for us as a civilization. We next consider what problems might accompany these benefits. While advanced topics such as The Singularity (Kurzweil, 2006) are worthy of wide debate in the coming years, our concerns here are about present and near future, practical applications of augmented intelligence. How these evolve and how we respond to them will set the stage for more advanced forms of Artificial Intelligence.

We live amid rapid changes of many kinds and augmented intelligence is one of many forces creating societal impacts. A 2016 survey of Chief Executive Officers on The Future of Jobs during the period 2015–2020 (Future of Jobs, 2016) identifies both demographic and socioeconomic drivers of change as well as technological drivers of change. In the technological change category, the respondents ranked the top nine drivers as:

1. Mobile Internet and Cloud technology
2. Advances in computing power and Big Data

3. New energy supplies and technologies
4. The Internet of Things
5. Crowdsourcing, the sharing economy, and peer-to-peer platforms
6. Advanced robotics and autonomous transport
7. Artificial intelligence and machine-learning
8. Advanced manufacturing and 3D printing
9. Advanced materials, biotechnology, and genomics

Source: Future of Jobs Report, World Economic Forum

While IT shows up in several ways on this list, artificial intelligence is near the bottom, with only 7% of respondents rating it as the most important change during 2015–2020. This may reflect the relatively near-term focus of the study. It may also be hard to distinguish among "artificial intelligence and machine-learning," "advances in computing power and Big Data," "The Internet of Things," and "advanced robotics and autonomous transport." Collectively, the area of IT is seen as the major technological source of change.

Starting from this observation, there is a wide range of societal impacts that might be considered, but among these some of the most significant are:

- The nature of progress
- The nature of work and the types of jobs to be performed
- The nature of education and continued development
- The right to know and understand
- The growth of complexity
- The structures of organizations

These are the subjects for this section.

Progress

Over time our perceptions of value evolve. Since *Homo sapiens* emerged, the most basic types of value have been water, food, and shelter. While information, especially commercial, political, and military intelligence, has always had value, it is only with the advent of the Worldwide Web that information has broadly acquired value as a raw material and has been produced on such a vast scale. In the previous section we have seen how the production, collection, and analysis of information have already produced major societal impacts. Such developments would have been hard to imagine fifty years ago, when large-scale computing was just getting started and its relevance to the average person, even in highly developed countries, was hard to perceive. Today a core proposition for the use of augmented intelligence is that information has value, just as gold has value and a Rolling Stones concert has value.

We might think of the emergence of information-as-value in terms of "the ascent of Maslow's hierarchy of needs" (1943), as shown in Figure 1.1, through which we have progressed from assigning value to our most basic needs to recognizing value in being able to satisfy ever more abstract needs. Work follows value, whether that value is recognized monetarily or otherwise. As society finds new sources of value—whether black tulips or Rolling Stones concerts—new jobs are created. Until the late 18th century, the vast majority of human beings—greater than 95%—were simply engaged in producing and processing food for themselves and for the other 5%. In terms of Maslow's Hierarchy, 95% of the population was primarily able to satisfy only the lowest two or three levels, while those constituting "the other 5%" were able to reach higher, with some reaching the topmost level of "Self-Actualization." We never lose the need to satisfy our physiological needs and the work of enabling the entire population to satisfy those needs also never disappears. But with technological advances, fewer workers are needed to meet those needs and the work itself becomes more abstract.

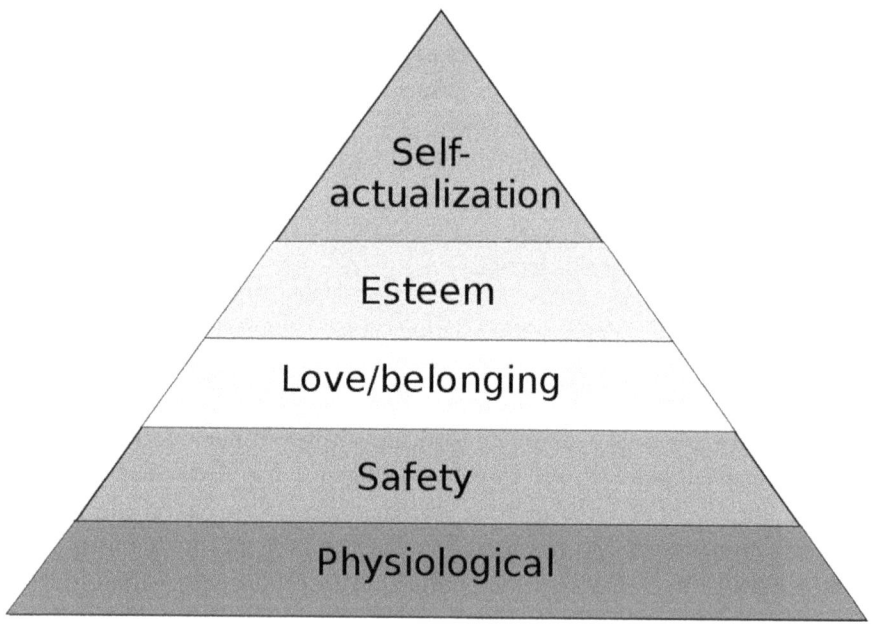

Figure 1.1: Maslow proposes a hierarchy of human aspirations and motivations.
Source: FireflySixtySeven—Own work using Inkscape, based on Maslow's paper, A Theory of Human Motivation., CC BY-SA 4.0, https://commons.wikimedia.org/w/index.php?curid=36551248.

"Progress" in this context means enabling ever-larger fractions of the population to move into jobs that allow them to satisfy their needs at the highest levels as well as the lowest levels of the hierarchy. We might visualize this as a distribution of global population ranging vertically over the hierarchy with a peak that is moving progressively upward and tails that extend to the base and summit.

The ascendance of information as a source of value has implications that will take some time to work out. The idea of information-as-value is relatively new for the general, global public and yet, as we ascend Maslow's hierarchy of human needs, information and the techniques and devices needed to create, store, and process information will become an ever larger part of our public, private, and personal lives.

Work and Jobs

The societal purpose of work is to produce some form of value. New types of jobs are created when new forms of perceived value emerge that require human skills to produce. Old types of jobs disappear or are changed when they are no longer perceived to produce value or when the value can be created in whole or in part by other means. In many cases the jobs that are displaced are replaced with jobs requiring higher skills. Thus up to the 19th century transportation infrastructure was built using armies of laborers, "navvies" in the case of canals, whose primary skill lay in heavy physical labor. These jobs were displaced in the 19th century by machinery such as the steam shovel, which required far less physical labor, but much greater skill in operating and managing complex machinery. Likewise in the late 20th century the adoption by large corporations and government organizations of early forms of augmented intelligence technology displaced armies of workers in manufacturing, accounting, and information services such telephone directory services. Yet the advent in 1971 of the Age of Information (Perez, 2003) created new jobs in numerically controlled machining, in manufacturing semiconductors, in managing an explosion of financial transactions, in collecting and managing vast databases of new types of information, and in creating software for these new uses. These new jobs increasingly demanded intellectual rather than physical skills.

The Future of Jobs (2016) report cited at the beginning of this section is a survey of Chief Executive Officers' opinions on the impacts of various factors on various kinds of jobs across many sectors. In some cases, new jobs will be created, for example, assessing climate change impacts using Big Data and advanced modeling. In other cases, old jobs will disappear, for example, general office and administrative jobs, with the work being performed by technology. A third possibility is that certain professional jobs such as physicians, lawyers, or policymakers will initially find their work enriched, as augmented intelligence enables them to harness far more information than previously or to reach conclusions far more quickly, but later find that augmented intelligence begins to displace the least skilled among them.

The Future of Jobs survey looks only at the net effect of a technology factor and a given factor is likely to have both positive and negative impacts. As noted earlier IT appears in various guises, but most of these are predicted to produce net job growth with Compound Annual Growth Rates (CAGRs) of 1.4% (robotics) to 2.9% (Big Data, processing power). However artificial intelligence is predicted to produce net job losses with CAGR of −1.6%. Further, in many cases where jobs are changed, rather than eliminated, the workers' role and the required skills will have changed. The survey considers this in terms of "skill stability"—the fraction of industry-specific skills that will become more or less relevant. This suggests that the most heavily impacted industry will be Financial Services & Investors (43% unstable) and the least impacted will be Media, Entertainment, and Information (27% unstable).

The largest single occupational impact is predicted to fall on office workers, much of whose routine work will be largely automated through the application of augmented intelligence. Blue-collar jobs have already been automated by robots to a large degree and so are less affected, although advances in robotics and additive manufacturing will continue this erosion. The surprising new impacts are in cognitive support for highly educated professionals such as physicians, attorneys, engineers, and government administrators. IBM Watson is betting heavily on "cognitive health" (Watson 1, n.d.) to integrate and assimilate the immense volume of clinical data that is now being collected in medical records and results that are being published in medical journals. This area is at present the Mount Everest of cognitive support, but may well be overtaken in the coming decade by the volumes of real-world data being collected from Internet of Things systems (n.d.), in which it is estimated that some 50 billion connected devices will be deployed by 2020 across industrial, municipal, medical, and military systems. Cognitive support may even extend to senior management tasks such as preparing company reports as was demonstrated (Fidler, 2015) by human teams whose work was choreographed by Amazon's Mechanical Turk process (n.d.).

Collectively, these transitions continue the trend of the last two hundred and fifty years in migrating work away from physical labor, whether growing food, mining coal, or shuffling paper, and toward the intellectual labor of applying human insight and creativity to information-based processes. In the best cases, this represents "progress" in the ascent of Maslow's Hierarchy, but the human cost of such transitions can be extremely painful for the workers affected and their families. The transitions appear at the time to be daunting. Who could have imagined that 18th-century farm workers would evolve into skilled factory workers? But that evolution lasted some hundred and fifty years, allowing time for new social structures to emerge—not overlooking the revolutionary periods in the mid-19th century and around the turn of the century—and for successive generations to adapt progressively to new roles. The social transformations of the Age of Information are progressing much faster, certainly too quickly for us to simply wait for the next generation to take on the emerging roles.

Societies' approach to help with these changes is through (re-)education and (re-)training.

(Re-)Education for the Age of Information

The notion of public education emerged in the late 18th century as societies recognized that new skills were required for the Industrial Age. The American Revolution coincided with the Age of Enlightenment, when developed nations began to throw off historical legacies of allegiance to monarchies, aristocracies, and churches and to embrace liberty, fraternity, equality, tolerance, and constitutional government. In the United States these new principles were embodied in the revolution and the provision of free public education was seen by the leaders of the revolution as a necessary support for a strong democracy (U.S. History, n.d.). Public education developed in the cities, but well into the 19th century, the vast majority of the population lived on the land producing food. The school year fit badly with the need for the children of farming families to help with animals and crops, so that by 1870 half of American children still received no formal education. Education for all only became a reality in the closing decades of the 19th century, as urbanization took off and the Industrial Revolution became complete, and factory managers realized they needed greater literacy and new skills in their workers.

Consider the basic concepts of the Age of Information—what is information, how is it produced, how is it consumed, how is it stored and transmitted, how does it create value, how is it protected, what rights do I have to access and own information, and so forth. A failure to teach these basic concepts broadly will exacerbate the existing deep inequalities in countries that are already leveraging augmented intelligence and also deepen the mistrust of governments and private organizations that rely on it.

Education continues to be a necessary support for a strong democracy, but the type of skills required and the rate of societal change require rethinking how this can be delivered. Being an effective member of society still requires, country by country, a foundational understanding of who are, where we are, what are our values, and how we arrived in the present state of the world. It also requires skills in language, science, and mathematics that have growing value as workers become involved in using and developing cognitive support systems based on augmented intelligence. These are matters that are well suited to classroom learning supported by continuing professional skill development throughout careers.

But the future workforce is increasingly required to have skills that are less easily taught and that evolve rapidly under the kinds of forces discussed above. The Future of Jobs (2016) survey referenced earlier contrasts the prioritized general skills needed in 2015 with those anticipated for 2020.

Table 1.1: Prioritized general skills for 2015 and 2020.

In 2015	In 2020
Complex problem solving	Complex problem solving
Coordinating with others	Critical thinking
People management	Creativity
Critical thinking	People management
Negotiation	Coordinating with others
Quality control	Emotional intelligence
Service orientation	Judgment and decision-making
Judgment and decision-making	Service orientation
Active listening	Negotiation
Creativity	Cognitive flexibility

Source: Adapted from Future of Jobs Report, World Economic Forum.

Few of these skills can be learned directly in the classroom. Rather they are absorbed through experiences such as team activities, science fairs, performance arts, and community service. Many of these educational activities have been eroded under the pressure to improve results on testable skills related to classroom learning, although new approaches to team-based and challenged-based learning are emerging (Challenge-driven Universities, n.d.). Nonetheless, the Industrial Revolution shows that through education we can re-equip entire societies for new kinds of work.

The value of such experienced-based learning erodes rapidly in a changing world, as illustrated in Table 1.1. Workers need support from coaches and mentors throughout their lifetimes to continue the development of these soft skills as the nature of work evolves and this may be provided in the future through social network tools similar to LinkedIn. In addition to human coaches and mentors, some of this coaching may come from augmented intelligence systems that can engage in dialogue over learning moments, and propose exercises and goals for development. Knack is an early behavioral analysis system of this kind (Knacks, n.d.).

A further consideration is what to teach? If all the world's information is available at our fingertips, what is the motivation to learn about it? First there is the need to develop and maintain the ability to learn as a skill in its own right. Skills such as observation, interpretation, memorization, and judgment remain essential in interpersonal communication and other situations where augmented intelligence is not available. They serve to anchor us in the real world. GPS navigation systems illustrate the risks of assuming we can simply rely on technology. Such systems are undoubtedly valuable in helping us to find our way through unfamiliar areas, but they leave us with no lasting impression of where we are. Worse, they inculcate an unwarranted degree of trust that the system will take us where we intend to go as opposed to where we ask it to take us (Milner, 2016). By neglecting to develop and use our own cognitive abilities, we risk becoming detached from the world around us and becoming instead dependent on the alternative reality created by such systems.

The Right to Know and Understand

All human beings produce and consume information to some degree and the growing importance of information as a source of value brings with it the need for new approaches to establishing ownership of and access to information. The Internet of Things, among other things, will serve to collect much of that data, but what mechanisms will exist to determine who shall have access to it? The last decade or so has seen the rise of Open Data (n.d.) at various levels of government, matched by the rise of civic organizations' use of this data (Code for America, n.d.), and the Open Science movement (n.d.). In the private sector there is little equivalent progress on societal impacts beyond the emergence of standards for financial and compliance reports of publicly held companies (XBRL, n.d.). An exception is the work of the Carbon Disclosure Project (n.d.) in publishing surveys of greenhouse gas emissions and similar environmental impacts.

In the (Re-)Education section earlier I noted the changing needs for primary, secondary, tertiary, and continuing education in the Age of Information. The application of augmented intelligence erects new barriers to transparency by separating how the world works from human cognition and embedding it in algorithms that are inaccessible and that may not be understood by any human mind.

Failure to provide broad educational support for this trend may leave many people adrift in a world beyond their comprehension.

I noted earlier that the growth of scale of a society is necessarily accompanied by a growth in the complexity, as direct interaction among individuals who know and trust one another evolves toward transactions among anonymous individuals and faceless public or private bureaucracies. The ability to create and operate complex procedures depends today, among other things, on augmenting the administrators with IT systems to manage the complexity, although in many governmental programs there is also a degree of ambiguity at the operational level that allows for human adaptation.

A result of this is, for example, that to apply for the U.S. Supplemental Nutrition Assistance Program (SNAP, n.d.) for food benefits, also known as food stamps, the applicants—some of whom do not speak English or Spanish, others who are barely literate, and few of whom have access to a computer or smart mobile telephone—are required to complete a twenty-three-page form and to provide substantial amounts of documentation. Bureaucracies worldwide impose such hurdles on those who wish to claim benefits as a way of throttling demand for perpetually underfunded programs. But in doing so they also confuse themselves, as the administrators, who are often well-intentioned toward the applicants, struggle to understand the many requirements and choices.

So the risk here is that we employ augmented intelligence to create systems that are beyond the understanding of some or all of their human users. Indeed, we already have such systems that even highly intelligent people cannot understand. An example cited earlier is in high-speed financial transactions, where the need to make complex, high-value decisions in much less than a millisecond requires the users to turn over responsibility for execution to the machines, sometimes with unexpected results. Other systems are beyond human understanding altogether, notably the global banking system. The failure to understand this system was a major contributor to the near collapse of the global banking system in October 2008. When such events do occur, the actions that central bankers take are to a large degree dictated by the computer models. Understanding will have to come later, if at all.

These trends toward ever greater complexity, particularly in dealing with national or global systems, whether public or private, have the effect of taking control out of human hands and placing it in systems that we have no choice but to trust. This problem extends to systems that must be used by those individuals in our societies who are the least able to cope with such complexity, whether through issues of literacy, dementia, or simply the effects of old age that leave them unable to comprehend how the system is supposed to work and what they are supposed to do to make use of it.

The author spent some months in 2008 in Abu Dhabi where the "net-zero" city of Masdar (n.d.) was beginning to be built. Masdar aims to develop an economy rooted in technologies for sustainability and hence its target citizens were PhD engineers. The author felt at home in this environment, but felt compelled to point out to the project's managers that even PhD engineers would be accompanied by young children and aged parents and that these people might well struggle to understand what was going on around them.

Hence as we employ ever more powerful augmented intelligence in public and private systems that touch on the lives of all members of our societies, we risk disenfranchising ever more of them. Apart from the hardship endured by those who must depend on such complex systems for food, healthcare, or employment, this lack of transparency further contributes to the perception that such systems are beyond human control. This alienation then generates demands for "small government" or for a rejection of government entirely and worsens the inequality between those who seem to be in charge of these systems and those who are dependent on them.

Organizational Structures

Prior to the Industrial Revolution, the main large-scale organizations were armies, governments, and religions. These organizations employed hierarchical approaches to managing large numbers of people and these were adopted for the management of the factories and mines that developed in the 19th century. The profession of manager was almost unknown and the main candidates for managers were noncommissioned army officers. Factories and mines were spatially concentrated assets, where the owners wished to extract the maximum value from the massive investments they had made. As a result the dominant industrial organizational model for the 19th and 20th centuries was both hierarchical and centralized.

In the Age of Information hierarchy and centralization are far less important, indeed centralization or concentration of assets may today be seen as a resilience issue. Both the means of value creation and the skills for organizing and executing value creation—that is, work—are far more widely diffused into society and IT provides instantaneous, global connectivity that further facilitates this diffusion. Organizations have reduced the layers of middle management as planning, monitoring, and coordinating roles have been displaced by Management Information Systems (n.d.). Firms have become less vertically integrated and have established global networks of suppliers. Yet IT is used to continue the concentration of information and decision-making to organizations' centers and to aggregate information produced by millions of consumers into the hands of small numbers of extremely large organizations.

An important trend in private enterprise is the emergence of platform business models such as eBay, Airbnb, and Uber that have few direct employees and few assets compared to the volumes of business they manage. With the exception of eBay, which is still primarily a pure marketplace, such platform models also rely heavily on augmented intelligence to predict demand, to manage supply, and to achieve optimum pricing. As a result, while the creation of actual value is highly distributed, the harvesting of knowledge value from the operations is highly concentrated. The model appears to be partially decentralized/bottom-up, but is in reality still centralized/top-down.

The value produced by augmented intelligence requires very large volumes of data, highly skilled analysts, and analytical tools. Even if individuals or small firms are able to retain ownership and control over the information that they produce, it is likely to be too small to yield detailed insights. On the other hand, no mechanisms exist today to allow groups of individuals or companies to pool their information without losing control of it.

The above examples are only a few of the many ways in which augmented intelligence is already having impact on societies around the world. As with other major technologies it brings both positive and negative effects and societies must consider how to deal with these.

Conclusion

In this chapter I have looked at a few of the roles of information in societies and a very small number of areas where augmented intelligence may create new problems as well as helping with today's problems. Aside from augmented intelligence, IT itself has had and continues to have profound social, economic, and political impacts that are the subject of heated debates. Many of these debates overlap with the issues discussed here for the impacts of augmented intelligence. Yes, it is likely that augmented intelligence will replace jobs through automation, but as *Homo sapiens* our response to that should be to use the opportunity to refocus on what cannot be automated, on deep creativity, on making decisions under uncertainty, and on creating the lasting value that only humanity can produce.

To summarize learning from the small number of examples considered above, on the positive side we may see:

- Recognition of the ownership by the individual of information that he or she produces and the right to control how that information is used

- Better ways to address challenges such as climate change, stability of the global financial network, and pandemics and generally understanding and providing better stewardship of the world around us
- Better social and diplomatic policies resulting from more holistic perspectives
- Improved explanation of complex situations leading to greater transparency and understanding by the individual of public and private policies
- Large numbers of creative jobs based on understanding human behaviors
- Improved medical outcomes from personalized medicine

While on the negative side we may see:

- Loss of control by the individual of information that he or she produces
- Diversion of human cognition away from the real world and into machine-based abstractions
- Irrevocable dependencies on and increased technological risks due to systems that no one understands
- Even greater complexity and obscurity in public and private processes
- Disenfranchisement of those who cannot cope with such systems and do not find meaningful work, thereby exacerbating social inequality
- Narrowing of the cognitive gene-pool of our artistic, scientific, political, and community activities

Like most engineers, the author believes that his work can create a better world, but he also acknowledges that new technologies often bring new problems. It is easy to be pessimistic about the benefits and costs of new technologies. No doubt every technological innovation has found opposition in some quarter. Nonetheless, it is also easy to be optimistic that augmented intelligence can enable us to continue the ascent of Maslow's hierarchy of needs that has raised hundreds of millions of people from the aching labor of farming and the horrors of industry and that will offer billions of others new opportunities for Self-Actualization.

Acknowledgments

The author thanks Daniel Araya for proposing the topic for this chapter and also gratefully acknowledges James Cortada, Michael Ecsedy, Rachel Kaplan, Sandy McDowell, and John Thomas for their guidance and thoughtful comments in this work.

References

Bloomberg Terminal, Investopedia. (n.d.). Retrieved from http://www.investopedia.com/terms/b/bloomberg_terminal.asp?partner=asksa

Carbon Disclosure Project. (n.d.). Retrieved from https://www.cdp.net/

Cave Painting. (n.d.). Retrieved from https://en.wikipedia.org/wiki/Cave_painting

Challenge-driven Universities, NESTA. (n.d.). Retrieved from http://www.nesta.org.uk/2016-predictions/challenge-driven-universities

Code for America. (n.d.). Retrieved from https;//www.codeforamerica.org/

Cohn, C., & Kayyali, D. (2014). The top five claims that defenders of the NSA have to stop making to remain credible. Retrieved from https://www.eff.org/deeplinks/2014/06/top-5-claims-defenders-nsa-have-stop-making-remain-credible

Collaborative Filtering. (n.d.). Retrieved from https://en.wikipedia.org/wiki/Collaborative_filtering

Collective Intelligence. (n.d.). Retrieved from https://en.wikipedia.org/wiki/Collective_intelligence

Complex Systems. (n.d.). Retrieved from https://en.wikipedia.org/wiki/Complex_systems

Cortada, J. (2016). *All the facts: A history of information in the United States since 1870.* New York, NY: Oxford University Press.

Diamond, J. (2013). *The world until yesterday: What can we learn from traditional societies?* New York, NY: Penguin Books.

Efficient Market Hypothesis. (n.d.). Retrieved from https://en.wikipedia.org/wiki/Efficient-market_hypothesis

Fidler, D. (2015, April). Here's how managers can be replaced by software. *Harvard Business Review.*

Francis Bacon. (n.d.). Retrieved from https://en.wikipedia.org/wiki/Francis_Bacon

Future of Jobs. (2016, April 26). Retrieved from https://www.weforum.org/reports/the-future-of-jobs

Global Systems Science and Policy. (n.d.). Retrieved from http://global-systems-science.eu/

Harrison, C., & Caglayan, A. (1997). *Agent sourcebook.* New York, NY: John Wiley.

Internet of Things. (n.d.). Retrieved from https://en.wikipedia.org/wiki/Internet_of_Things

John Searle. (n.d.). Retrieved from https://en.wikipedia.org/wiki/John_Searle

Knacks. (n.d.). Retrieved from https://www.knack.it/knacks

Kurzweil, R. (2006). *The singularity is near: When humans transcend biology.* New York, NY: Penguin Books.

Linear B. (n.d.). Retrieved from https://en.wikipedia.org/wiki/Linear_B

Lohr, S. (2016, February 28). The promise of artificial intelligence unfolds in small steps. *New York Times.*

Masdar City. (n.d.). Retrieved from http://www.masdar.ae/en/masdar-city/live-work-play

Maslow, A. H. (1943). A theory of human motivation. *Psychological Review, 50*(4), 370–396.

Mechanical Turk. (n.d.). Retrieved from https://www.mturk.com/mturk/welcome

Milner, G. (2016, February 11). Ignore the GPS. That ocean is not a road. *New York Times.*

MIS—Management Information System. (n.d.). Retrieved from http:/en/wikipedia.org/wiki/Management_information_system
MODA 1—New York City Mayor's Office of Data Analytics. (n.d.). Retrieved from http://www1.nyc.gov/site/analytics/index.page
MODA 2—New York City Citywide Data Sharing—The MODA DataBridge. (n.d.). Retrieved from http://www1.nyc.gov/site/analytics/initiatives/citywide-data-sharing.page
Open Data. (n.d.). Retrieved from http:/en/wikipedia.org/wiki/Open_data
Open Science. (n.d.). http:/en/wikipedia.org/wiki/Open_science
Parkes, D. C., & Wellman, M. P. (2015). Economic reasoning and artificial intelligence. *Science Magazine, 349*(6245), 267–272.
Patterson, S. (2011). *The quants: How a new breed of math whizzes conquered Wall Street and nearly destroyed it*. New York, NY: Crown Business.
Patterson, S. (2013). *Dark pools: The rise of the machine traders and the rigging of the U.S. stock market*. New York, NY: Crown Business.
Perez, C. (2003). *Technological revolutions and financial capital: The dynamics of bubbles and golden ages*. Gloucestershire: Edward Elgar Publishing.
Persons of Interest. (n.d.). Retrieved from https://en.wikipedia.org/wiki/Person_of_interest
Porter, E. (2016, April 26). The mirage of a return to manufacturing. *New York Times*.
Priest, D. (2016). Covert ops, 2011: Arlington, VA. *Lapham's Quarterly, IX*(1), 75–79.
Smithberger, M. (2016). America's $1 trillion national security budget. Retrieved from http://www.pogo.org/straus/issues/defense-budget/2016/americas-1-trillion-national-security-budget.html
SNAP—Supplemental Nutrition Assistance Program. (n.d.). Retrieved from http://www.fns.usda.gov/snap/supplemental-nutrition-assistance-program-snap
Theory of Mind. (n.d.). Retrieved from https://en.wikipedia.org/wiki/Theory_of_mind
Thomas, J. C. (2016). Turing's nightmares. CreateSpace Independent Publishing Platform.
Three Body Problem. (n.d.). Retrieved from https://en.wikipedia.org/wiki/Three-body_problem
Tianchi Competition. (n.d.). Retrieved from https://tianchi.shuju.aliyun.com/competition/index.htm?spm=5176.100065.111.2.oDm1zI&id=
Transdisciplinarity. (n.d.). Retrieved from https://en.wikipedia.org/wiki/Transdisciplinarity
U.S. History Public Education. (n.d.). Retrieved from http://www.ushistory.org/u/39a.asp
Watson 1—IBM Watson for Clinical Trial Matching. (n.d.). Retrieved from http://www.ibm.com/smarterplanet/us/en/ibmwatson/clinical-trial-matching.html
Watson 2—IBM Watson and Jeopardy! (n.d.). Retrieved from https://en/wikipedia.org/wiki/Watson_(computer)
Worldwide Web. (n.d.). Retrieved from http://webfoundation.org/about/vision/history-of-the-web/
XBRL. (n.d.). Retrieved from https://www.xbrl.org/the-standard/what/the-standard-for-reporting
Ziman, J. (n.d.). Retrieved from https://en.wikiquote.org/wiki/John_Ziman

CHAPTER TWO

The Future of Digital Cognitive Systems

Tool, Assistant, Collaborator, Coach, Mediator

JIM SPOHRER AND M. ABUL KALAM SIDDIKE

Introduction

Technology and organizations are two instruments that have been developed to augment the human intellect in order to make people smarter (Norman, 1993). In fact, Douglas Engelbart, an American engineer, and an early computer and Internet pioneer who invented the computer mouse, urged people to work quickly to "augment human intellect and address complex, urgent problems" (Engelbart, 1962, 1995). Herbert Simon, a Nobel Prize laureate and an American political scientist, economist, sociologist, psychologist, and computer scientist, took a multidisciplinary approach to decision making and identified "bounded rationality" as a condition that technology and organizations could mitigate (Simon, 1997). Following these thinkers, we argue in this chapter that digital cognitive systems, known as cognitive mediators, may someday address a range of problems associated with "bounded rationality" (Simon, 1997), "knowledge burden" (Jones, 2005), and "half-life-of-facts" (Arbesman, 2013).

We predict that most people will have cognitive mediators as a form of intelligence augmentation (IA), embedded in smart phones or equivalent technologies such as wearables and the environment. Cognitive mediators represent both the evolution of technological capability and the evolution of social trust. This evolution of digital cognitive systems extends from cognitive tool to personal assistant to collaborator to coach, and ultimately to cognitive mediator. After laying out the vision and building blocks required to build cognitive mediators, this chapter advocates for changes in workforce management and public policy in support of people-centered system redesign. This is to say, artificial intelligence (AI) for IA, rather than task-centered system redesign approaches, or AI for fully autonomous systems.

To understand the rise of cognitive mediators in society, a basic understanding of service science and T-shaped people are important foundations. Simply put, service science is about improving our ability to play win–win or positive sum games through a better understanding of sociotechnical system evolution and design. Sociotechnical systems of people and technology interconnected by value propositions are known as service systems. Service science is the study of the evolving ecology of nested, networked service systems, including their value cocreation and capability coelevation mechanisms (Spohrer & Maglio, 2008). In service science, labor specialization of workers is a value cocreation mechanism within an ecology, or populations of interacting entities in an environment. Adam Smith identified specialization as a key to labor productivity and the wealth of nations. A second type of value cocreation mechanism is Ricardo's Law or comparative advantage which applies to sociotechnical entities at multiscales including people, households, companies, cities, states, and nations. This second mechanism shows advantage for interactions between entities that follow the heuristic of doing a little more of what they do best, a little less of what they do least well, and trade to make up any deficits. Exploiting comparative advantage can lead to greater specialization of entities. Value cocreation mechanisms are sometimes referred to as nonzero-sum games, and it has been argued that human progress is based on the growing number and sophistication of such games or mechanism designs (Wright, 2001).

What are T-shaped professionals? The demand for eSkills is well documented (Orihuela, 2015). Less well documented is the benefits for long-term career success of T-shaped skillset and mindset. Skillset means the proficiency to use technical tools, while mindset means the lens to use in navigating life (Huhman, 2011). For example, data scientists are expected to know how to use Python and R—technical tools. However, to achieve long-term career success, mindset is used to navigate through challenges and toward opportunity. Today's T-shaped professionals are in contrast to I-shaped professionals of the past. During the 20th century, universities produced I-shaped graduates, deep in one area, and jobs changed relatively slowly. For I-shaped professionals, just one area of depth could easily last a decade, if not an entire career. Liberal arts graduates were the generalists, who could communicate with I-shaped professionals and help integrate their ideas to solve the problems of business and society. In this earlier time, most people specialized in either depth or breadth, and there were good jobs for both types of people that could span decades or more. In contrast to I-shaped professionals, T-shaped professionals are characterized by breadth as well as depth in one person. T-shaped breadth requires a type of boundary spanning ability. Boundary spanning is the ability to communicate across disciplines, systems, and cultures, as well as self-knowledge, or the "me" in the T (T Summit, 2016). This boundary spanning ability is often associated with empathy. Designs firms seek out T-shaped professionals with empathy not only for customers and their problems, but also empathy for other teammates pooling their knowledge to solve customers' problems (Hansen, 2010).

Why are T-shaped professionals so sought after? In the 21st century, T-shaped professionals are sought after because of the problem of complexity and the pace of change. Complexity means the number of areas of knowledge that must be combined to solve problems is growing. Almost every unsolved problem today requires engineers, managers, behavioral and social scientists, communicators, and policy-makers working together. For example, consider driverless cars—and what just one incident of a malfunction can create in terms of a problem to be solved. The pace of change is driven largely by rapid technological innovation, but demographic, social, economic, environmental, and regulatory changes also contribute. For example, storm surges along the coastline and flows of migrants that result from environmental change can dramatically impact regions and the work that people do from one year to the next. AI will have a dramatic impact on the types of jobs and skill requirements as well (Chui et al., 2015). Problem complexity places a premium on teamwork, and pace of change places a premium on adaptability. T-shaped professionals excel at teamwork and adaptability, over their I-shaped coworkers.

Understanding Cognitive Mediators

The goal of cognitive mediators is to facilitate value cocreation and capability coelevation interactions between entities at multiple scales. Cognitive mediators are inherently designed to interact many times faster than people interact with each other today. By systematically mapping and exploring value cocreation and capability coelevation opportunities, we envision that people using cognitive mediators will be part of smarter and wiser service systems. A smart service system can be viewed as a type of sociotechnical system in which most people are augmented with cognitive mediators to get and give service offerings more seamlessly, reducing service failures, and accelerating service recoveries. A wise service system goes beyond smart, to improve multiscale entity interaction opportunities, recursively improving individual and collective quality of life into the future (Spohrer, Bassano, Piciochhi, & Siddike, 2016).

Today, Apple's Siri, Google's Now, Amazon's Echo, IBM's Watson, and other cognitive tools are beginning to reach a level of utility that will provide a foundation for a new generation of cognitive collaborators and cognitive coaches. Nonetheless, cognitive mediators require a level of capability and trust to augment and scale expertise that is not only higher, but is built from cognition-as-a-service building blocks that do not yet fully exist (Kelly III & Hamm, 2013; Spohrer, 2016c; Spohrer & Banavar, 2015). Someday, as building blocks and trust improve, cognitive mediators will provide people with high-quality recommendations in order to help them make better data-driven decisions (Demirkan et al., 2015) These capabilities will help people to achieve deeper insights into huge amounts of structured and unstructured data, boosting both creativity and productivity (Spohrer & Banavar, 2015).

Big data is a natural resource and will continue to expand more and more rapidly, in part due to metadata connections added by cognitive systems. Cognitive mediators will have models of the world, their user, and other human and nonhuman entities they need to interact with. In fact, by 2035, cognitive mediators are expected to possess episodic memory systems that perform at superhuman levels compared to normal memory of events. Indeed, many engineers predict that by 2055, nearly everyone may have one hundred cognitive assistants that "work for them" (Spohrer, 2016c). Cognitive mediators and digital workers of each person will boost both the creativity and productivity of both customers (users) and providers (employees), leading to a merging of the marketing and communications function and the human resources functions in most firms. Almost all occupations including doctors, physicians, bankers, and policymakers will have well-developed cognitive assistants built from cognition-as-a-service building blocks to help augment and scale expertise (Spohrer & Banavar, 2015).

The Future of Cognitive Mediators

Cognitive mediators will build better and better models of their users and their users' digital workforce (Spohrer, 2016c). However, initially these software will operate as rudimentary social organisms, learning as apprentices (Forbus, 2016). Learning the roles and responsibilities of human culture will not be easy. Ultimately, as cognitive mediators develop increased capabilities they may provide "weak telepathy" (AI understands what you have in mind and why, and completes that action), "weak immortality" (even after your death, virtual selves can continue to interact with loved ones, friends, business associates, carry on conversations, carry out assigned tasks and others), "weak cloning" (duplicating individuals instantly as they are now, so that people might be in several places at once), and other capabilities that are only science fiction today (Lenat, 2016; Lenat 1979). With the help of a cognitive mediator, a young future-ready adult in 2055 could have the ability to rapidly rebuild societal infrastructure from scratch (Spohrer, 2016c).

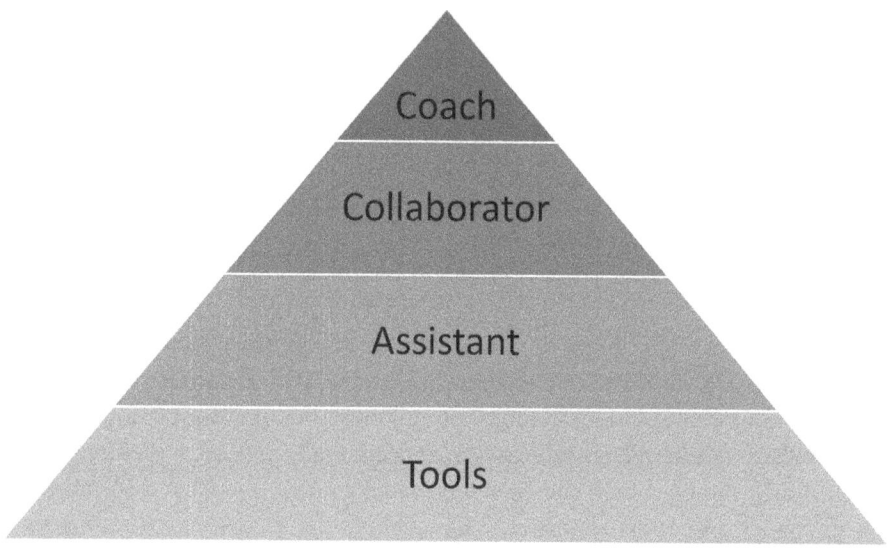

Figure 2.1: TACC hierarchy (tools, assistant, collaborators, and coach).

Cognitive systems can potentially progress from tools to assistants to collaborators to coaches, and be perceived differently depending on the role they play in a service system (see Figure 2.1). To be people-centered, this progression requires that cognitive systems recursively acquire more advanced models of their users in order to develop expert cognitive and social capabilities. Eventually, cognitive assistants will exist for all types of occupations and societal roles in service systems—and this will be the dawn of the era of smart, people-centered service systems. The ownership of cognitive systems and the personal data on which they will operate—as they build user models—will become an active area of legislation in coming years, as companies that produce intelligent personal assistants seek to monetize fully the benefits they create for customers (Spohrer, 2016c).

Recently, initiatives have been taken to utilize the power of cognitive computing in education and research. Deakin University in Australia, for example, used IBM's Watson Engagement Advisor to enhance student engagement and experience by providing a Student Advisor application, giving Deakin's students real-time, 24/7 answers to frequently asked questions (Eassom, 2015; IBM, 2014; Smith, 2014). Human assistive technologies, on the whole, can also be used to help research and process vast amounts of information. Indeed, applications like Watson Teacher Advisor hold great promise for strengthening teaching across the United States, with potential application in other areas of the world. As an example, a professor of AI at the Georgia Institute of Technology has already begun using AI as a teaching assistant (Korn, 2016; Maderer, 2016).

Changes in the Global Workforce

Disruptive changes to business models will have a profound impact on the employment landscape over the coming years (Araya, 2016; World Economic Forum, 2016). Table 2.1 shows the current top skills and future required skills.

Table 2.1: Top skills in 2020.

SN	Top skills in 2015	Top skills in 2020
1	Complex problem solving	Complex problem solving
2	Coordinating with others	Critical thinking
3	People management	Creativity
4	Critical thinking	People management
5	Negotiation	Coordinating with others
6	Quality control	Emotional intelligence
7	Service orientation	Judgment and decision making
8	Judgment and decision making	Service orientation
9	Active listening	Negotiation
10	Creativity	Cognitive flexibility

Source: Adapted from World Economic Forum, 2016.

According to the World Economic Forum Report (2016), current trends of skills could lead to a net employment impact of more than 5.1 million jobs lost to disruptive labor market changes over the period 2015–2020, with a total loss of 7.1 million jobs (two-thirds of which are concentrated in routine white collar office functions, such as office and administrative roles) and a total gain of 2 million jobs, in computer, mathematical, architecture, and engineering-related fields.

These negative projections are largely based on task-centric systems, and not people-centric systems. In fact, a redesigned approach that has a focus on augmenting human intellect with cognitive mediators coupled with a basic income guarantee and focus on entrepreneurship education could see a creation of many new value creating firms in support of an emerging fourth industrial revolution (Industry 4.0).

As the World Economic Report (2016) suggests, new and emerging job categories and functions are expected by 2020. In fact, two jobs types that stand out due to the frequency and consistency with which they are seen across all industries include data analysts, and sales representatives. Data analysts are expected to help companies make sense and derive insights from torrents of data generated by technological disruption. While specialized sales representatives will be key to translating innovation as every industry seeks to become skilled in commercializing and explaining their offerings to business or government clients and consumers. A particular need is also seen in industries as varied as energy and media, entertainment and information for a new type of senior manager who will successfully steer companies through new phases of change and disruption. Figure 2.2 shows this timeframe and its impact on industries and business models.

Technological disruption such as robotics and machine learning—rather than completely replacing existing occupations and job categories—are likely to

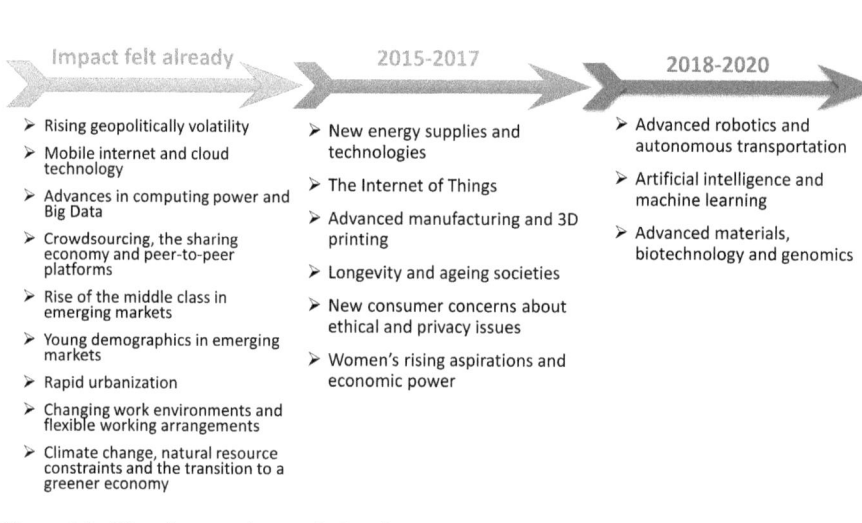

Figure 2.2: Timeframe to impact industries.
Source: Adapted from World Economic Forum, 2016.

substitute specific tasks previously carried out as part of these jobs, freeing workers up to focus on new tasks and leading to rapidly changing core skill sets in these occupations (Atalay et al., 2017). Even those jobs that are less directly affected by technological change and have a largely stable employment outlook (say, marketing or supply chain professionals) may require very different skillsets just a few years from now, as the ecosystems within which they operate evolve.

On average, by 2020, more than a third of the desired core skillsets of most occupations will be comprised of skills that are not yet considered crucial to the contemporary workforce. Overall, this includes social skills—persuasion, emotional intelligence, and teaching narrow technical skills. In essence, technical skills will need to be supplemented with strong social and collaboration skills (World Economic Forum, 2016). For this reason, there will be an acute need for future-ready innovators, with depth and breadth and the ability to work well within multidisciplinary, multisector, and multicultural teams.

Public Policy

As AI technologies mature and become a major source of competitive advantage for nations, firms, and individuals, the implications are both broad and deep for postindustrial societies and future generations of knowledge workers. The sciences that study natural and artificial (human-made) systems are advancing rapidly, with significant implications for the future of multiple disciplines including management, engineering, the social sciences, design, arts/humanities and public policy, as well as AI-core disciplines of computer science, cognitive science, and brain science. In the United States, the White House Office of Science and Technology Policy (OSTP) has recently published a request for information to solicit information from the public about AI (OSTP, 2016).

This section advocates for public policy in support of people-centered system redesign, or AI for IA, rather than task-centered system redesign. The ongoing evolution and redesign of business and society is enabled by better technology building blocks for enhancing human performance, including augmenting human intellect (Spohrer & Engelbart, 2004). For example, cognition-as-a-service building blocks are offered to the public by leading information technology (IT) firms today, and these are the basis for building AI-powered cognitive systems (Spohrer & Banavar, 2015).

Importantly, there is a problem with task-centered system redesign approaches that people-centered system redesign approaches can overcome. Simply put, task-centered system redesign leads to an autonomous machine-to-machine economy to produce all things with no need for people, since machines can perform the required tasks efficiently and effectively (Arthur, 2011). Consider, for example, that nature's ecosystem services operate without people (Wikipedia, 2016a).

In contrast, people-centered system redesign leads to an economy of growing opportunities for people to interact with each other and participate in communities of practice to improve quality-of-life generation after generation. Nevertheless, awareness of the limitations of people becomes a fundamental design constraint of this approach. For example, in the Federalist Papers, the founders of the United States argue about the design of a new form of government to protect individual freedoms and provide open mechanisms for orderly collective decision-making and change by and for the people, with awareness of the physical, mental, moral, and ethical lapses and limitations of people as a fundamental design constraint (Simon, 1996). Nobel laureate and cofounder of the field of AI, Herbert Simon also spoke of people's bounded rationality. Quoting Simon (1996):

> Moreover they did not postulate a new man to be produced by the new institutions but accepted as one of their design constraints the psychological characteristics of men and women as they knew them, their selfishness as well as their common sense. In their own cautious words (The Federalist, no. 55), "As there is a degree of depravity in mankind which requires a certain degree of circumspection and distrust, so there are other qualities in human nature which justify a certain portion of esteem and confidence."

A people-centered system redesign of business and society results in augmented intellect for all people in the form of personal cognitive mediators and occupational cognitive assistants. Augmented cognition can help to improve the performance of both the least-able and most-able members of a society. The least able should in fact benefit the most since they have the most Potential for Improved Performance (PIP) on tasks (Gilbert, 2007). We now turn to specific issues overlapping augmented intelligence and public policy.

Issue 1: Legal and Governance

In a world where everyone has a personal cognitive mediator and occupational cognitive assistant, there will be multiple regulatory concerns (Scherer, 2016). A primary legal and governance concern is likely to be data ownership, monetization, security and privacy. People do not have perfect memories, but cognitive systems might record everything (Gelernter, 1992). For example, if an employee changes companies and works for a competitor, what policy will remove privileged knowledge about a previous employer from the individual's cognitive systems? Industry is highly motivated to solve this challenge in an open and collaborative way.

AI impact on tort law could be significant, including design, manufacturing, warning, and warranty on cognitive machines, that access cognition-as-a-service components from onboard hardware or online cloud. Systems that learn and change in response to user experience will be a new area in tort law. In the far future, since self-aware cognitive systems become possible, there are many precedents for legal personhood based on limited-liability corporation model. Since building cognitive systems is still very hard, this is not an immediate concern—but it does speak to the need for a long-term roadmap for these types of systems with detailed models of the world and others.

A legal and governance issues roadmap that maps out these possibilities is needed.

Issue 2: Public Good

AI has enormous potential for public good. For example, the winning entry in the first IBM Watson university competition was a student team from UT Austin that created a cognitive app to help the homeless access local social services (Willis, 2015). Cognitive systems aimed at flagging and remediating anomalies in early childhood attention and literacy development have the potential for 2x to 10x economic impact, not to mention the impact on families struggling to raise children with behavioral issues arising from developmental challenges (Karoly et al., 2005; Pusiol et al., 2014). Industry has announced major investment in healthcare and education applications of AI. Other studies have documented the potential for saving lives and avoiding injuries with driverless cars.

An industry-by-industry public good roadmap is needed.

Issue 3: Safety and Control

Science fiction includes stories of AI out-of-control. Leading scientists and billionaire entrepreneurs have also voiced concerns. The public expects more than IT industry and government agency reassurances that such scenarios are unlikely given the current state of AI technology and capabilities. The public concerns are related to cybersecurity concerns and dependence on IT, in general, as described in Industry 4.0 proposals. Terrorist and criminals hacking into systems is a big concern. When industry AI-powered chatbots learn politically incorrect tweeting habits, concerns grow. Cyberwarfare, robot soldiers, and autonomous drone capabilities all are real public concerns. Just as police are wearing body cameras, for public accountability, more transparent and auditable cognitive and cyberphysical systems would help address these and other safety and control concerns of the general public. Hedge funds with tens to hundreds of millions of dollars or more being traded by AI systems, also fuel concerns about safety and control.

Finding proactive and effect ways to address these public concerns is a major need for industry, university, and government collaboration. As recently stated (Arbesman, 2016), "Neither fear nor awe is a productive response; both cut off questioning and the potential for gaining even a hint of understanding." Education and improved scientific understanding are the best antidotes to fear and awe in human culture. For sociotechnical systems, simulation tools will likely be essential.

Simulation tools that help educate the public about future pathways are needed.

Issue 4: Social and Economic

From people-centered system redesign perspective, the main social and economic challenge is transformation of work (Levy & Murnane, 2012). Engineers, who primarily adopt a task-centered system redesign perspective, automate tasks to eliminate work by people in established occupation. What remains, after tasks are automated, are interpersonal interactions, executive sign off for strategic choices, preference pooling for collective intelligence, personal-branding of heritage and creative items, as well as other activities where people compete for best practice performance, from sports to other types of work with a performance, creativity, or self-actualization component. People reputations (models of self and accomplishments) compete with themselves (earlier self) and those of others in select populations.

Adapting to rapid change is 90% mindset and 10% skillset, so new mindsets are needed (Dweck, 2006; KFF, 2016).

Issue 5: Research Questions

How does learning work in individuals, organizations, species, and ecosystems? How can the input to learning systems be represented? What are the learning algorithms? What are the range of capabilities that can be learned, and what limits levels of performance? Cognitive mediators need to build detailed models of their users. Cognitive assistants need to build details models of workers, and where they are on their novice to expert performance journey. Today, it takes about ten million minutes of experience for a person to develop to adulthood in society, and a whole life is closer to fifty million minutes of experience. Ten thousands hours of practice account for about a third of the variance in explaining novice to expert performance on a range of tasks, which translates to about two million minutes of life/living for a person working eight hour days on the task (Hambrick et al., 2014).

Computer science/AI researchers must truly learn to represent the diversity of minutes of experience in people's lives, if cognitive systems are to build accurate models of the world and others. Cognitive science/cognitive can model entities learning to some degree, but much more is needed. Brain-neurosciences are needed to understand process that happen in people, including when they are sleeping or subconsciously processing experiences.

Better experience representation and machine learning algorithms are needed.

Issue 6: Research Gaps

Within the people-centered system redesign approach, the goal is to augment human intellect, and to develop personal cognitive mediators for all people and to develop occupational cognitive assistants for all workers (Spohrer & Banavar, 2015; Spohrer & Engelbart, 2004). People should learn to build, understand, and work with these two types of cognitive systems. However, as stated above, there are fundamental research questions related to representing life experiences and learning capabilities to perform tasks based on those input experiences. People do it for a much broader range of experiences, capabilities, and tasks than machines, and this is essential for people to perform as social actors in a human culture, and become apprenticed to others with more capabilities to benefit from social learning. Better experience representation and machine learning algorithms are needed to understand the gaps between the performance of people and machines on tasks embedded in the diversity of real-life social contexts. Animals, such as dogs, may provide a lot of clues for closing research gaps related to experience representation and learning algorithms in social contexts (Forbus, 2016). Even more broadly, as part of the sociotechnical systems design loop, research gaps exist in all disciplines (Kline, 1995).

Better understanding of social learning is needed.

Issue 7: Higher Education

To keep up with the demand for AI skills, online courses are available from a number of top universities including Stanford, Berkeley, and MIT. In addition, leading firms offer faculty and students access to cognition-as-a-service on cloud platforms. These online courses and cognitive service platforms include basic components for machine learning, natural language processing, image recognition, robotics as well as use-cases and applications.

However, most courses and platforms require mathematics and computer science or programming skills as prerequisites, and the available data sets are not sufficiently developed to enable multidisciplinary students and practitioners to build, understand, and work with cognitive systems. Also, integrated computer science/AI, cognitive science, and brain-neurosciences curriculum to enable people-centered system redesign are nascent at best.

More inclusive courses to build, understand, and work with cognitive systems are needed.

Issue 8: Institutions

To encourage multidisciplinary AI research, government agencies, research institutions, universities, and foundations, can work together on a number of projects. First and foremost, since all these organizations have employees whose jobs will be impacted by cognitive systems, they can collaborate on a framework for the development of cognitive assistants for all occupations. The U.S. Occupational Information Network (O*Net) was established by the U.S. Department of Labor, and now is an open data set that maps the changing occupations across the economy. All disciplines across science, engineering, management, law, health care, and the arts are represented in this list of occupations that people fill in our American economy, from accountants to zoologists. A people-centered system redesign framework for cognitive assistants for all occupation will require understanding the interactions between people in various occupations, and the role cognitive assistants can play in improving the creativity and productivity of those occupation-to-occupation interactions. For example, IBM piloted a Cognitive Build initiative for all employees to collaborate in envisioning their transformed job roles in the cognitive era (IBM, 2016). As data becomes the most abundant and valuable natural resource, mining it for insights will become an aspect of all knowledge-worker jobs.

Second, engaging all departments in universities, not just technical areas, but law schools, management schools, public policy, social science, arts and humanities, and design schools should be made priority. For example, research faculty can use cognitive tools to process growing amounts of relevant data more efficiently and effectively. Teaching faculty can use cognitive tools to help students find and use the most relevant courseware to meet their needs. In additions, universities need to make sure students have the right mindset, not just skill set, to adapt to a world of accelerating change, and one where entrepreneurial mindset is needed in all jobs as work continually transforms.

Organizations should enable workers to reimagine their jobs in the cognitive era.

Issue 9: Data Sets

To advance the core sciences (computer science/AI, cognitive science/cognitive architectures, brain science/neural networks), open data sets are essential to enable researchers and learners. Ten million minutes of experience to adulthood in multiple cultures, and two million minutes of experience from novice to experts on multiple tasks are important data sets. Some progress had been made in collecting and framing these types of learning and development data sets for individuals, but much more work is needed (Ericsson, 2004; Roy, 2009). Even more broadly, human history is a data set of interest, since understanding the sociotechnical system design loop and innovation in terms of technological extension factors is important for both exploring possible futures, and reimaging alternative modularizations and pathways for rebuilding systems to make them more resilient (Kline, 1995).

Ten million minutes to adulthood and two million from novice to expert data sets are needed.

Issue 10: Prizes

The building blocks are getting better, and the incentives are getting better as well. Globally, over one-third of adults report they occasionally use smartphones, and over half of adults report they occasionally access the Internet (Poushter, 2016).

IBM, for example, has established a $5 million XPrize for the best use of AI to empower teams of people to tackle the world's grand challenges. The UNDP has identified seventeen global sustainability goals (e.g., no poverty, zero hunger, good health and well-being, quality education, gender equality, clean water and sanitation, affordable and clean energy, decent work and economic growth, industry, innovation, and infrastructure, reduced inequalities, sustainable cities and communities, responsible consumption, climate action, life below water, life on land, peace, justice and strong institutions, partnership for goals) (UNDP, 2016). Making progress requires global collaboration and national scale efforts ultimately involving the behaviors of billions of people. Billions of people making slightly different mundane decisions every few minutes of their lives add up. About one third of people on the planet are still working on their first ten millions minutes of life. How might access to a cognitive mediator help young people reach adulthood with a better model of the world, and how their decisions and actions impact the seventeen global sustainability goals?

If cognitive mediators can help improve knowledge of self and knowledge of the world, then perhaps they can improve decisions making of people. Qualcomm established a $10M XPrize for a tricorder device that will accurately diagnose 13 health conditions (12 diseases and the absence of conditions) and capture five real-time health vital signs, independent of a health care worker or facility, and in a way that provides a compelling consumer experience. The winners of the prize are expected to be announced in early 2017.

More prizes that inspire students and encourage prototype systems are needed.

Issue 11: Other Concerns—Trust

Trust is an important issue. Trust is essential for the adoption of AI in business and society. Cognitive assistants for all occupations and cognitive mediators for all people—augmented intellect available to all—is the goal of people-centered system redesign in the cognitive era of advanced AI technologies (Kelly & Hamm, 2013). The progression from cognitive tool to assistant to collaborator to coach to mediator, is in fact a progression of trust.

In the 19th century, people did not trust steam engines and "boilers." The problem was they often exploded (Wikipedia, 2016b). Over time the design and engineering improved, trust went up, and economic growth resulted. For example, consider just this one application of steam engine in America: "In 1850, a decade before the Civil War, the United States' economy was small—it wasn't much bigger than Italy's. Forty years later, it was the largest economy in the world. What happened in between was the railroads" (Arthur, 2011).

In the 21st century, people do not fully trust cognitive engines or "AIs." Knowledge, technology, and organizations are three ways people augment themselves to become smarter (Norman, 1993). However, knowledge, technology, and organizations must be trusted to spur economic growth. Advanced cognitive systems must become trusted social entities to be effective in our culture (Forbus, 2016). Only as trusted social entities can cognitive systems augment human intellect and interact with people to cocreate new knowledge, technology, and organizations.

The social sciences have an important role to play going forward. So far the trusted economic model (the API economy plus open business model) for secure cognitive transactions platform (Blockchain, crypto-ledger) is not in place. This is not a traditional scientific or technical research question, but it should be well designed from a people-centered systems redesign perspective. When this trusted economic platform is in place people will be better able to build, understand, and work with cognitive systems—they will have at last become trusted social entities; cognitive engines, like steam engines before, will transform the U.S. economy.

This section has argued for policy makers to adopt a people-centered systems redesign AI for IA. The resulting big change for society will be that everyone has a personal cognitive mediator and all occupations have cognitive assistants;

imagine everyone with a digital staff of workers to help them get more done. AI for IA (people-centered systems redesign) puts us on that pathway to the future. The progression from cognitive tool to assistant to collaborator to coach to mediator will happen gradually, since building cognitive systems is still very hard. The recommendations in this short document, if followed, will help us get there faster and safer.

Concluding Remarks: Future Research Directions

Table 2.2 summarizes this chapter and the progression from tool, assistant, collaborator, and coach, and eventually a trusted cognitive mediator. Cognitive mediators will help people boost the creativity and productivity of their interactions, and deal with complexity and the pace of change in a world in which data is a growing resource for all. Cognitive mediators will also have a great deal of information about the person they are bound to, including memories of all experiences and interactions. When people change employment from one company to another, governance policies that allow a cognitive mediator to forget confidential information will be required. Children will grow up with their cognitive mediators, and be encouraged by mentors to work on teams to tackle problems with no known solution, and in this way develop a T-shaped skillset and mindset.

Table 2.2: Cognitive mediators as tool, assistant, collaborator, and coach.

Nature	What will do for us
Tools	Data and information (as a tool will be able to process trillions of data and information)
Assistant	Knowledge (as an assistant cognitive mediator will have more knowledge about people)
Collaborator	Understanding (as a collaborator can understand people's situation and culture, conditions more than us)
Coach	Wisdom (as a coach can help our next generation build and rebuild from the scratch)

The only known way to become T-shaped is to participate in multidisciplinary project teams working on problems that have no known solutions, with mentors who encourage empathy and a growth mindset. For example, being part of a start-up, even if the start-up fails, as most will, is a great way to develop as a T-shaped professional. The "me" in the T is self-knowledge. T-shaped mindset requires self-knowledge, and a growth mindset (Dweck, 2006). A growth mindset is based on the belief that intelligence can be developed, leading to a desire to learn and a tendency to (a) embrace challenge, (b) persist despite obstacles, (c) see effort as a path to mastery, (d) learn from criticism, and (e) be inspired by others success. Working on multidisciplinary teams to solve problems with no known solutions is common in business, but rare in university settings. To produce more T-shaped graduates, education must evolve to be more project-based, and focus on work to solve problems with no known solutions versus a focus on individual projects with known solutions.

In the decades to come, students and professionals may very well be symbiotic with their cognitive mediators. Our cognitive mediators, depending on the context, will seem like a tool, an assistant, a collaborator, or a coach. If Moore's law holds, our personal cognitive mediators in 2035 will have the power of one human brain, but by 2055, many thousands of brains. Will human resource platforms like Jobly help us put those thousands of brains to good use? The problem will not simply be, what should I do to earn a living, but, what purpose should I direct my cognitive mediator toward to inspire the next generation to build it better?

The best way to predict the future is to inspire the next generation to build it. Our personal cognitive assistants may know us so well that they can represent us in many of the routine interactions with other people's cognitive assistants. Surely, as the capabilities and models of those they assist grow, they will be providing an income stream for their owners.

As cognitive mediators become routine, what can we hope for, and what should we aspire to achieve? What will be expected of individuals for them to be considered responsible members of society and to have earned the rights as citizens of what is likely to span multiple bodies in our solar system? Certainly, more will be expected than knowing reading, writing, and arithmetic, passing a driver's test, and being able to find a job and a basic living wage. It seems reasonable that a young adult in the future, with the help of a cognitive mediator and a small team of others equally equipped, could have the ability and the experience to rapidly rebuild societal infrastructure from scratch (Spohrer, Giuiusa, Demirkan, & Ing, 2013). The ability to understand the world, to work from raw materials, and to achieve the level of 3D printers in leveraging personal assistants equipped with the sum of societal knowledge—this would be a test worthy of future citizenry. It is a very high bar, but it is also an aspiration to use the knowledge responsibly.

How can we achieve cognitive mediators for everyone? People-centered systems redesign is already happening—knowledge is being chunked, modularized, and distributed through networks that support rapid rebuilding (Spohrer, 2016b).

The cognitive tools are already helping people both with knowledge-intensive expert thinking and with complex communication (Spohrer, 2016a).

In the future, we predict that cognitive mediators will be as common as smart phones are now in 2016 (i.e., more than one-third of adults globally have used a smart phone). From now until then as a broad collection of AI technologies from natural language processing to machine learning evolve in capability, a progression from tool to assistant to collaborator to coach will occur for software systems. Make no mistake, this is a progression in trust, not simply technology. In the future, we predict that cognitive mediators will be trusted by people to interact on their behalf in many contexts and for many purposes. In fact, in the future, some people, with a bit of humility, may even admit that their cognitive mediators know them better than they know themselves. How might this come about? What skills will people need to responsibly use cognitive mediator (advanced AI) technology? How might this technology be misused? How might cognitive mediator technology lead to not just smarter people with more rights and capabilities, but wiser people with more responsibilities and constraints? Future work will continue to explore the notion of cognitive mediators for T-shaped professionals from a service science perspective.

Acknowledgments

Jim Spohrer would like to acknowledge the inspiration provided by his colleague, friend, and mentor Douglas C. Engelbart (1925–2013). Images courtesy of SRI International and DEI (Douglas Engelbart Institute), and special thanks to Christina Engelbart (DEI).

References

Araya, D. (2016, November 16). Augmented intelligence: Educating skilled labor for the machine age. Brookings Blog. Retrieved from http://www.brookings.edu/blogs/brown-center-chalkboard/posts/2015/11/16-augmented-intelligence-educating-skilled-labor-machine-age-araya

Arbesman, S. (2013). *The half-life of facts: Why everything we know has an expiration date*. New York, NY: Penguin.

Arbesman, S. (2016). *Overcomplicated: Technology at the Limits of Comprehension*. New York: Penguin.

Arthur, W. B. (2011, October). The second economy. *McKinsey Quarterly, 4*, 90–99. Retrieved July 6 from http://www.fullertreacymoney.com/system/data/images/archive/2011-10-10/TheSecondEconomy.pdf

Atalay, E., Phongthiengtham, P., Sotelo, S., & Tannenbaum, D. (2017). The Evolving US Occupational Structure. Discussion paper; 2017 Sep 21. Retrieved from https://ssc.wisc.edu/~eatalay/APST_task.pdf

Chui, M., Manyika, J., & Miremadi, M. (2015, November). Four fundamentals of workplace automation. *McKinsey Quarterly*, 1–9. Retrieved from http://www.yourworkplace.ca/wp-content/uploads/2013/08/Four-fundamentals-of-workplace-automation.pdf

Demirkan, Bess, H. C., Spohrer, J., Rayes, A., Allen, D., & Moghaddam, Y. (2015). Innovation with smart service systems: Analytics, big data, cognitive assistance and the internet of everything. *Communications of the Association for Information Systems, 37*, 733–752.

Dweck, C. (2006). *Mindset: The new psychology of success*. New York: Random House.

Eassom, S. (2015). IBM Watson for education. Retrieved from http://insights-on-business.com/education/ibm-watson-for-education-sector-deakin-university/

Engelbart, D. C. (1995). Toward augmenting the human intellect and boosting our collective IQ. *Communications of the AC,. 38*(8), 30–32.

Engelbart, D. C. (1962, October). Augmenting human intellect: A conceptual framework. Original SRI Summary Report AFOSR-3223, Contract AF 49(638)-1024, SRI Project No. 3578 (AUGMENT, 3906). Doug Engelbart Institute. Retrieved from http://www.dougengelbart.org/pubs/augment-3906.html

Ericsson, K. A. (2004, October 1). Deliberate practice and the acquisition and maintenance of expert performance in medicine and related domains. *Academic Medicine, 79*(10), 70–81.

Forbus, K. D. (2016, March 1). Software social organisms: Implications for measuring AI progress. *AI Magazine, 37*(1).

Gelernter, D. (1992). *Mirror worlds: Or the day software puts the universe in a shoebox … How it will happen and what it will mean*. Oxford Paperbacks.

Gilbert, T. F. (2007). *Human competence: Engineering worthy performance*. Hoboken, NJ: John Wiley & Sons.

Hambrick, D. Z., Altmann, E. M., Oswald, F. L., Meinz, E. J., Gobet, F., & Campitelli G. (2014, August 31). Accounting for expert performance: The devil is in the details. *Intelligence, 45*, 112–114.

Hansen, M. (2010, January 21). DEO CEO Tim Brown: T-Shaped Stars: The backbone of IDEO's collaborative culture: An interview with IDEO CEO Tim Brown. *Chief Executive Magazine*. Retrieved from http://chiefexecutive.net/ideo-ceo-tim-brown-t-shaped-stars-the-backbone-of-ideoae%E2%84%A2s-collaborative-culture/

Huhman, H. (2011, August 26). Skillset vs. mindset: Which will get you the job? *U.S. News & World Reports Careers*. Retrieved from http://money.usnews.com/money/blogs/outside-voices-careers/2011/08/26/skillset-vs-mindset-which-will-get-you-the-job

IBM. (2014). Codename: Watson teacher advisor, Corporate Responsibility Report. Retrieved from http://www.ibm.com/ibm/responsibility/2014/communities/education-in-communities.html

IBM. (2016, July 6). IBM cognitive build: Frequently asked questions. Retrieved from https://cognitivebuild.bluefundit.com/help

Jones, B. F. (2005). The burden of knowledge and the 'death of the renaissance man': Is innovation getting harder? NBER Working Paper, No. 11360.

Karoly, L. A., Kilburn, M. R., & Cannon, J. S. (2005). *Early childhood interventions: Proven results, future promise*. Report MG-341-PNC. Santa Monica, CA: Rand. Retrieved September 14, 2014 from http://www.rand.org/publications/MG/MG341

Kelly, III J., & Hamm, S. (2013). *Smart machines: IBM's Watson and the era of cognitive computing*. New York, NY: Columbia University Press.

KFF. (2016, July 6). Kern Family Foundation—Entrepreneurial Mindset, Retrieved from http://www.kffdn.org/entrepreneurial-mindset/

Kline, S. J. (1995). *Conceptual foundations for multidisciplinary thinking*. Palo Alto, CA: Stanford University Press.

Korn, M. (2016, March 6). Imagine discovering that your teaching assistant really is a robot. Students mostly couldn't tell 'Jill Watson' wasn't human; 'Yep!'. *Wall Street Journal*. Retrieved from http://www.wsj.com/articles/if-your-teacher-sounds-like-a-robot-you-might-be-on-to-something-1462546621

Lenat, D. B. (2016). WWTS (what would Turing say?). *AI Magazine*, 37(1), 97–101.

Lenat, D. B., Hayes-Roth, F., & Klahr, P. (1979, June). Cognitive economy. Rand Report N-1185-NSF. Retrieved from http://www.rand.org/content/dam/rand/pubs/notes/2008/N1185.pdf

Levy, F., & Murnane, R. J. (2012). *The new division of labor: How computers are creating the next job market*. Princeton, NJ: Princeton University Press.

Maderer, J. (2016, May 9). Artificial intelligence course creates AI teaching assistant: Students didn't know their TA was a computer. Georgia Tech News Center. Retrieved from http://www.news.gatech.edu/2016/05/09/artificial-intelligence-course-creates-ai-teaching-assistant

Norman, D. A. (1993). *Things that make us smart: Defending human attributes in the age of the machine*. New York, NY: Basic Books.

Orihuela, R. (2015, June 4). Help wanted: Black belts in data. *Bloomberg Businessweek*. Retrieved from http://www.bloomberg.com/news/articles/2015-06-04/help-wanted-black-belts-in-data

OSTP. (2016, July 10). Request for information: Preparing for the future of artificial intelligence. Retrieved from https://www.whitehouse.gov/webform/rfi-preparing-future-artificial-intelligence

Poushter, J. (2016, July 6). Smartphone ownership and internet usage continues to climb in emerging economies. Pew Research Center. Pewglobal.org. Retrieved from http://www.pewglobal.org/2016/02/22/smartphone-ownership-and-internet-usage-continues-to-climb-in-emerging-economies/

Pusiol, G., Soriano, L., Fei-Fei, L., & Frank, M. C. (2014). Discovering the signatures of joint attention in child-caregiver interaction. *Proceedings of the 36th annual cognitive science conference*. Retrieved September 14, 2014 from http://vision.stanford.edu/pdf/guido14.pdf

Roy, D. (2009, July 6). New horizons in the study of child language acquisition. *Proceedings of Interspeech 2009*, Brighton, England. Retrieved from http://www.media.mit.edu/cogmac/publications/Roy_interspeech_keynote.pdf

Scherer, M. U. (2016, May 30). Regulating artificial intelligence systems: Risks, challenges, competencies, and strategies. *Harvard Journal of Law and Technology*. 29(2).

Simon, H. A. (1996). *The sciences of the artificial*. Cambridge, MA: MIT Press.
Simon, H. A. (1997). *Administrative behavior: A study of decision-making processes in administrative organizations*. New York, NY: The Free Press.
Smith, S. (2014). EDUCAUSE 2014: What IBM's Watson could bring to higher education. Retrieved from http://www.edtechmagazine.com/higher/article/2014/10/educause-2014-what-ibm-s-watson-could-bring-higher-education
Spohrer, J. (2015, February 15). From cognitive computing to wise computing: AAAS Annual Meeting, San Jose, CA USA. Retrieved from http://www.slideshare.net/spohrer/wise-computing-20150215-v3
Spohrer, J. (2016a). Innovation for jobs with cognitive assistants: A service science perspective. In D. Nordfors, V. Cerf, & M. Senges (Eds.), *Disrupting Unemployment: Reflection on a Sustainable, Middle Class Economic Recovery* (pp. 157–174). Kansas City, MO: Ewing Marion Kauffman Foundation.
Spohrer, J. (2016b). Keynote: Engineering grand challenges & solving them (with a little from the future: Our very polite cognitive mediators). Engineers for a Sustainable World: Design-Educate-Build, Berkeley, CA, USA. Friday April 8, 2016. Retrieved from http://www.slideshare.net/spohrer/spohrer-esw-20160408-v4
Spohrer, J., & Banavar, G. (2015, December 1). Cognition as a service: An industry perspective. *AI Magazine, 36*(4), 71–86.
Spohrer, J., Bassano, C., Piciochhi, P., & Siddike, M. A. K. (2016). What makes a system smart? Wise? *Proceedings of AHFE Human-Side of Service Engineering (HSSE) Conference*, Orlando, FL.
Spohrer, J. C., & Engelbart, D. C. (2004, May 1). Converging technologies for enhancing human performance: Science and business perspectives. *Annals of the New York Academy of Sciences, 1013*(1), 50–82.
Spohrer, J., Giuiusa, A., Demirkan, H., & Ing, D. (2013, September 1). Service science: Reframing progress with universities. *Systems Research and Behavioral Science, 30*(5), 561–569.
Spohrer, J., & Maglio, P. P. (2008, May 6). The emergence of service science: Toward systematic service innovations to accelerate co-creation of value. *Production and Operations Management, 17*(3), 238–246.
T Summit. (2016). What is the "T"? Retrieved from http://tsummit.t
UNDP. (2016, January). A new sustainable development agenda. United Nations Development Programme (UNDP) Policy and Program Brief. Retrieved July 6 from http://www.undp.org/content/undp/en/home/sdgoverview/
Wikipedia. (2016a, July 6). Ecosystem services. Retrieved from https://en.wikipedia.org/wiki/Ecosystem_services
Wikipedia. (2016b, July 6). List of boiler explosions. Retrieved from https://en.wikipedia.org/wiki/List_of_boiler_explosions
Willis, J. (2015, July 6). Students will use prize money for social services app. *Daily Texan*. Retrieved form http://www.dailytexanonline.com/2015/01/22/students-to-use-award-money-for-mobile-app

World Economic Forum. (2016). *The future of jobs: Employment, skills and workforce strategy for the fourth industrial revolution.* Retrieved from http://www3.weforum.org/docs/WEF_Future_of_Jobs.pdf

Wright, R. (2001). *Nonzero: The logic of human destiny.* New York, NY: Vintage.

Dedication: Douglas C. Engelbart
Father of the mouse and augmentation theory

Figure 2.3: Dedication to Douglas C. Engelbart.[1]

---

1   Figure 2.3 image descriptions (start upper left, and go clockwise)
Image 1 is: Two photos merged:

(a) Portrait of Doug Engelbart holding the mouse 2008 (c)SRI / Source: SRI timeline (click on Legacy tab) photographer Scott Bramwell;

(b) inset of Doug's hand holding the mouse circa 1995 (c)DEI / Source: DEI's History in Pix—Mouse section photographer Ballard Engelbart

Image 2 is: Screenshot of 1968 Demo / (c)SRI / Source: DEI gallery: 1960s Historic Photo: Demo Screenshot

Image 3 is: Photo of 1967 computer-supported meeting at Doug's SRI lab /(c)SRI / Source: DEI gallery 1960s Historic Photos: 1967 Meeting

Image 4: Photo Ballard and Doug Engelbart 1951 / (c)DEI / Source: DEI Doug's 85th: Happy Birthday Memories

CHAPTER THREE

Augmented Intelligence

Work and Class in the Age of Machine Intelligence

DANIEL ARAYA AND KEVIN STOLARICK

Even as mounting demand to advance human capital has triggered a wide-ranging debate about the kinds of skills needed to drive postindustrial economies, fears remain about the future of work (Araya, 2014). Knowledge-based economies are said to be moving into a "Machine Age" (Brynjolfsson & McAfee, 2014) in which advanced technologies are now transforming labor across a range of industries. But how has technology actually impacted the skills and requirements of knowledge workers over the past two decades? Is technology enabling newer and more creative forms of labor or is it simply subsuming human labor entirely? This chapter examines workplace data in the United States in order to better understand the impact of technology on labor over the past two decades.

Analyzing empirical data from the U.S. Occupational Information Network (O*Net), this study explores employment characteristics nationally and across metro regions for three common occupations: Graphic Designers, Credit Analysts, and Statisticians. Based on this analysis, we suggest that the trajectory of work in the 21st century is changing. Indeed, we believe that the digitization of labor is likely to further increase the demand for creative skills. While the next wave of automating technologies will likely displace a wide range of occupations, it remains the case that technology is complementary to many forms of creative work (Christensen, 1997).

At the same time, class-based occupational structures are significantly impacting the value of creative work. Simply put, not all creative labor is valued equally. What is obvious is that differences in the class of an occupation are driving salary increases in some professions and not others. To be sure, this overlaps a broad economic shift rooted in the capacities of technology to augment certain kinds of work (Englebart, 1962; Drucker, 1969; Schumpeter, 1976 [1942]). Technology is not the whole story, however. Adjusting for inflation, wages in the United States have not increased since the mid-1970s. Even as wages have remained flat, the lion's share of wealth generated over the past three decades has accrued to a very small elite. Nonetheless, our research suggests that there remains significant opportunity for professional work across a range of creative occupations, particularly work that overlaps entrepreneurial innovation.

Technology and Underemployment

As the 2013 study by the Oxford Martin School suggests, nearly half of all occupations in the United States could be displaced through technological automation over the next two decades (Frey & Osborne, 2013). To be sure, knowledge economies are highly computational. In contrast to the perception that it is only low-skilled labor that is vulnerable to automation, theories on technological unemployment now argue just the opposite (Brynjolfsson & McAfee, 2011; Moravec, 1988). As *Moravec's paradox* suggests, it is knowledge-based labor that is the most highly susceptible to computerization. Even as some factory automation remains specialized and expensive, it is cognitive labor (work based on precise, well-understood procedures) that is most easily codified and performed by machines (Zuboff, 1988).

As this "computational knowledge economy" expands and matures, it is facilitating structural changes in the U.S. labor force. And as Brynjolfsson and McAfee (2014) point out, the accelerating impact of technological automation will soon become a daunting challenge. Much as the Industrial Revolution transformed physical labor, the Computational Revolution is now transforming cognitive labor (Beniger, 1986). In the United States, the overarching policy response to this economic transformation has been to focus on leveraging education to manage against labor redundancy. But rising underemployment across a range of industries may make this strategy less tenable.

Few would argue against the notion that underemployment has become a serious problem. In fact, less than 82% of working-age Americans participate in the labor force (McAfee & Brynjolfsson, 2016). Twenty-five million households (the bottom fifth of the income ladder) now earn $18,000 or less annually (Kenworthy,

2014). Recent data from the U.S. Bureau of Labor Statistics (2014) indicate that civilian labor force participation has been declining since 2009:

> Over the past three decades, labour's share of output has shrunk globally from 64% to 59%. Meanwhile, the share of income going to the top 1% in America has risen from around 9% in the 1970s to 22% today. Unemployment is at alarming levels in much of the rich world, and not just for cyclical reasons. In 2000, 65% of working-age Americans were in work; since then the proportion has fallen, during good years as well as bad, to the current level of 59%. (Economist, 2014)

Where OECD (2013) countries have emphasized the need for promoting competitive proficiencies overlapping advanced STEM (science, technology, engineering, math) skills, one wonders whether this kind of skills-based training will be sufficient to the challenges of technological displacement. Notwithstanding the fact that the official unemployment rate is just 4.9%, most economists concede that the real figure is much higher. In fact, according to the Bureau of Labor Statistics (BLS), the U-6 rate (*total unemployed, plus all persons marginally attached to the labor force, plus total employed part time for economic reasons*) measures unemployment at 10%. If we add in people who have given up looking for work altogether, the number is higher still.

What is especially perplexing about this economic restructuring is that productivity gains appear to be decoupling from jobs and income (even as new wealth is overwhelmingly consumed by the owners of capital). Notwithstanding the fact that the principle of workplace automation has not fundamentally changed since the dawn of the computer era, the costs of automation have fallen dramatically. This exponential decline in computing costs is in turn fueling an ever-expanding substitution of fixed capital (computers) for labor.

Looking at the Data

The real question to be asked is: How has technology actually impacted the skills of knowledge workers over the past two decades? Is the exponential advance of technology enabling newer and more innovative forms of labor, or is it simply subsuming human labor entirely? Looking at O*Net data in the United States, we explore various features of contemporary professional employment. Examining the data on three prominent occupations: Graphic Designers, Credit Analysts, and Statisticians, we consider: (i) average share of regional employment (for regions with any employment reported); (ii) share of regional employment for the region with the highest share in that occupation; (iii) total regional employment for the region with the highest total employment in that occupation. So, in effect, for each occupation we consider: (i) average employment; (ii) greatest concentration; (iii) largest total employment.

The Geography of Work

We begin by examining the data for each of the three occupations focusing on the variation in the distribution of each group across metropolitan regions and over time. All three occupations have seen at least some growth in both total numbers and in the share of employment, with Statisticians and Graphic Designers making up a larger average share of regional employment. However, Credit Analysts and Statisticians have both seen wages rise (relative to inflation), while Graphic Designers have actually seen real wages decline.

(1) Graphic Designers

Looking at the data, we find that Graphic designers have become broadly dispersed nationally with the average share increasing even as the share in the largest region has contracted. For the most part, Graphic Designers are fairly uniformly distributed at about 0.11–0.12% of the total workforce. The share increased a little over time, but there is not a lot of variation among the various regions. Although the largest regions saw a big leap in employment in graphic design in the mid-2000s, this was mostly due to the changes in the way the regions were defined. The regions with the most graphic designers are the regions that have the most employees in general—that is, the largest metros. For example, New York, Los Angeles, Chicago, and Washington D.C. are consistently among the top 5 locations employing the most graphic designers. As the actual regions became larger (with new metro definitions), so the number of designers increases.

(2) Credit Analysts

There has been little change in the shares and numbers for Credit Analysts over the past 17 years.[1] However, in terms of locations with the highest share of employment of Credit Analysts, there has been some geographic shift. In fact, recently, North Carolina (Charlotte and Winston/Salem) has become a prominent center for Credit Analysts even as New York and Jersey City declined. While New York remains a substantial center of employment with regard to total number of Credit Analysts, they simply do not make up as large a share of New

York City's total employment. Atlanta has become prominent in recent years as a metro with large total employment and Phoenix is pretty consistently in the top 5 metros. While the regions with the largest number of Credit Analysts seem to grow in size roughly equivalent to overall population growth, the largest share seems to decline. Taken as a whole, the difference between the average share (around 0.045%) and the share in the highest regions (around 0.12–0.24% for the five highest) indicates that these jobs are more concentrated in a smaller number of regions.

(3) Statisticians

The vast majority of Statisticians work in Washington D.C, and state capitals. Washington D.C. consistently employs 3–4 times as many Statisticians as the region with the second highest number. The graphs do show that the average share has increased over time, but the share in the region with the highest share (D.C.; Olympia, WA; Jefferson City, MO; Durham, NC) has not changed very much. The growth in total employment (in DC) has basically kept pace with overall employment growth, which is why the highest share has not really changed much. Among the regions with the highest share, Statisticians make up 0.05–0.30% of the total workforce while the average regional share is 0.02–0.03%. So, like Credit Analysts, Statisticians are concentrated in a smaller number of metros throughout the United States.

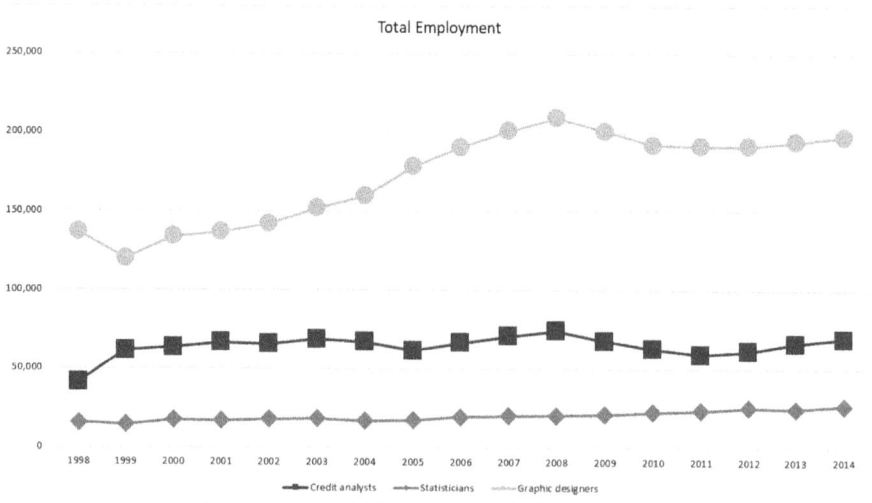

Figure 3.1: Total employment.
Source: Author.

AUGMENTED INTELLIGENCE | 67

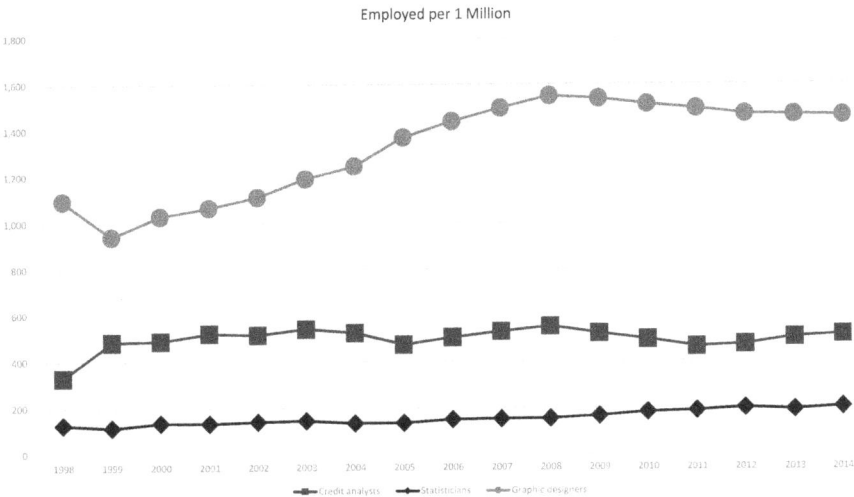

Figure 3.2: Employed per 1 million.
Source: Author.

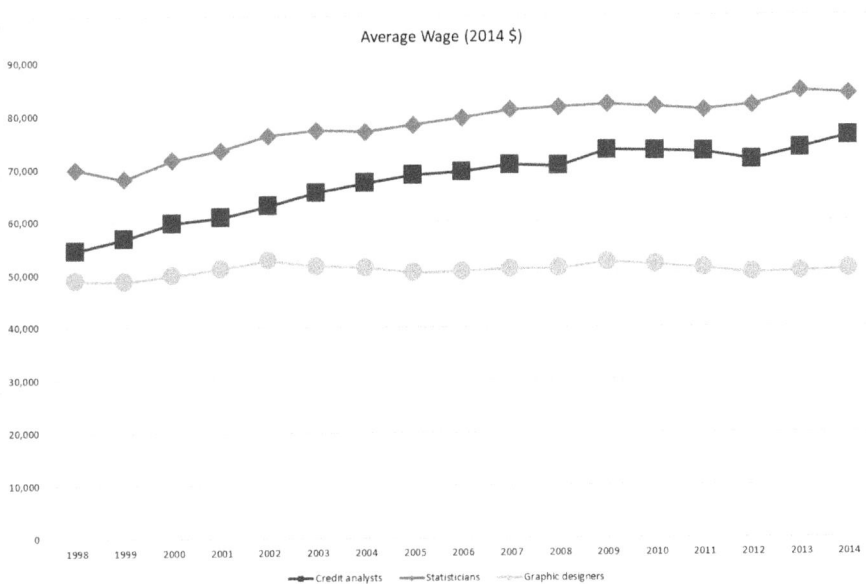

Figure 3.3: Average wage (2014 $) A.
Source: Author.

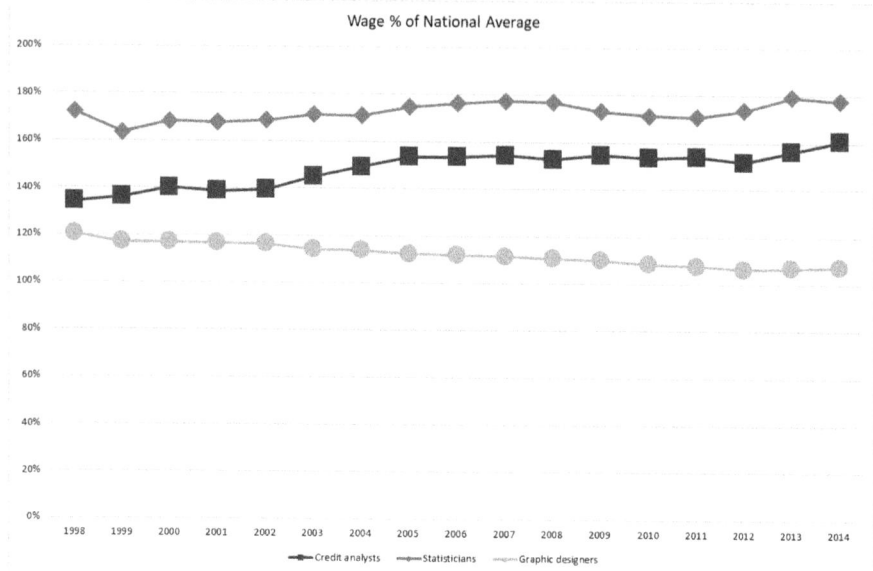

Figure 3.4: Wage % of national average A.
Source: Author.

Figure 3.5: Average of regional share of employment.
Source: Author.

AUGMENTED INTELLIGENCE | 69

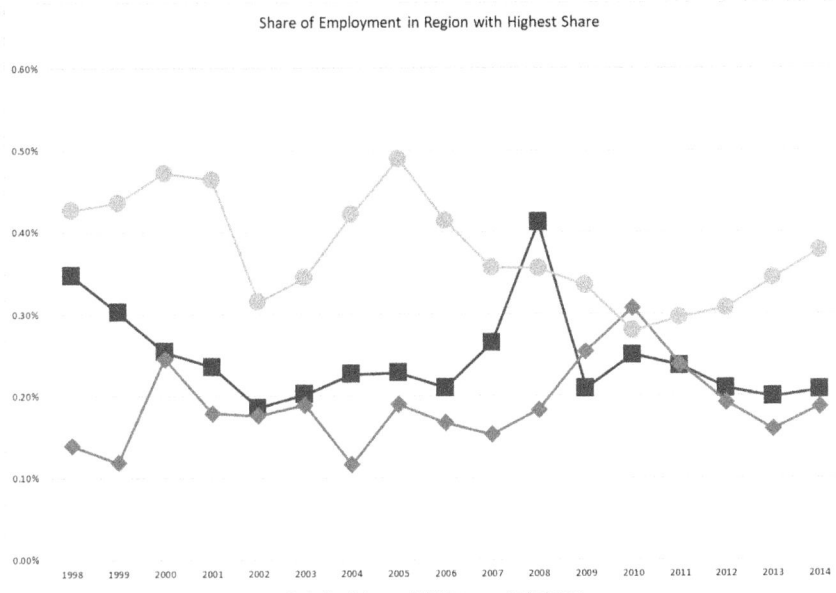

Figure 3.6: Share of employment in region with highest share.
Source: Author.

Figure 3.7: Total employment in region with highest employment.
Source: Author.

Defining the Occupations in This Study

In order to properly define the occupations used in this study we have included O*Net's working description of each profession. Table 3.1 shows those descriptions and how they have changed over time.

Table 3.1: Defining the occupations in O*Net.

O*Net releases	Years	O*NET-SOC Code	Title	Description (changes are highlighted)
3.1–14.0	2000–2008	13-2041.00	Credit Analysts	Analyze current credit data and financial statements of individuals or firms to determine the degree of risk involved in extending credit or lending money. Prepare reports with this credit information for use in decision making
15.1–20.0	2009–2014	13-2041.00	Credit Analysts	Analyze credit data and financial statements of individuals or firms to determine the degree of risk involved in extending credit or lending money. Prepare reports with credit information for use in decision making
3.1–14.0	2000–2008	15-2041.00	Statisticians	Engage in the development of mathematical theory or apply statistical theory and methods to collect, organize, interpret, and summarize numerical data to provide usable information. May specialize in fields, such as biostatistics, agricultural statistics, business statistics, economic statistics, or other fields
15.1–20.0	2009–2014	15-2041.00	Statisticians	Develop or apply mathematical or statistical theory and methods to collect, organize, interpret, and summarize numerical data to provide usable information. May specialize in fields such as biostatistics, agricultural statistics, business statistics, or economic statistics. Includes mathematical and survey statisticians

* in 2008, two additional "suboccupations" for statisticians were also identified—since we don't have employment/wage data for them only the main occupation (Statisticians) was used in the analysis.

O*Net releases	Years	O*NET-SOC Code	Title	Description (changes are highlighted)
14.0–20.0	2008–2014	15–2041.01	Biostatisticians	Develop and apply biostatistical theory and methods to the study of life sciences
14.0–20.0	2008–2014	15–2041.02	Clinical Data Managers	Apply knowledge of health care and database management to analyze clinical data, and to identify and report trends
3.1–20.0	2000–2014	27–1024.00	Graphic Designers	Design or create graphics to meet specific commercial or promotional needs, such as packaging, displays, or logos. May use a variety of mediums to achieve artistic or decorative effects

Table 3.2 shows the descriptions of the O*Net Data occupation content model. The content model forms the basis for more specific information about occupations, as well as changes to specific elements of occupations over time.

Table 3.2: Descriptions of O*Net data occupation content model.

Element ID	Element name	Description
1	Worker characteristics	Worker characteristics
1.A	Abilities	Enduring attributes of the individual that influence performance
1.B	Interests	Preferences for work environments and outcomes
1.C	Work styles	Personal characteristics that can affect how well someone performs a job
2	Worker requirements	Worker requirements
2.A	Basic skills	Developed capacities that facilitate learning or the more rapid acquisition of knowledge
2.B	Cross-functional skills	Developed capacities that facilitate performance of activities that occur across jobs
2.C	Knowledge	Organized sets of principles and facts applying in general domains
2.D	Education	Prior educational experience required to perform in a job
3	Experience requirements	Experience requirements
3.A	Experience and training	If someone were being hired to perform this job, how much of the following would be required?

(*Continued*)

Table 3.2: (*Continued*).

Element ID	Element name	Description
3.B	Basic skills—entry requirement	Entry requirement for developed capacities that facilitate learning or the more rapid acquisition of knowledge
3.C	Cross-functional skills—entry requirement	Entry requirement for developed capacities that facilitate performance of activities that occur across jobs
3.D	Licensing	Licenses, certificates, or registrations that are awarded to show that a job holder has gained certain skills. This includes requirements for obtaining these credentials, and the organization or agency requiring their possession
4	Occupational requirements	Occupational requirements
4.A	Generalized work activities	Work activities that are common across a very large number of occupations. They are performed in almost all job families and industries
4.B	Organizational context	Characteristics of the organization that influence how people do their work
4.C	Work context	Physical and social factors that influence the nature of work
4.D	Detailed work activities	Specific work activities that are performed across a small to moderate number of occupations within a job family
4.E	Intermediate work activities	Work activities that are common across many occupations. They are performed in many job families and industries

Two work activities (4.A), "Interacting with Computers" and "Thinking Creatively" and one work context (4.C), "Degree of Automation" are considered for this study. Information on each work activity for all occupations from the most recent year available and over time for the three focus occupations is presented. Looking at the data on Interacting with Computers, for example, the level and importance of this work activity is highly correlated across all occupations and is correlated with average salary—which has increased over time for all three occupations. The Degree of Automation has both increased and decreased over time across the three occupations but has slightly increased on average across all occupations—with no jobs reported at the highest levels for automation in either 2000 or 2014.

"Thinking Creatively"

For the work activity, *Thinking Creatively*, this analysis also divides the occupations among Florida's (2002) classes of labor–creative, service, working, farming/fishing/forestry (final one not reported). Again the importance and level are highly correlated among all current occupations, and the product of the two is correlated with average wages. But, that correlation weakens considerably when the occupations are divided into the four classes. Only within the service class is the correlation between importance and level of *Thinking Creatively* weak but positively and significantly related to average wages. Within occupations, creative thinkers are not rewarded more for greater creativity. Among the three occupations examined in this study, the product of importance and level for *Thinking Creatively* rose for Graphic Designers but was more mixed for the other two occupations. When combined with the earlier average wage results for Graphic Designers, the result is that over time on average, Graphic Designers have had to increase their level of *Thinking Creatively* but have done so for less money.

"Interacting with Computers"

Examining the data on the work activity, *Interacting with Computers*, this study covers 2000–2014 (there are some mid-year releases) for all three occupations. In the early 2000s (at the beginning of O*Net) this activity was described as:

> Controlling computer functions by using programs, setting up functions, writing software, or otherwise communicating with computer systems.

The "level" of work activity (scored 1–7, with level 0 scored if the activity is not part of the occupation) as shown by Table 3.3:

Table 3.3: "Level" of work activity.

Anchor value	Anchor description
1	Using computers to produce standard correspondence, graphic materials, and business related information.
1.5	Key entering employee personnel information. Editing correspondence on word processing equipment.
4	Writing software to keep track of parts in inventory. Setting up the payroll on computer for a large employer.
6.5	Setting up a new computer system for a large, multinational company. Programming a high speed computer to evaluate scientific information.
7	Using computers to develop very complex, high-speed data linkages and operating systems.

This work activity for each occupation was also scored on "importance" (1–5). While *level* referred to work performance, *importance* was geared toward how important that activity was to the job. The standard for researchers using O*Net data is to multiply level and importance to develop a single composite score (0–35). This becomes important because all of the various job components are scored in a similar manner. But, since this study also wants to look at the separate level and importance scoring as well as the product, separate scores are significant for considering how a single occupation has changed, while the product of the two is useful for comparing multiple occupations using a single number.

By 2002, the work activity description for *Interacting with Computers* had changed to:[2]

> Using computers and computer systems (including hardware and software) to program, write software, set up functions, enter data, or process information.

The level (still 0–7) was then scored by Table 3.4:

Table 3.4: "Level" of work activity in 2002.

Anchor value	Anchor description
2	Enter employee information into a computer database
4	Write software for keeping track of parts in inventory
6	Set up a new computer system for a large multinational company

The graph below shows the scatterplot of importance and level for *Interacting with Computers* for all occupations in 2014. In that year, not a single occupation was scored with a level of 0, but 43 of 954 occupations scored 0.75 or less. Three occupations (Stonemasons; Helpers—Painters, Paperhangers; and Mine Shuttle Car Operators) had the lowest average importance score of 1.04. A clear and strong relationship between level and importance for *Interacting with Computers* is obvious (correlation 0.927, it is not quite linear), but the increasing variation (the "V" shape to the scatter) as both level and importance increase, demonstrating why both should be considered.

The highest importance (5) is for Database Administrators and Web Administrators, and the highest level (6.13) is assigned to Computer Systems Engineers/Architects and Database Architects. A couple of outliers are also shown and they are informative to understanding changes in the trajectory of work. Creating fiber-optic cable (Extruding et al.) requires a higher level of interaction with computers than expected given its lower importance. While baristas and cafeteria clerks

(Counter Attendants et al.) have a lower level of interaction but a higher importance. Both Cashiers and Retail Salespersons have an importance/level relationship that is in line with the other occupations. It is possible that these two are simply outliers—just a confluence of coincidence around how the several people that scored those jobs interpreted the anchors (shown above). But, the wage data at least indicates there might be something to this. Counter attendants make slightly more than other Fast food workers ($19,820 vs. $19,210) but less than other food workers ($21,980). And Extruding Operators ($34,090) make more than other Miscellaneous Textile Workers ($33,610) but less than other Production Occupations ($35,490). The mismatch between level and importance could be creating a small salary boost compared to other similar jobs but a reduction compared to the broader employment sector. To be sure, these are pretty small effects to identify from just two outliers.

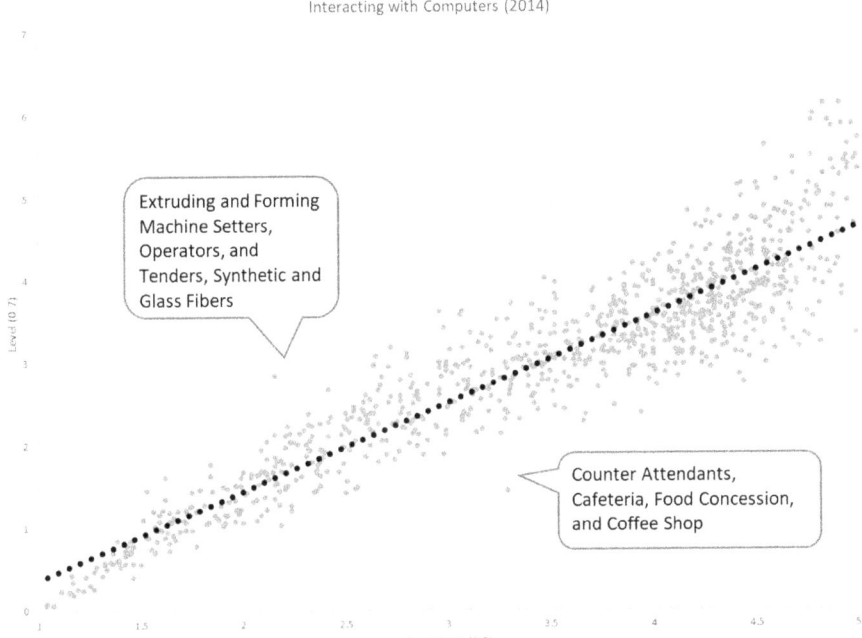

Figure 3.8: Interacting with computers (2014) A.
Source: Author.

Examining the 2014 data overall, there is an apparent relationship between *Interacting with Computers* (level × importance) and average wage. The correlation is strong but not as pronounced (0.559). It is slightly stronger for level (0.560) than for importance (0.538), but always positive and significant. Clearly, wage differentials are not simply explained by computer interaction. Nonetheless, computer interaction does contribute to salary (or at least is positively related to salary) in a small way on an economy-wide basis.

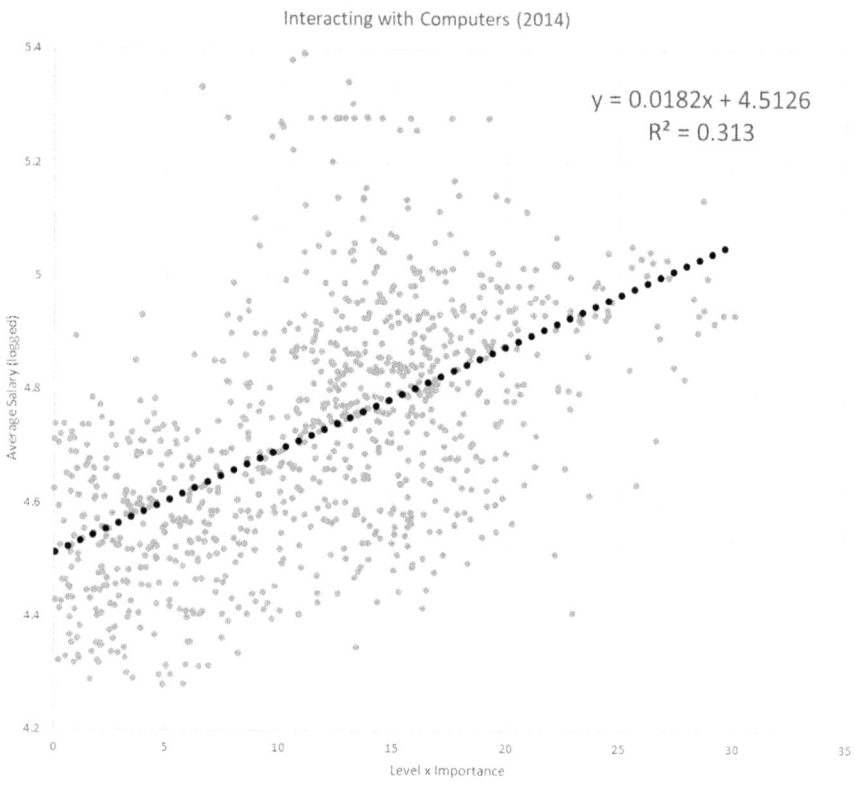

Figure 3.9: Interacting with computers (2014) B.
Source: Author.

The graph below shows the level x importance for our three occupations over time. And, the scores have generally grown. The recent drop in Statisticians is interesting. It may just be noise, but it may also indicate that slightly less intensity in the activity is needed (i.e., computers are doing more). Significant increases in the early 2000s for Credit Analysts and Graphic Designers were matched in the mid-2000s for Statisticians. The order of importance for Interacting with Computers is always: Statisticians, Graphic Designers, Credit Analysts. But, these are occupations that all score fairly strongly on this work activity. In 2014, the scores (as a product of level and importance) for our three occupations were:

Statisticians—23.2; Graphic Designers—18.5; Credit Analysts—14.6. The average for all occupations is 11.6, but for Engineers & Designers the average is 18.5, and for Computer & Mathematical occupations, the average is 24.8. For Financial Professionals, the average is 15.4, indicating that Credit Analysts score below many other financial professionals.

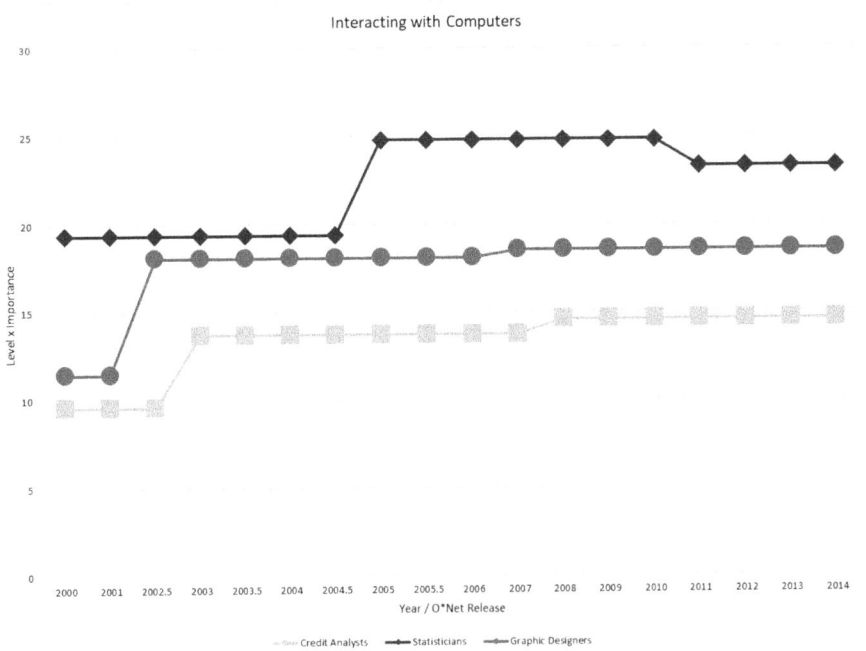

Figure 3.10: Interacting with computers C.
Source: Author.

Looking at each occupation in turn we can see how both the level and importance have changed. They are graphed as a percentage of their maximum value since they have different maximums.[3] Also shown is the product of the two (graphed using the secondary/right axis). For these graphs, X is the product of plus and triangle and uses the right hand axis. Interestingly, importance dropped for Credit Analysts when level increased, but we don't see that happening with the other two occupations. For Statisticians, both level and importance are fairly high, and importance more so—importance averaging 4.5 out of 5 (90%) and level averaging 4.9 out of 7 (70%). For Graphic Designers, importance is also fairly high (average 4.5 out of 5, 90%) but level is not as high (average 3.9 out of 7, 56%). Looking at the 2014 numbers for all occupations, you see something similar—importance averages 3.5 out of 5 (70%), while level averages 3.0 out of 7.0 (43%).

So, computers are generally important to work even if the extent to which they are used (remember level is about ability not frequency) is not as great. Perhaps it would be appropriate to say that the O*Net data supports calling occupational interaction with computers a "necessary evil."

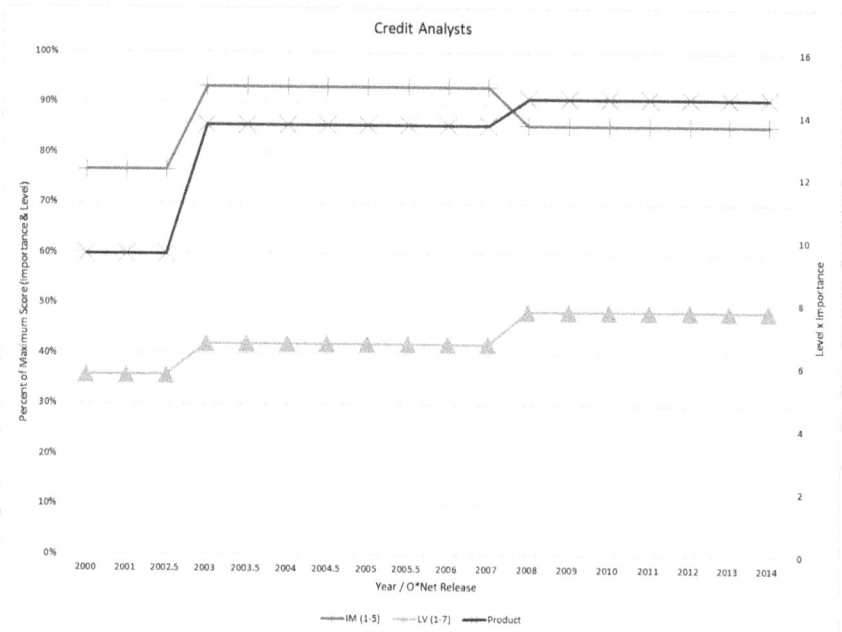

Figure 3.11: Credit analysts A.
Source: Author.

"Degree of Automation"

Next this study examines the data on the *Degree of Automation*. This is a description of job context, which means that it describes features about the context in which the job is performed. Context includes things like relationships, physical work conditions, required attire, location (inside/outside), etc.

Jobs are rated on degree of automation on a 1–5 scale:

1. Not at all automated
2. Slightly automated
3. Moderately automated
4. Highly automated
5. Completely automated

Here are the ratings over time for our three occupations:

AUGMENTED INTELLIGENCE | 79

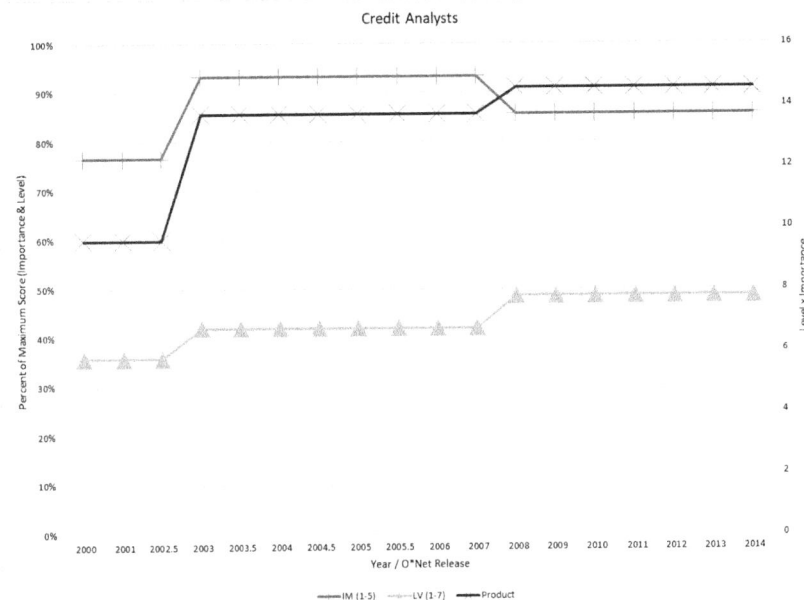

Figure 3.12: Statisticians A.
Source: Author.

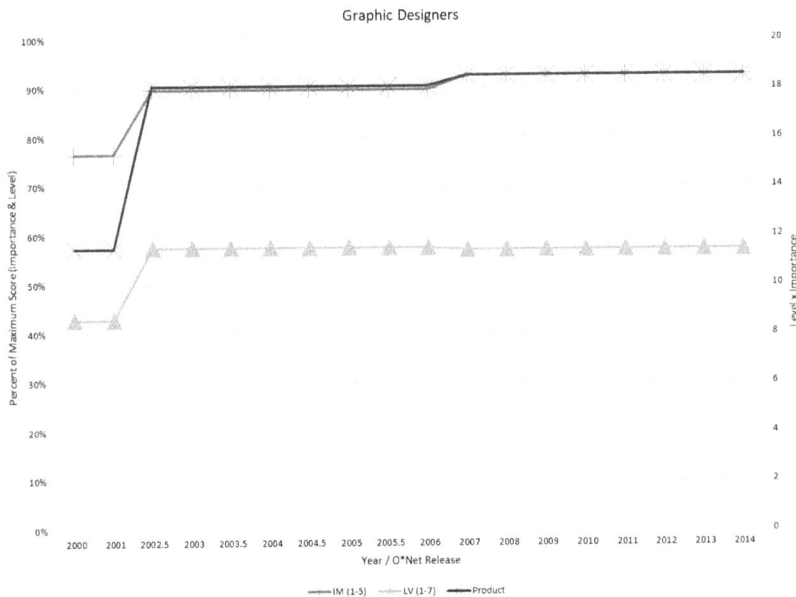

Figure 3.13: Graphic designers.
Source: Author.

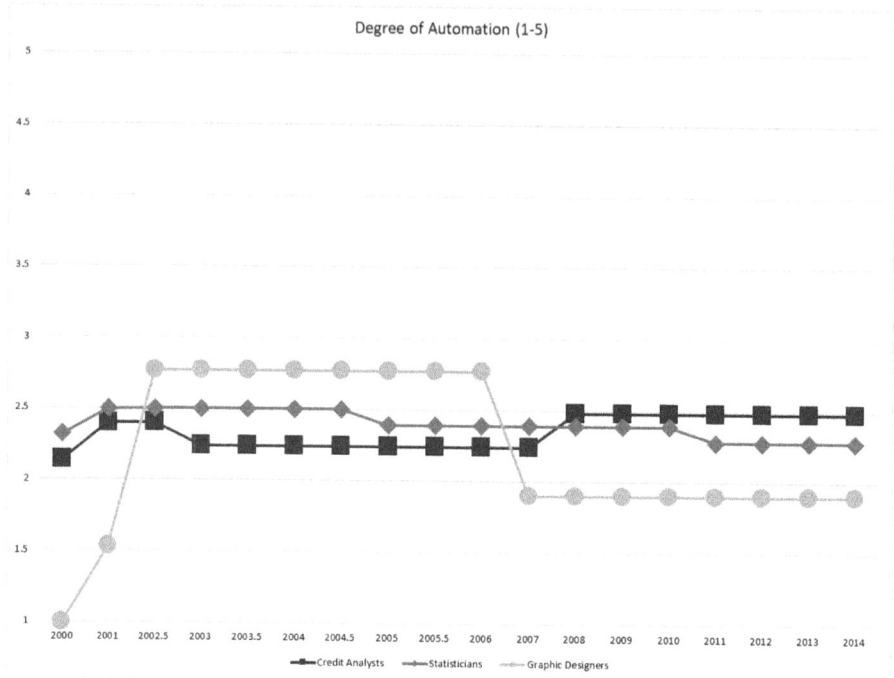

Figure 3.14: Degree of automation (1–5).
Source: Author.

The three occupations are not very automated (between slightly and moderately). However, the increase in automation for Graphic Designers (between 2000 and 2006) followed by a correction downward is likely explained by a shift in the value of design. The initial computerization for design jobs almost certainly gave way to an understanding that good design was done by skilled designers and not computer programs: Computers changed the way work was done—pencil and paper gave way to bits and bytes, but the value-added in terms of design thinking and design practice has remained constant.

Taken as a whole, no trend appears to demonstrate that these three occupations have become any more automated over the past 15 years.[4]

However, looking at all occupations (overall), the average score does increase from 1.8 to 2.2 (there is an adjustment for a change in the scale between O*Net 3.1 (2000) and O*Net 20.0 (2014)). The median score also changed from 1.57 to 2.16—so that also increased slightly. And, the standard deviation didn't really change. So, over time, there was some upward drift of jobs to higher levels of automation—but not that much. Indeed, the variation in the level of automation across all jobs remains consistent across the years.

In 2000, no jobs scored a 6 or 7 (the highest scores in that year) on degree of automation and only 18 of 900 (2.0%) jobs scored more than 5. By 2014, there were still no jobs in the highest two categories (4 or 5), and only 13 of 954 (1.4%) scored higher than 3.5.

So, the intensity of automation even in a select few jobs has not really increased. While the average job could only move a little, the "high end" could have shifted more but that doesn't seem to be the case. So, taken with the earlier results—while interaction with computers did go up, automation has not really increased significantly across all U.S. occupations.

Looking at this data, it is difficult to find empirical evidence to support the argument that automation is now transforming work. While it may indeed be the case that massive levels of automation are on the horizon, the evidence at present does not support this thesis. Rather, it is clear from the data that the automation of the U.S. labor force has simply not happened (yet).

"Thinking Creatively"

Thinking Creatively is another work activity (4.A) we examine in this study. The "Thinking Creatively" anchors span a range of 1–7 and include:

1 Change the spacing on a printed report
4 Adapt popular music for a high school marching band
6 Create new computer software

The first four graphs are for all occupations from the O*Net 20.0 (2014) data, examining importance and level: importance x level and average annual salary (logged). The second versions are the same but differentiate the four classes outlined by Florida (2002): creative (circle), service (triangle), working (small square), farming/fishing/forestry (large square, not shown separately). For each class, the correlation between level and importance stays at around 0.90.

Much as the work activity *Interacting with Computers* indicates, there is a strong, positive correlation between level and importance (0.930). There is also a fairly strong positive correlation between level x importance and wages (0.553). Not surprisingly, the creative class scores the highest on level and importance of *thinking creatively*. The working and service classes are more spread out along the range of values. Separate graphs are provided for each.

Wages are related to on-the-job creativity. Looking by occupational class, the results are much more mixed. It looks as if the relationship between creativity and wages is accounted for by class. The correlation between the two is still positive for the service class, but for the creative and working classes the correlation isn't very strong or significant. Looking at all jobs, creativity is related to wages but once divided into classes (albeit based somewhat on creativity) the relationship is not as strong.

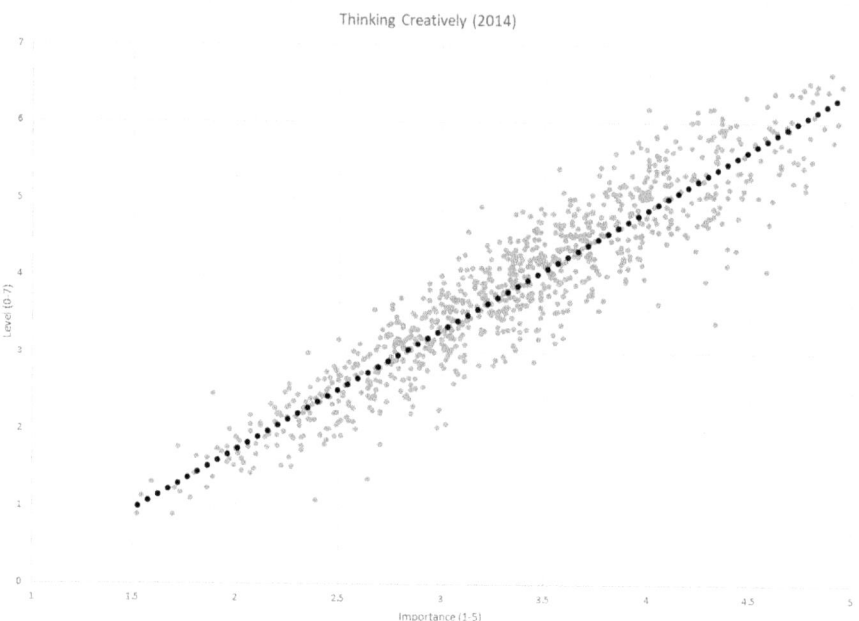

Figure 3.15: Thinking creatively (2014) A.
Source: Author.

Returning to our three occupations and looking over time, the data becomes interesting.

The first graph examines the product (level × importance) for all three occupations over time. While Statisticians declined in creativity during the mid-2000s, the occupational category increased significantly toward the end of the decade. Graphic Designers, on the other hand, continually rise in this work activity, indicating that creativity remains critical. Credit Analysts rise slightly and then drop slightly (alongside the 2008 financial crisis).

Looking at importance, level, and product for each job separately, we see that Credit Analysts increase in the early 2000s in both level and importance but then both decreased in 2008. For Graphic Designers level rose (so more creative thinking was needed) while the importance of creative thinking to the job stayed at nearly 5 out of 5 (it couldn't increase any more).

It is hard to say for sure, but it is possible that the slight decrease in creative thinking for Credit Analysts could actually be the result of technology making

AUGMENTED INTELLIGENCE | 83

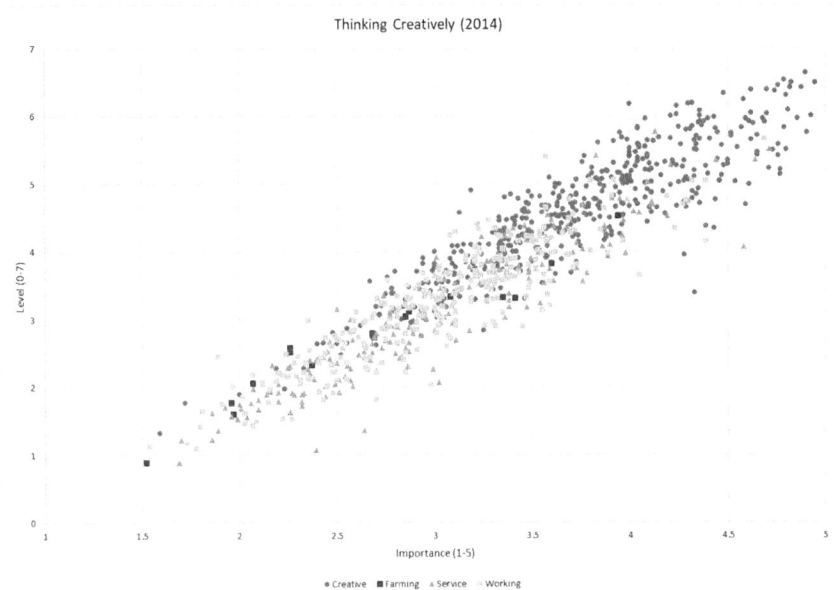

Figure 3.16: Thinking creatively (2014) B.
Source: Author.

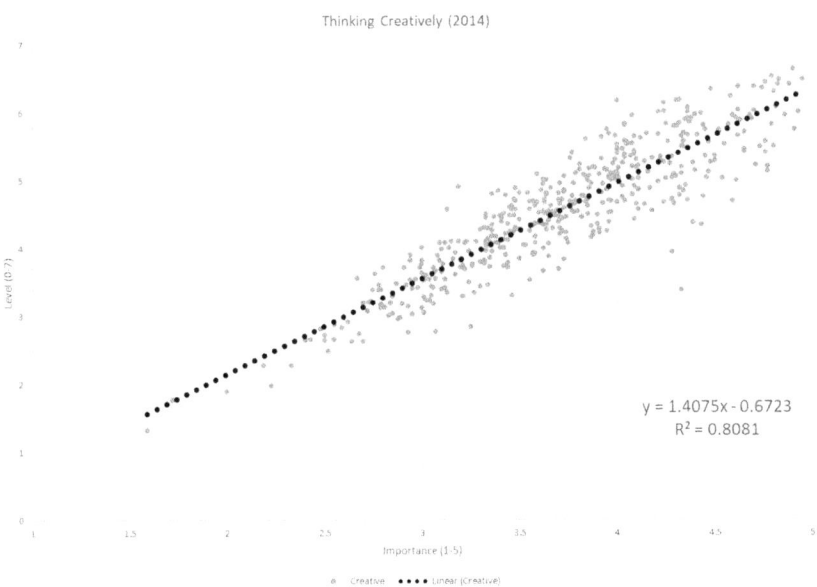

Figure 3.17: Thinking creatively (2014) C.
Source: Author.

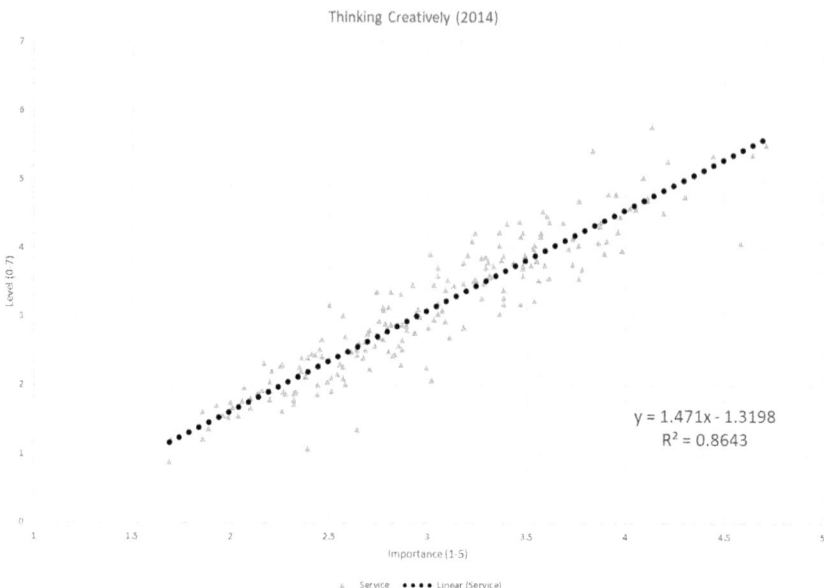

Figure 3.18: Thinking creatively (2014) D.
Source: Author.

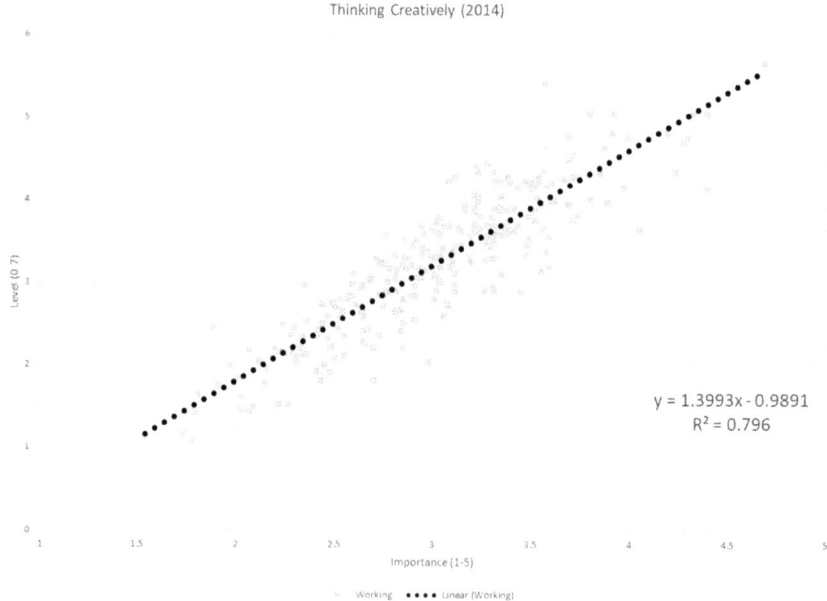

Figure 3.19: Thinking creatively (2014) E.
Source: Author.

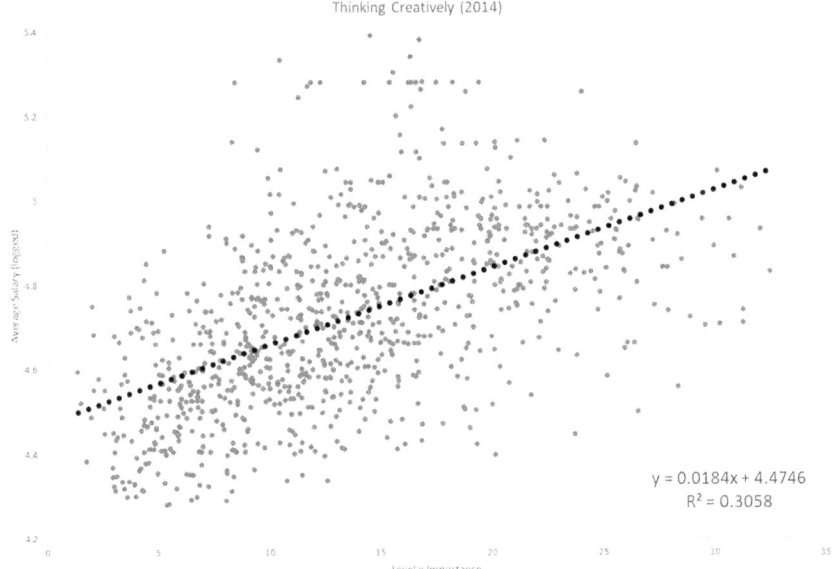

Figure 3.20: Thinking creatively (2014) F.
Source: Author.

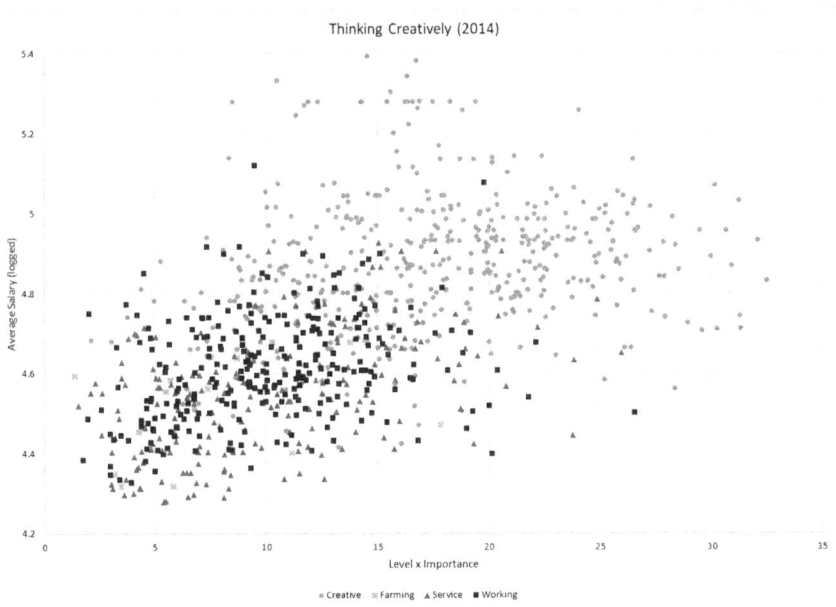

Figure 3.21: Thinking creatively (2014) G.
Source: Author.

86 | DANIEL ARAYA AND KEVIN STOLARICK

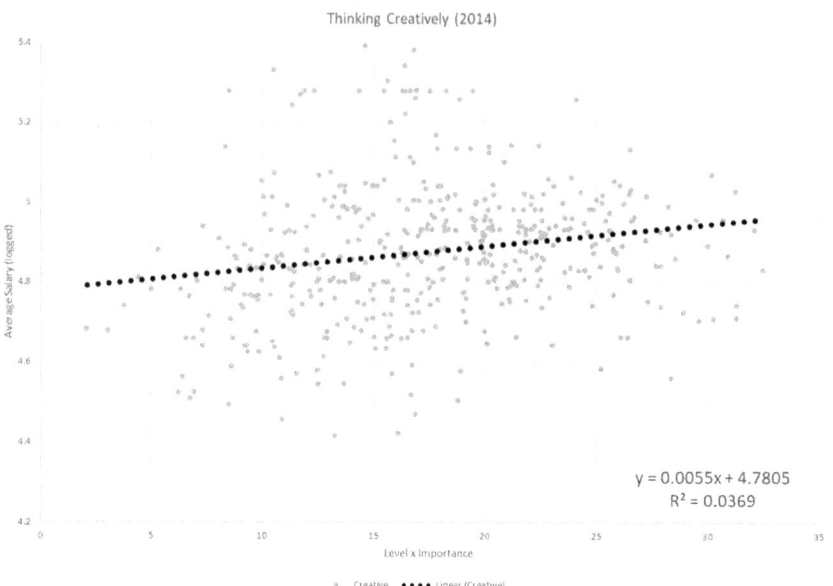

Figure 3.22: Thinking creatively (2014) H.
Source: Author.

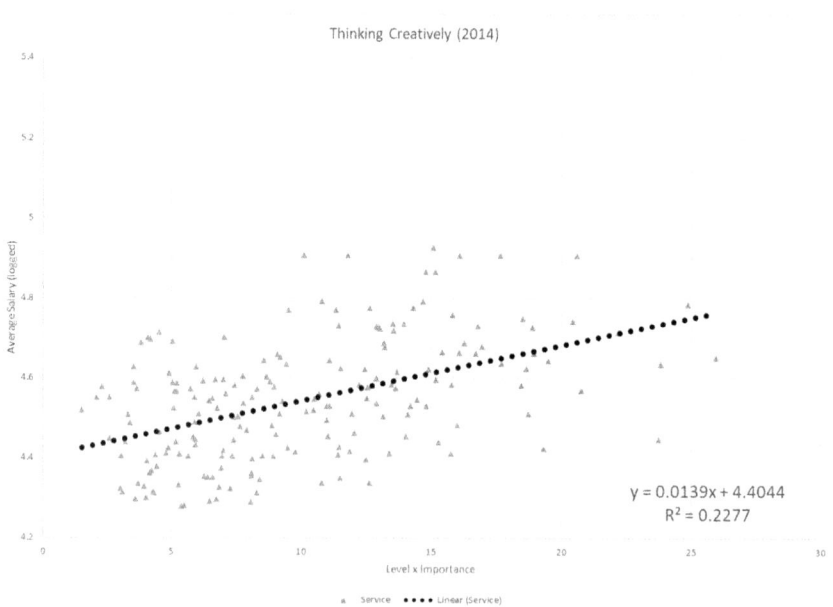

Figure 3.23: Thinking creatively (2014) I.
Source: Author.

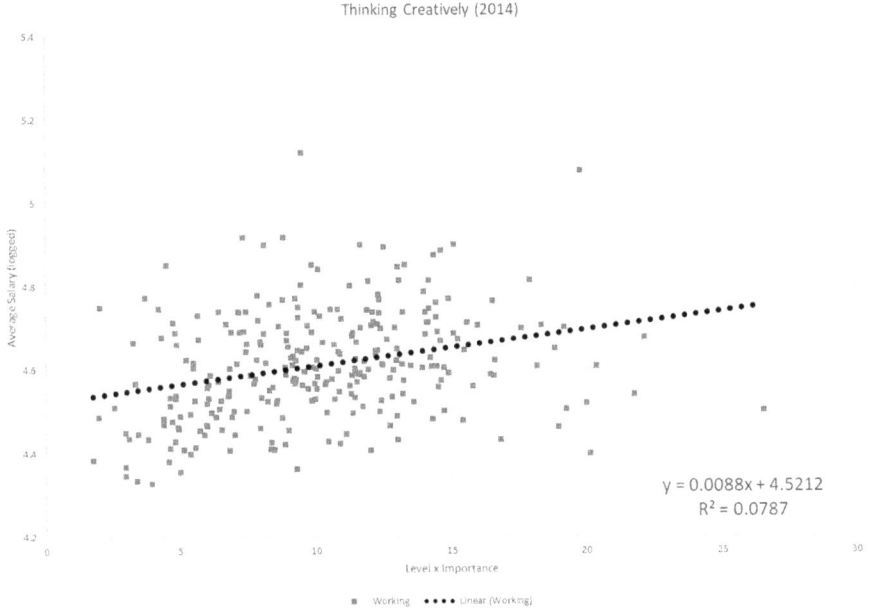

Figure 3.24: Thinking creatively (2014) J.
Source: Author.

more of the decisions—the job requires less creative thinking because the machine (software) is doing more of it. However, when this is linked to the earlier salary results—it is a bit troubling. Credit Analysts and Statisticians have seen their salaries increase, while Graphic Designers have lost ground on wages. In fact, on a "per creative activity" basis, Graphic Designers have lost even more ground despite requiring increasing levels of creativity. That is to say, Graphic Designers are required to be more creative but for less money. Salary graphs are repeated here for comparison.

The Commoditization of Creativity

As this data makes clear, postindustrial economies are increasingly dependent on creativity and creative labor even as technology becomes more foundational to work. At the same time, there would appear to be little relationship between the degree of "creative thinking" and wages across classes of work. This implies that "creativity" as a driver of wages is being treated as a binary and not as a continuous variable. Building on the case of Graphic Designers, for example, it would seem that many kinds of creative labor are increasingly devalued even as creative work becomes foundational to the global economy.

88 | DANIEL ARAYA AND KEVIN STOLARICK

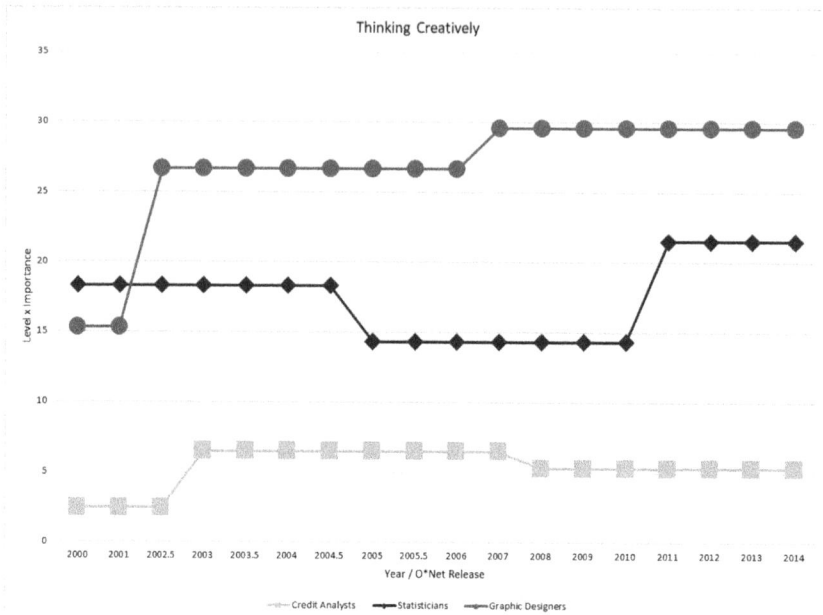

Figure 3.25: Thinking creatively (2014) K.
Source: Author.

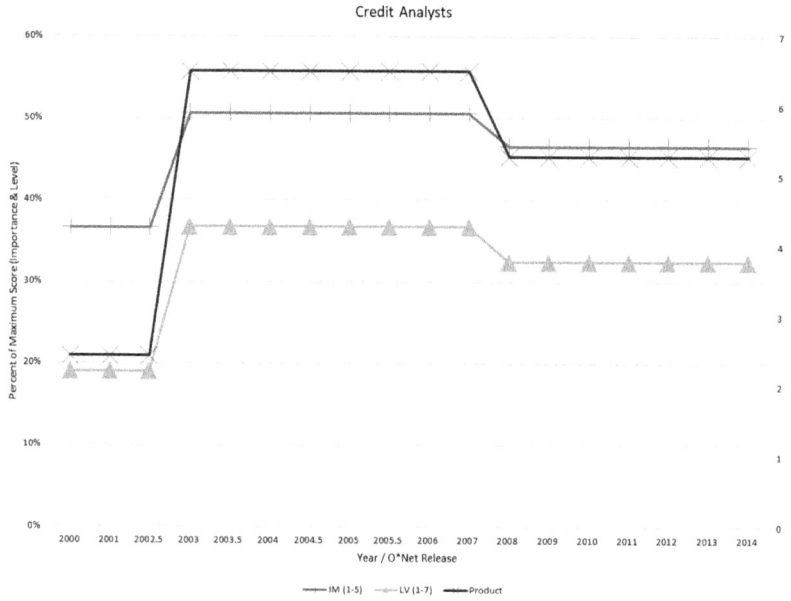

Figure 3.26: Credit analysis B.
Source: Author.

AUGMENTED INTELLIGENCE | 89

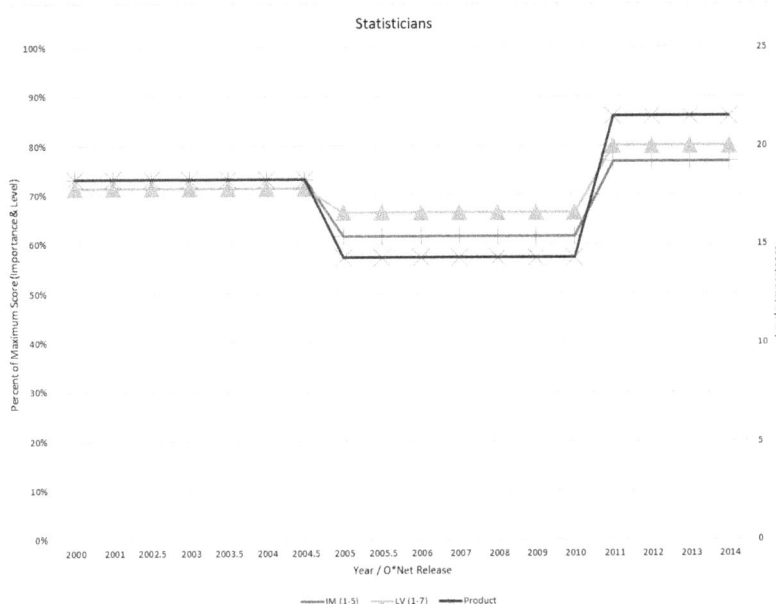

Figure 3.27: Statisticians B.
Source: Author.

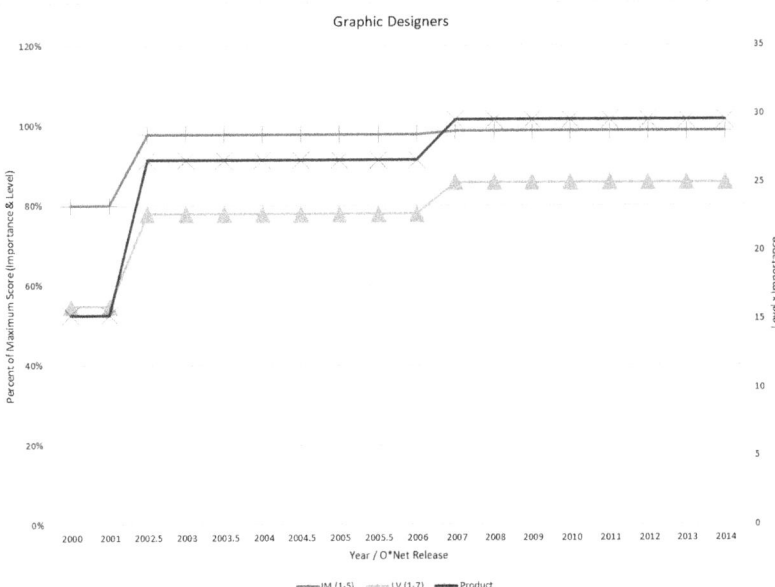

Figure 3.28: Graphic designers.
Source: Author.

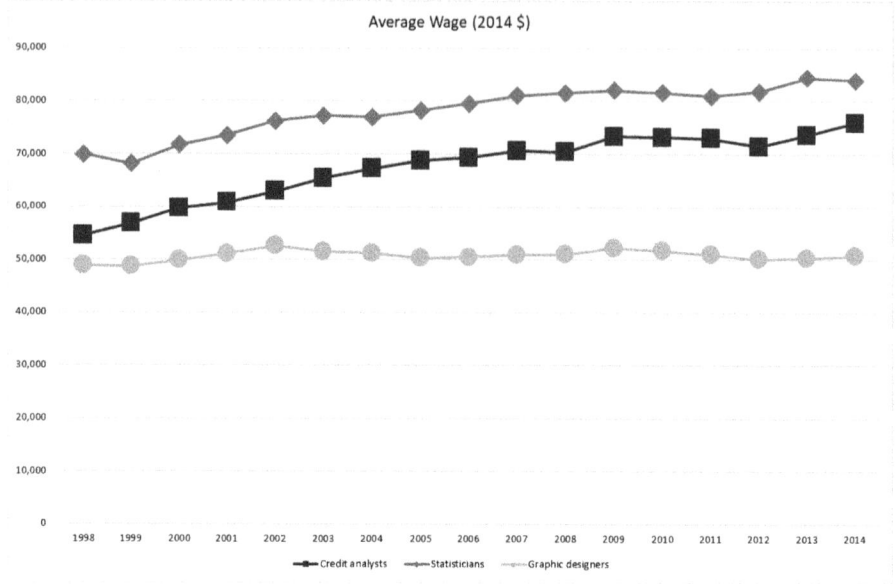

Figure 3.29: Average wage (2014 $) B.
Source: Author.

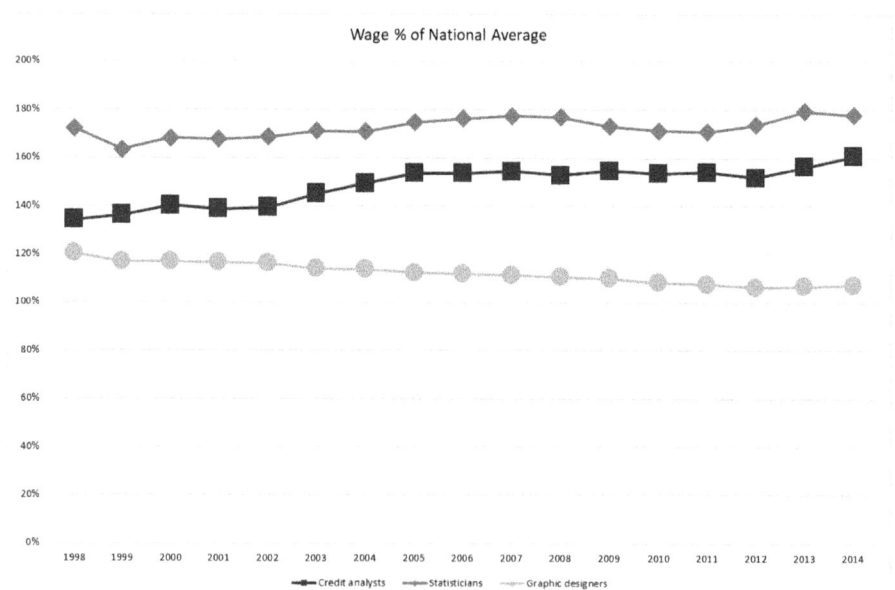

Figure 3.30: Wage % of national average B.
Source: Author.

This overlaps a broad economic shift rooted in the capacities of technology to augment certain kinds of work. But as this study concludes, technology is not the whole story. Even as wages have remained flat, the lion's share of wealth generated over the past three decades has accrued to a very small elite. One hypothesis is that the commoditization of creativity and a glut of labor supply are together driving down wages. In other words, if a given occupation is deemed "creative," workers earn a higher salary. If an occupation is not, workers earn a lower salary. If creative work and concomitant wages are seen as a binary, then the value given to elite creative work over commoditized labor is producing new tiers within a postindustrial creative economy (Florida, 2002).

In this sense, creativity as a substantial force of social and economic transformation is also characteristic of a new class structure. In fact, one could argue that a proletarian creative class is emerging as a kind of commoditized labor. While on the one hand, we are seeing the rise in importance of creative work, on the other hand, this creative labor is being met by downward pressure all the way through the postindustrial value chain. This translates as an increasingly precarious labor force in the form of the so-called "precariat" (Standing, 2014). This may help to explain some of the wage differentials occurring across the U.S. labor force.

Even as creativity and innovation are perhaps the only factors of production that cannot easily be programmed or automated, widening inequality within the US labor force suggests that not all creative labor is treated equally. Indeed, the more creative work is needed, the less it may be actually valued. Without a more nuanced appreciation of the value of creativity that a worker brings to his or her job—and a variation in wages based on a variation in creativity, the more likely we are to continue seeing this trend in future studies.

The most consistent policy response to growing inequality within OECD[5] countries has been to focus on educational reform. Education is largely viewed as key to developing human capital and thereby expanding economic growth. But where human capital theory offers value to educational reform in the short term, it may offer less value to rethinking education systems over the long term. Postindustrial societies would be wise to construct policies that adapt creative labor to accelerating computationally driven automation systems while being careful to mitigate ongoing efforts to reduce (creative) workers to basic labor.

One area for further research is the impact of technology in this commoditization of creative work. Brown et al. (2012), for example, describe this commoditization in terms of "digital Taylorism." That is, the use of technology for rapidly translating creativity and innovation into routine commercial practices. Like industrial Taylorism, technology is accelerating productivity for the purposes of advancing efficiency and reducing costs. Unlike simple mechanical Taylorism, however, digital technologies are also enabling the extraction and codification of creativity in new ways.

Nonetheless, our research suggests that there remains significant opportunity for professional work across a range of creative occupations, particularly work that overlaps entrepreneurial innovation. Regardless of technological automation or class-based polarization in the labor force, it would seem likely that the value of creative work will increase as digital technologies become a more predominant feature of work. The reason for this is that creative occupations are the least susceptible to automation because of the current limitations of information technologies. In this sense, we believe that social and economic policies supporting creativity are the best strategic resources for managing against underemployment. This interpretation is supported by research from the British think tank Nesta (Bakhshi et al., 2015), as well. In their view, policies supporting creative work remain the only long-term solution for mitigating technological automation.

Conclusion: Creative Work and Augmented Intelligence

What is the future of work and learning in the age of machine intelligence? Is technology enabling newer and more creative forms of labor or is it simply subsuming human labor entirely? What this study suggests is that even as knowledge-based economies adapt to a "Machine Age," creativity remains fundamental to work across industries (Araya & Peters, 2010; Chiu, 2012). Put differently, even as the capacity of computers to replicate tasks that are well defined is high, the capacity of computers for creativity and innovation remains low.

The data show that the usage of computers in occupations has increased over time, and the level of usage and importance of computers to jobs are strongly related. Both are also strongly related to wages. Yet, the degree of automation is still not that high in the U.S. labor market. While automation may be happening, it is not showing up in current occupational data.

At the same time, creativity as an important job-based factor is also on the rise and is related to wages. But, class-based occupational structures are significantly impacting the value of creative work. Put simply, not all creative labor is valued equally. What is obvious is that differences in the class of an occupation are driving salary increases in some professions and not others. Rather than ignoring these problems, researchers and policymakers will need to consider the design of effective policies and practices to mitigate ongoing labor stratification (Brynjolfsson & McAfee, 2011; Araya, 2014). This suggests the need for bold policy experiments that leverage technology in concert with education and training systems that support creative work and learning with a specific focus on the underlying class of workers.

Note about the data

For the O*Net data, the database has official releases and then updates. When there was an update in a given year, only the update was used. So there is a release 5.0 and a 5.1—only 5.1 was used. The date used in this analysis is the date up one year from the release data. So, for example, O*Net 5.0 was released on 4/1/2003 and 5.1 on 11/1/2003. I only used the 5.1 release and said it was for the year 2002.5. 5.0 was the 2002 data. Given the processing time for these, that makes the most sense. So, given this, 18 O*Net databases were used (3.1 to 20.0). And, there is no 2.0, and 1.0, which is called O*Net 98—was redone to become 3.0, updated as 3.1. The upshot of all this is that for O*Net data, we start with 3.1 (released in 2001 but using 2000 data) and go to 20.0 (released in 2015 but for 2014 data). It ends up being 18 O*Net releases covering 2000–2014 (so there are some years with multiples. Each release is only included once.

Notes

1. The OES employment numbers have some issues for this group and do not seem to be counted properly. It looks like there is probably another in 2008 (Phoenix seems to have too many—they didn't report a number for 2009 so there were clearly problems, but Phoenix was one of the metros that consistently had both fairly high shares and total numbers).
2. It has not changed since 2002.
3. Note that not every occupation is reevaluated with every release of the database so some of the consistency is artificial, as scores are not updated. Generally, scores are updated every 3–5 years.
4. Again, recognizing that O*Net scores are only being updated every 3–5 years or so.
5. Organization for Economic Cooperation and Development.

References

Araya, D. (2014). *Rethinking US education policy*. New York, NY: Palgrave.
Araya, D., & Peters, M. (2010). *Education in the creative economy: Knowledge and learning in the age of innovation*. New York, NY: Peter Lang.
Autor, D. (2014). Polanyi's paradox and the shape of employment growth. NBER Working Paper No. 20485. Retrieved from http://www.nber.org/papers/w20485
Bakhshi, H., Frey, C. B., & Osborne, M. (2015). Creativity vs. robots: The creative economy and the future of employment. Nesta.
Beniger, J. R. (1986). *The control revolution: Technological and economic origins of the information society*. Cambridge, MA: Harvard University Press.
Bereiter, C. (2002). *Education and mind in the knowledge age*. Mahwah, NJ: Lawrence Erlbaum Associates.

Brown, P, Lauder, H., & Ashton, D. (2012). *The global auction: The broken promises of education, jobs, and incomes.* New York, NY: Oxford.

Brynjolfsson, E., & McAfee, A. (2011). *Race against the machine: How the digital revolution is accelerating innovation, driving productivity, and irreversibly transforming employment and the economy.* New York, NY: Digital Frontier Press.

Brynjolfsson, E., & McAfee, A. (2014). *The second machine age: Work, progress, and prosperity in a time of brilliant technologies.* New York, NY: W. W. Norton & Company.

Bureau of Labor Statistics. (2014, June 9). Labor force statistics from the current population survey. Retrieved from http://data.bls.gov/timeseries/LNU01300000

Chiu, R. (2012). *Entrepreneurship education in the Nordic countries: Strategy implementation and good practice.* Oslo: Nordic Innovation Publication.

Christensen, C. M. (1997). *The innovator's dilemma: When new technologies cause great firms to fail.* Boston, MA: Harvard Business School Press.

Drucker, P. (1969). *The age of discontinuity: Guidelines to our changing society.* New York, NY: Harper & Row.

Economist. (2014). Coming to an office near you: The effect of today's technology on tomorrow's jobs will be immense—and no country is ready for it. Retrieved from http://www.economist.com/news/leaders/21594298-effect-todays-technology-tomorrows-jobs-will-be-immenseand-no-country-ready

Englebart, D.C. (1962). *Augmenting human intellect: A conceptual framework.* Summary Report AFOSR-3233. Menlo Park, CA: Stanford Research Institute.

Florida, R. (2002). *The rise of the creative class: And how it's transforming work, leisure, community and everyday life.* New York, NY: Basic Books.

Frey, C. B., & Osborne, M. A. (2013). The future of employment: How susceptible are jobs to computerisation? Retrieved from http://www.futuretech.ox.ac.uk/sites/futuretech.ox.ac.uk/files/The_Future_of_Employment_OMS_Working_Paper_1.pdf

Kenworthy, L. (2014). America's social democratic future: The arc of policy is long but bends toward justice. *Foreign Affairs, 93*(1), 86–100.

McAfee, A., & Brynjolfsson, E. (2016). Human work in the robotic future. *Foreign Affairs.* Retrieved from https://www.foreignaffairs.com/articles/2016-06-13/human-work-robotic-future

Moravec, H. (1988). *Mind children: The future of robot and human intelligence.* Cambridge, MA: Harvard.

OECD. (2013). *OECD skills outlook 2013: First results from the survey of adult skills.* Paris: Author. Retrieved from http://skills.oecd.org/documents/OECD_Skills_Outlook_2013.pdf

Schumpeter, J. (1976 [1942]). *Capitalism, socialism and democracy.* New York, NY: Harper & Row.

Standing, G. (2014). *The precariat: The new dangerous class.* New York, NY: Bloomsbury.

Zuboff, S. (1988). *In the age of the smart machine: The future of work and power.* New York, NY: Basic Books.

CHAPTER FOUR

This Is Your Brain on Code

Embodied Intelligence Augmentation and the Evolution of Conflict

RODRIGO NIETO-GÓMEZ

Introduction

> Computers are like bicycles for the mind.
> —Steve Jobs

Within the mythology of digital innovation, the opening epigraph of this chapter has become an axiom about the power of computing technologies as augmentation devices. Like many axioms, it is in reality a paraphrase that our collective intelligence has simplified to represent an important idea with more eloquence than its original formulation. But in this case some of the context lost from that original formulation matters. This is what Steve Jobs said in 1980, at the dawn of the Personal Computer era to define computers as cognitive augmentation devices:

> Scientific American, I think it was, did a study in the early seventies on the efficiency of locomotion. What they did was for all different species of things on the planet, birds and cats and dogs and fish and men and goats and stuff, they measured how much energy does it take for a goat to get from here to there, right?, ... and the condor [...] took the least amount of energy to go from here to there, and men didn't do so well, it came out with a rather unimpressive showing about a third of the way down the list. But fortunately, someone at Scientific American was insightful enough to test men with a bicycle, and men with a bicycle won, twice as good as the condor all the way up

the list. What it showed was that man as a tool maker has the ability to make a tool to amplify an inherent ability that he has … in general what we are doing is that we are building tools that amplify a human ability. (Steve Jobs rare footage 1980, 2011)

This Silicon Valley-esque explanation of technological augmentation is important because it matches almost perfectly to what armed forces call "force multipliers": "A capability that, when added to and employed by a combat force, significantly increases the combat potential of that force and thus enhances the probability of successful mission accomplishment" (DoD, 2007). This similarity makes transparent the relationship between these "bicycles for the mind" and conflict.

From the prehistoric spear to the thermonuclear bomb, human conflict can be framed as a constant toolmaking process to augment the force of the parties involved. As new tools are invented, new sources of tension emerge: An army using bicycles moves faster than an opposing army without bicycles. Human conflict has been a constant race to create better and more lethal multipliers for our muscles and, when those multipliers find their way into civilian use, they have also changed society in unforeseeable ways.

Through the study of two very different innovations: First, a ballistic weapon system that commoditized an important fighting skill and, second, a brain–computer interface that modifies the original blueprint of the *Homo sapiens*, this chapter explores how the emergence of a specific kind of augmentation that I call embodied intelligence augmentation accelerates and reshapes human conflict.

As the progressive embodiment of intelligence augmentation technologies advances, the pain points produced by them also multiply. Some of those conflicts are easy to nowcast as they are already visible if we know where to look. I will concentrate on those. Others will be surprising, unpredictable, and, therefore, very different to anything described on in this chapter.

The goal of this analysis is not to trigger precautionary-principle fears against embodied intelligence augmentation. On the contrary; like the canary in a coalmine, by explicitly analyzing two visible conflicts derived from the very early stages of embodied augmentation, we will develop the foundation for a framework to understand the challenges and inform regulatory actors so that we might move beyond the hype and beyond the fear.

Embodied Intelligence Augmentation, Explained

Force multiplication is the main reason why humans build tools. Through cognitive superiority and the dexterity that came initially from having an opposable thumb, humankind increased its capabilities to perform tasks well beyond its biological limits. With these tools, we live healthier lives, we move faster and farther and we produce abundance where the natural state of things (i.e., the nonforce-multiplied state of things) would be scarcity.

Whereas the heavy machines of the industrial revolution multiplied the force of our muscles (bicycles for our legs), the computer revolution has multiplied our intellectual abilities beyond our biological limitations: intelligence augmentation or bicycles for our minds.

To be clear, intelligence augmentation does not presuppose (although it does not preclude either) a merger between man and machine. The smartphone that defines the computer experience of the first two decades of the 21st century is already an intelligence augmentation device that we carry in our pockets.

In fact, Doug Engelbart, the father of augmentation research, described the process of augmentation in terms of developing the right Human–Computer Interfaces and the organizational processes for humans to leverage those computing artifacts in order to solve complex situations in the context of the office space.

He identified four means to augmentation: Artifacts, Language, Methods, and Training. A well-trained human with good methods, an appropriate language and the right computer artifact is, for Engelbart, an augmented human (Engelbart, 1962). This is as true at the office as on the battlefield.

Your knowledge of spelling and grammar has been augmented by a spell checker; your math skills have been augmented by Excel, and your sense of orientation augmented by Waze. Equally important, collaborative tools like Slack or Google docs have likely already augmented the collective intelligence of your organization.

As the first example will demonstrate, cognitive skills useful in violent conflict can also be multiplied by a mix of artifacts, language methods, and training: marksmanship, situational awareness, or survival capabilities are a few examples of these skills.

This first generation of augmentation technologies was the "desktop" version of augmentation. Thanks to the constant improvement of computational capacity and interface development, augmented intelligence technologies are now moving beyond that first generation of desktop augmentation, originally showcased by Engelbart in 1968 during his famous "mother of all demos" (Engelbart, 1968). The second generation of augmentation technologies is different because of a constant push toward a closer coupling with the human body that Frank Biocca calls "progressive embodiment."

For Biocca, progressive embodiment is "a steadily advancing immersion of sensorimotor channels to computer interfaces through a tighter and more pervasive coupling of the body to interface sensors and displays" (Biocca, 1997).

This progressive embodiment of the human relation with certain force multipliers brings intelligence augmentation closer to a "cyborg" status. Whereas Engelbartian augmentation has already taken place and we have been living in a digitally augmented civilization for decades, cyborg-like augmentation is still in its infancy, but well on its way. Smartphones, wearables, cochlear and neural implants, brain interfaces, and augmented reality displays are all steps toward a closer embodiment of the interface with the human body, blurring the dividing line between the two.

Case 1.—The Transhuman Sicario

> NEO: Can you fly that thing?
> TRINITY: Not yet.
> She pulls out a cellular phone.
> INT. HOVERCRAFT—Tank is back at the controls.
> TANK: Operator.
> TRINITY (V.O.): Tank, I need a pilot program for a military M-109 helicopter.[1]
> Tank is immediately searching the disk drawers.
> TRINITY (V.O.): Hurry!
> His fingers flash over the gleaming laser disks, finding one that he feeds into Trinity supplement drive, punching the "load" commands on her keyboard.
> EXT. ROOF (MATRIX)—DAY—Trinity's eyes flutter as information surges into her brain, all the essentials of flying a helicopter absorbed at light-speed.
> TRINITY: Let's go.
> —Original Matrix Script ("The Original Matrix Script, part 27," n.d.)

You cannot download a marksmanship program to your "supplement drive" to become a perfect sharpshooter (yet), but you do not need to. TrackingPoint, a gun manufacturing startup, introduced in 2015 the first generation of precision-guided firearms with what the company calls "RapidLok"™. A system that auto locks onto the target and "snaps" to it. The computer assisted tracking device "paints" an augmented reality dot to the center of mass in the scope's digital display and by connecting the tracking system to the trigger, the computer, not the human, releases the trigger at the right time, independently of any involuntary movement by the marksman or the target. Just like in the Matrix, this augmentation technology eliminates human error at the moment of the shot.

The task left to the human is to first select and "paint" the target and second, align the crosshairs with the painted dot. The computer will wait until the ideal conditions are present, and release a perfect shot.

TrackingPoint's marketing materials proudly state how, thanks to their technology, "You can make shoots that used to be humanly impossible." (TrackingPoint

Precision Guided Semi-Auto Series, 2014). This marketing tagline represents perfectly the concept of embodied intelligence augmentation: With intelligence augmentation, you can do things that used to be humanly impossible. Because of progressive embodiment, you can do them at the firing range or on the battlefield.

Precision-guided guns like those designed by TrackingPoint are not an incremental improvement of current scopes. Instead, they represent a new kind of augmented intelligence shooting system that multiplies the capacity to perform a task well beyond humankind's cognitive limits. They are a new step within the embodied augmentation process where laser rangefinders, ballistic computers, inertial measurement systems, wifi antennas, gyroscopes, and accelerometers are encased within the weapon system to enhance the intelligence of the human/machine system.

Guns themselves are an interesting kind of "wearable" force multiplier. They are the result of a technological process that begun in the 13th century, with the miniaturization of big artillery cannons to create the category of hand-held ballistic weapons. As a consequence of this incremental innovation process, humans became capable of embodying technology in their belt holsters that multiply the force and lethality of what they can propel with their hands.

Now, computer technologies are not multiplying the force of those ballistic projectiles, but the accuracy of the shooter, transforming perfect marksmanship from an ability that has to be learned, to a commodity that can be bought. This commoditization of a key cognitive skill of military forces opens the door to a singular kind of augmentation conflict. While I will use the context of the war on drugs as a point of reference, the same issues are valid wherever there is an ongoing violent armed conflict, especially against asymmetric adversaries with poor training capabilities.

The hitmen of Mexican and Colombian drug cartels receive the name of sicarios. They are the enforcement arm of the criminal mafias, and the cartels depend on them to project power against other cartels and against governments. Although always brutal on their use of force, the performance of sicarios is very irregular.

Like military forces, they too depend on force multipliers to increase the probability of accomplishing their missions, and if they have almost unlimited access to some force multiplication capabilities like heavy weapons (assault rifles, machine guns, mortars and even rocket propelled grenades), other elements of force multiplication, like effective training, have been more difficult to obtain.

A key element of military training is fire weapon operation and marksmanship. TrackingPoint technology is a kind of embodied intelligence augmentation that erases this key cognitive advantage that currently tilts the balance of power in favor of well trained military forces. An augmented sicario, that is, a sicario using precision-guided firearms, versus a nonaugmented American Navy Seal, has a more level playing field. Furthermore, as the market develops, precision-guided firearms will improve exponentially (we have seen that happening for other precision targeting systems, like those of fighter jets) while the human brain and human training will not.

Tradable resources cannot be the source of a competitive advantage as any competitor can purchase them too. Therefore, as the diffusion of precision guided firearms progresses, marksmanship will become irrelevant or at least less important as a cognitive advantage.

Also, with new technological affordances come new vulnerabilities. As weapons become intelligent, the capacity to influence, jam or alter the human–computer interaction becomes a target for adversaries.

During the 2015 DefCon conference, Runa Sandvik and Michael Auger demonstrated how to "root" any Trackingpoint rifle wirelessly, without any previous access to the weapon (*DEF CON 23—Runa Sandvik, Michael Auger—Hacking a Linux-Powered Rifle*, 2015). Once hacked, the system could be jammed, or the target altered, making the sharpshooter hit a different target.

On the one hand, embodied intelligence augmentation has improved the capacity of any human being to perform the cognitive task of long-range shooting with transhuman accuracy, transcending the limitations of the human body. An augmented sicario of the Juarez cartel (or a group of them) will therefore have a meaningful competitive advantage against other sicarios without augmentation, and against American law enforcement and military forces despite their superior training, but nonaugmented sicarios or law enforcement agencies may buy the same augmentation technology, leveling the playing field.

On the other hand, this new kind of embodied intelligence has created a new set of vulnerabilities associated with the potential gains that can be obtained by interrupting the interaction between the human and the augmentation technology. Perfect marksmanship can now be hacked.

Not unlike the first generation of desktop intelligence augmentation, embodied intelligence augmentation displaces the center of gravity of conflict from the linear natural limits of the human biology and training, to the exponential cycles of computer software and hardware development and information assurance.

The future special forces team to be deployed to capture the criminal mastermind of the 2030s will need to have a technology mix and a concept of operations to use that technology that will be radically different to those employed to capture el Chapo Guzman (again) in 2015. Every sicario defending this future Capo could be a transhuman shooter, as they will be capable of shooting accuracy that, to paraphrase TrackingPoint's own marketing materials, will go beyond of what it used to be "humanly possible."

However, those transhuman sicarios will be hackable, and the more they embody and need augmentation technologies, the more those vulnerabilities will be a critical risk to their success.

Case 2.—Hacking Umwelts One Cochlear Implant at a Time

Floating in CerebroSpinal Fluid, your consciousness resides inside the darkness of your skull, experiencing a virtual reality (VR) world. Your brain is attached to a series of wired bioreceptors (your senses) that feed your mind with data that is then processed in real time in order to construct the environment you perceive. Being intelligent is, at least in part, to be able to process those signals and make sense of the world to influence it in a deliberate fashion (Deary, 2000).

You think you "see" the "real" world through your eyes, but your visual sensors only capture a small selection of the light that is present (missing everything infrared or ultraviolet). In fact, you do not even "see" reality "as is." Instead, from two separate, limited, and inverted signals coming from each eye, your visual cortex artificially constructs your visual environment in one of the most complex high order functions your brain can perform. The world you see, or for that matter, the one you touch, smell, hear, or feel, is the synthetic result of complex calculations performed by your brain, using a discrete selection of signals that are only a small subset of the available data. Eagleman gives a name to this small sample of data we call reality: The Umwelt (German for environment). This is how he defines it: "the small subset of the world that an animal *[you]* is able to detect is its umwelt. The bigger reality, whatever that might mean, is called the umgebung" (German for surrounding) (Eagleman, 2015).

You already live inside of a kind of organic "Matrix" as your umwelt is only a virtual abstraction of the total umgebung, uploaded to your consciousness through living receptors wired directly to your brain and bounded by what those receptors can perceive. Interacting with that abstraction and transforming it are high order cognitive functions that can be technologically augmented.

Such umwelt augmentation has important social implications because we experience the world through our senses and, therefore, cultural norms, and identities are sensorial in nature: Language, music, dance, cinema, cuisine, literature, to cite some examples, are all experienced through one or multiple sensorial receptors. Because of this, our culture, our sense of belonging, our social intelligence, and our individual and social identities are all umwelt dependent.

As these and many other key cognitive abilities are dependent on how the umwelt is constructed, changes in sensorial capacities through umwelt expansion are another important path for embodied intelligence augmentation taking place through the research and development of Brain–Computer Interfaces.

This is a path to cognitive amplification that triggers alterity challenges and conflict, as I will now explain using the example of the first truly mainstream Brain–Computer Interface: the cochlear implant.

Thus far, the only way for your consciousness to perceive the world, the only inputs for your carbon-based brain/computer, have been the biological receptors given to us by evolution. The development of the cochlear implant is the first Brain–Computer technology to successfully change this, although other technologies with similar objectives are in different stages of development.

Cochlear implants are the most commercially successful Brain–Computer Interface for sensorial embodied augmentation. While

> humankind has been devising ways to aid the senses for centuries (eye-glasses date back to about 1300), … the cochlear implant represents the first device that actually replaces sensory receptors in the human body. … A cochlear implant is not a hearing aid. Not even a really, really good hearing aid. Devices like hearing aids and eyeglasses can only enhance or augment a sense organ. A cochlear implant actually replaces the cochlea, the magnificent organ in the inner ear where "hearing" really takes place and where the mechanical energy in sound waves is finally transformed into electric signals. (Henshaw, 2012, p. 7)

It may be surprising to read, but we actually have more than 5 senses because the organs that create our umwelt have multiple receptors. We have different ways of "touching" (i.e., temperature perception, vs pressure perception) and we also "see" the world with different light receptors (i.e., rods for night vision vs cones for day vision). Furthermore, humans perceive direction and movement through the vestibular sense and this sense of equilibrium is created by an organ different from the nose, tongue, eyes, skin, or the auditive part of the ears. The vestibular labyrinthine, while located in the inner ear, is as different from the auditive ear as the nose is from the eyes, even though eyes and ears are located in the same area of the face.

After analyzing many of the different receptors contained in the human body, Henshaw (2012, p. 9) identified a total of nine different senses: vision, hearing, smell, taste, touch, balance, temperature, proprioception (body awareness), and pain. Any of those senses is a potential candidate for the progressive embodiment of augmentation technologies (or, in the case of pain, deliberate suppression) by Brain–Computer Interfaces and other senses not on the list, like electroreception (perceiving electric currents) or a biosonar could be equally developed using artificial sensorial organs (Jebari, 2014).

The objective of that augmentation would be to either increase sensorial range or to create a new channel to perceive an expanded umwelt. Any of our current biological senses have a limited range of performance or, in technology terms, senses have "specifications" (or "specs") that define the boundaries of the human umwelt. For example, human ears and wolf ears have different specs, human eyes do not have the depth perception of the eagles' eyes, nor does human skin conducts information like the skin of an electric eel. Thus far, this range of performance has been a fixed value, but Brain–Computer Interfaces are making it possible to change that.

The biological senses also have a spatial limit. That is, perception using those receptors is limited by their physical position relative to the source of data. Therefore, the human umwelt is not only limited by the specs of the receptors, but also by their location. Because the sensors travel with our brains on the same vessel, our artificially constructed umwelt is limited in the same way reach is limited by the length of the arm.

Even the tools that allow humans to see or hear things happening far away are restricted by this spatial limitation. While a television or a VR headset are force multipliers that afford a person to see things happening far from her location, these devices still interact locally with the biological eyes and they do not replace them (they are like hearing aids, not like cochlear implants). The brain still receives the signal from the eyes, even when using an Oculus Rift to immerse ourselves on a VR environment. Those signals are still generated close to the eyes for the eyes, even if they display events far away and out of our line of sight.

While there is some degree of differentiation between specs among different individuals (e.g., some people have better sight or better hearing than others), most human beings use the same channels to create their umwelt. The exception to this rule are those individuals that, due to accident or illness, lack one or more of those channels and therefore learn about the world through a different kind of umwelt.[2]

Until the development of the first Brain–Computer Interfaces, if one of those sensors was missing there was little we could do to restore the missing functionality. Consequently, people with a missing or impaired sense adapted to the lack of an input channel by developing alternative ways to interface with a human world built mostly for people with an umwelt different to theirs. As part of that adaptation, people with disabilities have evolved a series of communities and cultures based in no small part on the shared understanding of a "minority umwelt."

Deaf culture (with capital D) is an example of these cultures that unite individuals with a "minority" umwelt. The World Federation of the Deaf define Deaf culture in the following way: "Deaf people as a linguistic minority have a common experience of life, and this manifests itself in Deaf culture. This includes beliefs, attitudes, history, norms, values, literary traditions and art shared by Deaf people" ("Deaf culture," n.d.)

The development of the cochlear implant, a kind of embodied augmentation technology, has triggered the first (but certainly not the last) cultural identity conflict based on the capacity of a bionic technology to augment the amount of umwelt channels, affecting cognitive experiences.

As this neuroprosthetic created the medical capacity to restore a channel through the use of a permanently embodied computer, some Deaf culture advocates decided to oppose it on the basis of a kind of bioidentity struggle:

> Deaf culture advocates, …, are strongly opposed to research geared at "curing" deafness and are particularly opposed to placing cochlear implants in children. They assert that members of their minority group "are in no more need of a cure for their condition than are Haitians or Hispanics." To many members of the Deaf cultural community, cochlear implants represent "the ultimate denial of deafness, the ultimate refusal to let children be Deaf." (Tucker, 1998, p. 8)

This opposition is now a political movement. For example, business conferences to promote innovation on cochlear implant technologies often encounter protesters outside of the building (Ringo, 2013) like it happens during symposiums for other politically contested technologies.

The chirurgical umwelt augmentation of children who cannot hear is at the heart of the conflict:

Throughout the 1980s and the early 1990s, Deaf people mobilized to protest the use of cochlear implants. In particular, they objected to the choice being made on behalf of young children to insert the implant. These critics reject the very idea of trying to find a "cure" for deafness. Indeed they have compared it to genocide. They argue that deaf people should not be thought of as disabled but as members of a minority cultural group. (Sparrow, 2005, p. 135)

This conflict line is clear: On one side of the divide, cochlear implants are the most widely accepted, and so far, the most technologically successful form of biohacking. On the other side, Deaf culture groups are the first organized bioconservative opposition to umwelt augmentation based on the defense of a "natural" (i.e., nonaugmented) cultural bioidentity.

Cochlear implants are cyborg technologies in the original sense of the word. They represent the final step in a progressive embodiment process, coupling the human body and the interface, beyond immersion, merging them completely.

Children who lack that natural channel for sound will experience learning and cognition in irrevocably different ways if they embody a cochlear implant or if they do not. This cognitive asymmetry is at the core of the conflict that juxtaposes a bioconservative Deaf Culture stance against the chirurgical biohacking of children's sound sense through Cochlear augmentation. It is the first case of an identity conflict based on the bionic expansion of the human umwelt for cognitive reasons.

Although these embodied computers only reestablish a missing channel most people are born with, the bioidentity conflict they generated casts a light into the future of augmentation alterity and conflict.

For example, the Naida CI Q70 announced in 2013 by Advanced Bionics is a sound processor for cochlear implants that offers a series of improvements not only when compared to previous generation models, but also when compared to a biological human ear ("Advanced Bionics Announces FDA Approval of the Naída CI Q70 Sound Processor," 2013).

In particular, people using this embodied technology have gained the capacity to break the previously described spatial limitation of the biological senses because their bionic cochlea is bluetooth enabled and can experience digital sound independently of point of origin. As long as the bluetooth signal can reach the receptor, augmented cochlear users can hear the waves of the ocean in exactly same way if they are at the beach or if they are at the International Space Station. The listening experience would be exactly the same.

More practically, they can perform cognitive functions like enjoying music or conducting business over the phone without needing an extra device (i.e., earphones or a phone) as the digital sound is transmitted directly to their artificial cochlea.

What this means is short of magical:[3] Their augmented body can now perceive digital signals present in the umgebung that a biological ear cannot perceive.

Children and adults who embody this augmentation technology have not only recreated a channel similar to the biological ear, but they have gained a sensorial capability that is not available to those without the implant. Almost like a new sense, they can perceive digital sound sources without intermediation in ways a biological ear cannot: If the source of sound is a bluetooth signal, a person with a biological ear would be deaf and incapable of learning the content of that signal without an external prosthetic (i.e., a bluetooth receiver, plus some earphones), but a person that embodies a cochlear implant can receive and make sense of that signal like he or she would do for any other sound.

As Brain–Computer Interfaces and neuroprosthetics research advances, the opportunities for bioidentity conflict (including violent conflict and hate crimes) will expand as the progressive embodiment of intelligence augmentation technologies challenges perceptions of what a "normal" body can do, sense, learn about, or even look like.

People with embodied intelligence augmentation devices will perceive the world differently and will also learn to intervene in their environment using channels unavailable to nonaugmented individuals.

As a thought experiment, if you have a functioning biological ear, imagine being in a room with three people dancing to a music you cannot hear. The bluetooth signal is there, but you do not have the appropriate receptor to integrate it to your umwelt. You cannot follow the rhythm or learn the lyrics. The three dancers have a cochlear implant, so those digital signals are available to them but not to you. How does that make you feel?

Just like the bioconservative Deaf culture advocates react with defiance to the use of cochlear implants in children because biohacking their umwelt alters their membership to that minority culture, umwelt hacking will challenge the dominant human bioidentity in multiple and unforeseeable ways, as the specs of our biosensors start to seem limited when compared to other technological enhancements.

As direct communication is established between our biological brain and our augmentation technologies, humans, for the first time in the history of the species, will stop sharing a common umwelt. Because our cognitive abilities are, as demonstrated before, intertwined with our perception of reality, this may create a sense of otherness not only with respect to how other human beings look, but also with respect to how we experience our reality compared to them.

As some embrace embodied intelligence augmentation technologies and some do not, this unequal pace of adoption will create more opportunities for identity-based conflict.

Conclusion: Resistance Is Futile

> An athlete using this prosthetic blade has a demonstrable mechanical advantage (more than 30 percent) when compared to someone not using the blade [...] As a result, Oscar Pistorius is ineligible to compete in competitions organized under IAAF rules
> —INTERNATIONAL ASSOCIATION OF ATHLETICS FEDERATIONS (IAAF)

In 2008, Oscar Pistorius was banned from participating at the Olympic Games because his prosthetic legs were deemed as too good, giving him an unfair competitive advantage on the race track. While four years later the Olympic authorities reversed the ruling and allowed him to run the 400 meters (he placed last), the case of "Blade Runner," as Pistorius became known because of the kind of prosthetic legs he uses are called blades, is the first documented case of a ruling body (the IAAF) classifying an individual using a prosthetic technology as unfairly enhanced when compared to other human beings.

As a kind of force multipliers, the prosthetic blades belong to the same category of bicycles, but unlike bicycles, their level of embodiment makes them more than an optional accessory, but an essential component of a human/machine being.

Embodied intelligence augmentation technologies, like the ones described in this chapter, belong to the category of "bicycles for the mind," but they are more like Pistorius' blades than like bicycles. Without a bicycle, the owner still can go from point A to point B, albeit slower and using more energy. In contrast, even though TrackingPoint is not implanted in the human body, an untrained sniper could not perform superhuman gunshots at all, making the augmentation technology essential. This interdependence is even more evident in the case of the cochlear implant, as it is literally a part of the body of the wearer. In all these cases, the merger between the cognitive skills and the tool is so deep that without the technology, the person loses cognitive abilities.

As described in this chapter, intelligence augmentation can be achieved in multiple ways. Some may impact directly the way the brain functions by increasing IQ scores, some may provide better embodied interfaces to interact with artificial intelligences through augmented reality, and some others may increase the umwelt of individuals through artificial receptors, allowing them to interact and modify their environment in novel ways.

A consequence for all these cases is that a bioconservative opposition may well emerge to challenge the transhumanist advantage that the augmentation technologies provide. This is exactly what the Olympic committee has been doing for years, fighting against the technologically assisted enhancement of physical performance.

As Bartlett describes, "Technology is often described as 'neutral.' But it could be more accurately described as power and freedom. For the transhumanists, technology provides the ability to stride across the universe, to live forever. For the anarcho-primitivists, it is a tool used to oppress and control others, to become less than human" (Bartlett, 2015, p. 237). It does not matter which of these two groups is right (probably none is), what matters is that these sociological representations will determine their heuristics used to judge the adoption or rejection of augmentation technologies.

Embodied intelligence augmentation is the new battlefield for the culture wars to come. These culture wars will be and in fact are being translated into legislative advocacy and regulatory initiatives to fight for and against augmentation.

As we legislate about the progressive embodiment of intelligence augmentation technologies, we will be regulating more than electronic devices. In fact, this legislation will be regulating the bioidentity of humankind and intervening in alterity conflicts triggered by the desires of different people to embody these technologies at a different rate of adoption, or not embody them at all. It is not an exaggeration to say that given the impact of intelligence augmentation technologies in the expression of human consciousness, legislating about them is to legislate what it means to be human.

Today, we regulate digital technologies and biotechnology at different speeds. At the time of the publication of this chapter, governments regulate medical research aggressively, slowing innovation in the name of risk management, but code development is mostly unregulated. Nevertheless, in a world where embodied intelligence augmentation technologies can and are merging with the human body, the difference between hardware and software development and medical research is not as clear as it used to be, and this opens the door to interesting paradoxes: For example, a medical procedure to enhance a biological ear would be heavily regulated, but uploading new code to a cochlear implant or even replacing the sound processor to produce the same enhancement would not.

Equally, we regulate cognitive skill augmentation in very irregular ways. There is no active regulation in the United States, for example, to control the proliferation of precision guided weapon systems. Should this kind of code development be treated differently from other kinds of code?

Is it ethical to limit the proliferation of a cognitive skill? Is it a good idea to empower public agencies to decide what cognitive abilities can be legally acquired through augmentation?

Like all technologies, embodied intelligence augmentation follows some variant of the technology adoption cycle. There are the early adopters of the technology, and there are laggards who actively resist it (Rogers, 2010). Unlike other technologies, though, this uneven rate of adoption is producing human beings with different capacities to perceive and transform the environment in a process not unlike a kind of cyborg speciation.

As altered perception leads to different kinds of creative expression, new cultures will emerge that are completely dependent on specific kinds of umwelt perception.[4] The membership to these cultures will be singular because no human will be able to join them without embracing embodied augmentation.

While body modification has been used for millennia as a mechanism for identity formation and group membership, it affected only the body's appearance but did not provide any kind of cognitive advantage. With the progressive embodiment of intelligence augmentation technologies, humanity is now confronted by a behavior that not only modifies the aesthetics of the human body, but expands its cognitive abilities.

Even without an increase in IQ, expert systems coupled with embodied interfaces can have a dramatic impact on the performance of cognitive tasks.

The first retinal implants have been successfully installed ("Bionic eye implant world first—BBC News," n.d.). While the technology is still in its infancy, it already produces some magical consequences similar to those of the cochlear implant. People with retinal implants can perceive the world from an angle independent of the location of their eyes, or even with their eyes closed. They can, if they wish, have eyes in the back of their heads, or at the other side of the room. They can look at odd angles, or, combining the two cases presented in this chapter, they could have direct communication to a TrackingPoint rifle mounted remotely, turning them into lethal assassins with very little training needed.

Will we be asking those augmented individuals to "check their microchips at the door" when applying for a job, taking any kind of test (e.g., a plumbing or driver's license) or when entering a government building? What if augmentation cannot be unplugged?

Will we protect the bioidentity of the unenhanced human body through legislation by limiting who can legally get a sensorial or neural implant?

Will the use of implants by individuals who have access to all the biological channels of the human umwelt be considered to be a cosmetic surgery?

If two individuals are applying to the same job and one uses augmented technologies that give her a demonstrable advantage, is it discriminatory to give the job to the enhanced person?

Is hacking a cochlear or a retinal implant a cybercrime or a biocrime?

We are rapidly moving from a world in which the use of prosthetics has been a handicap, to a world in which embodied intelligence augmentation technologies can provide a competitive advantage and the potential for triggering identity conflicts.

The proliferation of augmentation technologies cannot be stopped because it progressive embodiment is not an independent phenomena, but an intrinsic component of interface development.

Embodied augmentation technologies are not bicycles for the mind. Instead, they are more like the prosthetic blades that provide demonstrable cognitive advantages to the individuals who by choice or necessity (or even by the choice made by others, as is often the case with children using cochlear implants), merge their biological self with a synthetic technology. They provide skills that alter the balance of power between adversaries, and they produce a sense of otherness that creates conflict among those who use them and those who do not. With many of those technologies in the advanced stages of development, it is not too early to proactively identify solutions to the conflicts produced by embodied intelligence augmentation.

Notes

1. For the cyberpunk geeks (like myself) or the aviation enthusiasts (like myself, again), in the movie the scene was changed. Instead of a M-109, Trinity flies a B-212 helicopter.
2. There is another exception: some people born with a genetic mutation may actually possess an augmented umwelt when compared to others. Tetrachromats, for example, are individuals born with a fourth visual receptor that allows their eyes to perceive 100 times more colors than a common human eye. Compared to them, the average human being is color blind (Jameson, Highnote, & Wasserman, 2001).
3. Arthur C. Clarke famously said that "any sufficiently advanced technology is indistinguishable from magic."
4. Electroreception: https://en.wikipedia.org/wiki/The_Secret_Sense.

References

Advanced Bionics Announces FDA Approval of the Naída CI Q70 Sound Processor. (2013, August 28). Retrieved April 12, 2016 from http://www.advancedbionics.com/com/en/system/footer/about_us/corporate_news/2013/naida_us.html

Bartlett, J. (2015). *The dark net: Inside the digital underworld*. Melville House.

Biocca, F. (1997). The Cyborg's dilemma: Progressive embodiment in virtual environments. *Journal of Computer-Mediated Communication, 3*(2).

Bionic eye implant world first—BBC News. (n.d.). Retrieved April 17, 2016 from http://www.bbc.com/news/health-33571412

Deaf culture. (n.d.). Retrieved April 12, 2016 from http://wfdeaf.org/our-work/focus-areas/deaf-culture

Deary, I. J. (2000). Simple information processing and intelligence. In R. Sternberg (Ed.), *Handbook of intelligence* (pp. 267–284). Cambridge: Cambridge University Press.

DEF CON 23—Runa Sandvik, Michael Auger—Hacking a Linux-Powered Rifle. (2015). Retrieved from https://www.youtube.com/watch?v=PEpuEprQ5VU

DoD. (2007). Joint Special Operations Task Force Operations (Version Joint Publication 3–05.1). Department of Defense. Retrieved from https://fas.org/irp/doddir/dod/jp3_05_01.pdf

Eagleman, D. (2015). The umwelt. Retrieved February 2, 2016 from http://www.eagleman.com/blog/umwelt

Engelbart, D. (1962). Augmenting human intellect: A conceptual framework. Stanford Research Institute. Retrieved from http://www.dougengelbart.org/pubs/augment-3906.html

Engelbart, D. (1968). The mother of all demos. USA. Retrieved from https://www.youtube.com/watch?v=yJDv-zdhzMY

Henshaw, J. M. (2012). *A tour of the senses: How your brain interprets the world*. Baltimore, MD: JHU Press.

Jameson, K. A., Highnote, S. M., & Wasserman, L. M. (2001). Richer color experience in observers with multiple photopigment opsin genes. *Psychonomic Bulletin & Review, 8*(2), 244–261.

Jebari, K. (2014). Sensory enhancement. In J. Clausen & N. Levy (Eds.), *Handbook of neuroethics* (pp. 827–838). London: Springer.
Ringo, A. (2013, August 9). Understanding deafness: Not everyone wants to be "fixed." Retrieved April 12, 2016 from http://www.theatlantic.com/health/archive/2013/08/understanding-deafness/278527/
Rogers, E. M. (2010). *Diffusion of innovations* (4th ed.). New York, NY: Simon and Schuster.
Sparrow, R. (2005). Defending deaf culture: The case of cochlear implants*. *The Journal of Political Philosophy, 13*(2), 135–152.
Steve Jobs rare footage 1980. (2011). Retrieved from https://www.youtube.com/watch?v=0lvMgMrNDlg
The Original Matrix Script, part 27. (n.d.). Retrieved January 29, 2016 from http://thematrixtruth.remoteviewinglight.com/html/original-matrix-script-27.html
TrackingPoint Precision Guided Semi-Auto Series. (2014). Retrieved from https://www.youtube.com/watch?v=Pmteh_NChOQ
Tucker, B. P. (1998). Deaf culture, cochlear implants, and elective disability. *The Hastings Center Report, 28*(4), 6–14.

CHAPTER FIVE

Intelligence Augmentation

Uploading Brain into Computer: Who First?

YANA B. FEYGIN, KELLY MORRIS, AND ROMAN V. YAMPOLSKIY

Introduction

As we write this chapter there are teams of researchers around the world working toward the creation of a "Brain Simulation Platform," that is, software that will map the human brain, down to a minute level of detail (see https://www.humanbrainproject.eu). This kind of research has incredible implications for many scientific fields of study. Indeed, the completion of these projects will also represent the completion of the first two criteria set forth by Anders Sandberg and Nick Bostrom in their paper "Whole Brain Emulation: A Roadmap" (Sandberg & Bostrom, 2008), which would imply that we will be well on our way toward our first functional brain emulation. With the likely achievement of, at least a simplistic version, of whole brain emulation, we must begin to consider some implications for the future. The goal of whole brain emulation is the eventual use of the technology to emulate a human mind. For this reason, we must consider who the first person we choose to emulate will be. That means we must determine what traits will result in the best emulation, and, once these traits have been enumerated, what process should be used to find a person who possesses these traits and is willing to undergo the uploading procedure.

In this chapter we consider the criteria and selection process other groups have used in selecting their subject(s) and glean from these, desirable attributes and procedures. Humanity is pushing the envelope, planning the creation of digital versions of ourselves. In this, the question of "who first?" is not trivial, but quite the opposite. Indeed, the answer will set the tone and the trajectory for future artificial superintelligence (Yampolskiy, 2015), and consequently the quality of our collective future (Sotala & Yampolskiy, 2015). It is our view that we cannot take this decision lightly, rather we must attempt to set aside cultural bias/differences, and make a choice together, as a global community.

Whole Brain Emulation

Whole brain emulation also referred to as "uploading" (Hanson, 1994) or sometimes "downloading" is a process in which the structure of a brain is scanned in such a way that a software model could be created from that scan (Sandberg & Bostrom, 2008). This software representation would be to such a level of sameness, that when the program is run, it will behave in an identical fashion to the original brain. This is to say, the brain emulation will be a one-to-one emulation of the original. Emulation in this context refers to a computer program producing the same behavior as another program, by copying its low-level functions, achieving the desired outward behavior by copying that which causes that outward behavior. This differentiates emulation from simulation, in that simulation just endeavors to copy the outward behavior, a *reactive* process, whereas emulation is a *proactive* process (Sandberg & Bostrom, 2008).

In this chapter, we will be operating under the assumption that the resulting mind emulation will achieve a level of detail that is indistinguishable from the original brain, and will therefore inherit the traits of the individual to whom the original brain belonged. We are also assuming that the mind emulation is dynamic, and will therefore continue separately from that individual and be shaped by its own experiences.

Why It Matters Whom to Upload First

As stated above, whole brain emulation will result in a one-to-one emulation of the original brain, therefore that emulation will begin its existence as an exact replica of the original personality. It will possess their memories and experiences, up to the point of the procedure. It will behave with their personality traits, internal value system, and everything about us that makes us an individual so that the emulation will possess (be an exact operational copy) of the original person. For this reason, it is imperative that researchers demonstrate rigorous and thoughtful intentions when selecting the first individual(s) to be emulated. The first person(s) emulated will set the tone of a wholly new experience for our global community, and will either magnify or mitigate the possible side effects of a substrate independent mind.

Safety

It is inevitable that whole brain emulation will lead to superintelligence. Once a sufficient approximation of our own intelligence is created, what is to stop that entity from surpassing its creator's capacity for problem solving, it will be "born" with perfect, infallible memory, and the ability to process information, that would take hours, in a fraction of a second. It will, most likely, have access to the Internet and all the information stored therein (Yampolskiy, 2012). Therefore, it will inevitably become more intelligent than the brightest among us, more intelligent than we can comprehend at this moment. Hopefully this new superintelligent being will be benevolent, grateful to those that gave it "life." However, it is easy to imagine the opposite occurring. Indeed, it seems a high probability that at some point this entity will become malicious toward its creators (Yampolskiy, February 12–13, 2016).

The creation of a computer-based approximation of human intelligence opens the door to some serious questions concerning humanity's safety. It is not difficult for one to imagine a military application for such a device. A weapon, with the intelligence of a human, without the need for sleep, or rest of any sort. This application would change, forever, the way wars are fought. It would be utopian to think that we would remove the human element from our conflicts, simply pitting one nation's technology against another's! No, if history is any indication of future application, we can be assured that the incorporation of digital warriors in our conflicts will only make them bloodier, more clandestine, and with far-reaching effects on the civilians in close proximity to that violence.

Personality

Even though personality is a difficult concept to define on paper, we all have an innate understanding of the concept. It would behoove us to delineate criteria for higher level functions, to make sure that some negative attributes will not manifest in the human emulation. We will certainly want to eliminate anyone who deviates significantly from normal behavior patterns, especially if those deviations manifest in destructive and/or negative interactions with his or her fellows. It would be desirable to find a mind donor who possesses characteristics that could be considered passive, has an aversion to conflict, and a strong affinity for intrapersonal relationships.

Values

Let us define values as Schwartz and Bardi do in their article *Value Hierarchies Across Cultures: Taking a Similarities Perspective*. Values are "… desirable, transsituational goals, varying in importance, that serve as guiding principles in people's lives" (Schwartz & Bardi, 2001). In the social sciences, scholars have found 10 motivationally distinct types of values which comprehensively encompass the core values of human society across cultures, and philosophical and religious beliefs (Schwartz & Bardi, 2001). These are—Power: Social status and prestige, control or dominance over people and resources. Achievement: Personal success through demonstrating competence according to social standards. Hedonism: Pleasure and sensuous gratification for oneself. Stimulation: Excitement, novelty, and challenge in life. Self-direction: Independent thought and action choosing, creating, exploring. Universalism: Understanding, appreciation, tolerance, and protection for the welfare of all people and for nature. Benevolence: Preservation and enhancement of the welfare of people with whom one is in frequent personal contact. Tradition: Respect, commitment, and acceptance of the customs and ideas that traditional cultures or religions provide the self. Conformity: Restraint of actions, inclinations, and impulses likely to upset or harm others and violate social expectations or norms. Security: Safety, harmony, and stability of society, of relationships, and of self (Schwartz & Bardi, 2001).

Let us now introduce the concept of *subjective well-being*, research in this field looks to quantify how a person evaluates their life, both in the moment they are being evaluated and over an extended period of time (Diener, Oishi, & Lucas, 2003). It has been found that subjective well-being can be broken down into two main aspects, one that is cognitive and focuses on a person's sense of satisfaction with life in general, and one that is affective, and quantifies a person's feeling of happiness or sadness (Lilach Sagiv, 2000). In the research done by Sagiv and Schwartz (2000), they have determined that achievement, stimulation, and self-direction from the set of 10 values correlates to a positive sense of subjective well-being, while traditional values tend to correlate more negatively, and conformity and security correlated negatively with a person's sense of happiness (the affective aspect of subjective well-being) (Lilach Sagiv, 2000). Interestingly, power, security, and conformity values were found to have very little, if any correlation to subjective well-being, suggesting that they are neither cause nor predictor of one's sense of positivity about life and person (Lilach Sagiv, 2000; Sagiv & Schwartz, 2000).

With this in mind, we would certainly like to select an individual who is experiencing a high sense of subjective well-being, and has been experiencing that consistently over an extended period of time. Therefore, we should look for individuals who are found to experience high levels of achievement, self-direction, and stimulation, while feeling less motivated by traditional values and power. For our unique purposes, it would be desirable to find an individual who is also motivated by values of universality and benevolence, seeding the emulation with a sense of social justice and honesty.

Previous Work/Literature Review

Humanity will likely depend completely on the nature of the internal organization and the personality traits of the emulated brain. Consequently, it is vitally important to choose the brain wisely. The election would be similar to deciding what sort of god we would like to have for ourselves. In this section we survey the history of humanity's "firsts" from leadership selection to space exploration, all the way to DNA donation.

Leadership Selection

So how do we choose the president of the United States? How about Supreme Court justices? Or perhaps the United Nations secretary general? In the cases of the president (at least the U.S. president), other than age, residency and citizenship requirement, no specific requirements exist. This may work in the case of a large country with at least a few checks and balances on power, but we would not recommend a popular election to decide on the first person to upload. In the case of supreme court justices, according to Norman Dorsen in his article, "The Selection of U.S. Supreme Court Justices" (Dorsen, 2006), argues that the requirement is a balance between knowledge and understanding of constitutional law, "… the most valuable judicial qualities of competence, impartiality, empathy and wisdom" (Dorsen, 2006). These qualities are more along the lines of what the first uploaded brain should possess.

In the case of selecting a secretary general for the UN, the criteria and qualifications for appointment are purposefully vague so as not to disqualify someone based on a structure that is unnecessarily rigid. Included in the requirements are the following: administrative and executive qualities, leadership qualities, and moral authority, political judgment, communication and representation skills, and … "overall qualities which demonstrate to the world at large that personally the candidate 'embodies the principles and ideals of the Charter to which the Organization seeks to give effect'" (*UN Preparatory Commission Report*, December 23, 1945). These are qualities that are undoubtedly important to the human race, but are not sufficient for accomplishing any of the goals that would make whole brain emulation a necessary risk. The human chosen for the first and maybe second uploads must also be a competent researcher in a field of interest. This would make the selection similar to that of Project Mercury, the process of choosing the first human beings to go into space.

First Astronaut

Project Mercury was the first American "man-in-space" program, which began in 1958 and was completed in 1963. The objectives of the project were to "orbit a manned spacecraft around the Earth, investigate man's ability to function in space, and to recover both man and spacecraft safely" (*Project Mercury*, 1956). The Mercury Project and the initial Apollo missions used similar criteria when selecting their first crew members.

Applicants to the Mercury, Gemini, and initial Apollo programs were all volunteers and required to have significant experience as pilots of high-performance aircraft. These machines were similar in nature to the spacecraft, "consist[ing] of complex propulsion, electrical, mechanical, and hydraulic systems" (North, 1965). The applicants were required to have backgrounds in science or engineering and, as the field was narrowed to a reasonable size, given training in digital computer theory, guidance and navigation, astronomy, and geology (North, 1965). It was the goal of the program, and a requirement for each individual to "be able to perform all the piloting duties on the command module without the aid of the others" (North, 1965). Interestingly, in the Gemini and Apollo missions, the applicants were further narrowed to be no more than six feet to accommodate the limited size inside the space craft. An age restriction was implemented, applicants could be no more than 34 years, "to maximize the amount of time a man can actively participate in a flight crew ..." (North, 1965).

Those that met the above criteria and were selected to move forward in the process were subjected to "a one-year indoctrination program" which contained approximately 570 hours of classroom activity (North, 1965). After the completion of the classroom activities that comprise the indoctrination program, each person was assigned a specialty, and 75% of their time devoted to that specialty. The remaining time was spent in simulations, flying aircraft, and survival activates (North, 1965).

As we determine who will be the best person(s) to be uploaded first, we can draw upon some of NASA's procedures. First of all, it must be stated that those considered for mental donation should be volunteers. In most of the "developed world," this would be a given, but we hope to have volunteers from across the globe, and of course the willing and informed consent of all who are considered must be guaranteed! We should also consider a "training" period for prospective donors as we narrow the list of candidates. NASA used this time to make sure their team was educated and confident in every aspect of the mission they were meant to accomplish. We could use a "training" period to get to know each potential donor better. If we are going to create an eternal version of an individual we should know that individual at least as well as each astronaut knew their space craft and mission. Furthermore, and possibly more important, a period of immersive learning could give each potential donor the time to really come to terms with the repercussions of the choice they are making. This would allow for possible withdrawal before the actual procedure becomes imminent so that the research team might start the process of selection anew.

NASA elected to instate an age limit on their candidates, so as to get a substantial career out of each. This was made necessary by the amount of training each astronaut required to become "space ready." While we do not necessarily require any time from our mental donor after the procedure is complete, the question of an age restriction on volunteers is a prudent one to consider. It has been well documented, that after a certain point in our aging process our mental capacity tends to decline. The mental donor selected for uploading should be determined to be in their mental prime or in that stage of development when learning comes most easily. Therefore we propose that an age limit, on both ends of the spectrum, should be instated. For the lower end of the range, we consider age of majority, globally this ranges from 15 to 21 (*Age of Majority*, Retrieved May 6, 2016). To allow for a more mature ability to make such a decision we suggest 21. For the upper limit we consider the age restrictions placed on pilots, 65 years (*Fair treatment of Experienced Pilot Act*). This seems reasonable considering the mental faculties required to operate a machine as complex as a plane.

First DNA to Be Profiled

Sequencing the human genome was a mammoth accomplishment for humanity. The Human Genome Project (HGP) was an internationally collaborative event, culminating in the complete mapping of the human gene sequence, or genome (see genome.gov). For this research to take place, subjects had to be selected to provide the raw material for the research teams to begin their work. For research of this kind, the benefits and risks to these subjects must be weighed, prior to any experimentation taking place. The benefits of the HGP are significant: a more thorough understanding of our basic biology, and, by default, our diseases. It was assumed that with the completion of the project, therapies for genetic diseases would be more effective, easier to create, and possible methods of prevention would result. Interestingly, the project would not directly benefit the volunteer donors, clinically or financially. Those that chose to divulge their genetic make-up would have to do so out of a sense of altruism (Collins & Patrinos, 1996).

The risks for these altruistic donors may, at first, seem minimal. However, the information resulting from the HGP was made available through a public database, and containing information with the potential to reveal disease susceptibility/propensity. If it were possible for the donor to determine which sequence was their own, this knowledge may cause them distress depending on the results of their sequence. If this information were found out by the general populous or the individual's employer, insurer, etc., they could suffer discrimination and/or embarrassment. It was therefore, imperative to the project to keep their donors identity confidential, not only by standard procedure in maintaining confidentiality, but also, ensuring that a large enough group of donors was obtained to ensure each individual's anonymity (Collins & Patrinos, 1996). It was also determined that staff of laboratories involved in the project would be prohibited from donating DNA, due to a concern that staff members would feel pressured to donate, along with a greater level of difficulty to maintain confidentiality (Collins & Patrinos, 1996).

Informed consent is a major part of acquiring human subjects, and for the HGP, this issue proved to be less straight forward than for other human-subject-based research projects. The nature of the research made anonymity and confidentiality impossible to absolutely guarantee for large-scale DNA sequencing, along with the individual's inability to withdraw their genetic library from the public database, should they later wish to (Collins & Patrinos, 1996).

The HGP's work raises an interesting parallel to the selection process for any first choice for emulation. While it was the HGP's major concern that the confidentiality of their donor's information not be breached, confidentiality is an impossibility for our donor. This raises a number of concerns for that person, unwanted celebrity being among the more benign. More seriously, it is probable there will be a significant number of individuals who are adamantly opposed to creating artificial life of any kind. These individuals may engage in peaceful demonstrations or they may lash out at the person after whom, the emulation is modeled.

The notion that donors to the HGP would be unable to remove their DNA library from the public database raises the questions "will it be possible for an individual to retract their uploaded mental information once the emulation is functioning as a separate individual?" This is an issue we must deal with as fully as possible before beginning our selection process. We must be capable of making the options very clear to our volunteers. Unfortunately, it is impossible to disclose an exhaustive list of the risks to the individuals considering volunteering. We cannot know what the results of our research will be used for in the future. With this in mind it is imperative that we obtain informed consent from each individual who puts their name forward to be considered. It may be wise to reference the HGP's informed consent form when creating one for the purpose of selecting candidates for Uploading.

The HGP raises a very interesting and valid concern involving members of their own staff's ability to donate to the project. We agree that all persons and family members of those involved with the research process, in any capacity, should be barred from being considered for mental donation. As mentioned in the above synopsis, a sense of pressure to volunteer would be inevitable. Not to mention, the pressure one would feel if working to emulate a friend, coworker, or family member, it would certainly be impossible for the team to remain objective in such a circumstance.

Xenotransplantation and the Declaration of Helsinki

The medical field has had the most hands-on experience with research involving human subjects, and should be looked to for guidance regarding volunteer selection and the treatment of those volunteers. In fact, from the field of medicine we get the *Declaration of Helsinki,* a concise document that spells out the "ethical guidelines for physicians and other participant in medical research" (Carlson, Boyd, & Webb, 2004). The declaration begins with the following self-definition: "The World Medical Association (WMA) has developed the *Declaration of Helsinki* as a statement of ethical principles for medical research involving human subjects, including research on identifiable human material and data" ("World Medical Association Declaration of Helsinki. Ethical principles for medical research involving human subjects," 2001).

Under this definition, our research into uploading clearly falls under the umbrella of research the Declaration of Helsinki is meant to influence. Arguably, any research done on the resulting human emulation would also fall under its guidance in so far as the emulation would be identifiable human data. It is important that we familiarize ourselves with its principles before beginning any research involving human subjects.

According to the FDA, xenotransplantation is "any procedure that involves the transplantation, implantation or infusion into a human recipient of either (a) live cells, tissues or organs from a nonhuman animal source, or (b) human body fluids, cells, tissues or organs that have had *ex vivo* contact with live non-human animal cells, tissues or organs" (Siegel, 2002). The controversial nature of xenotransplantation research, along with the many unknowns that accompany experimentation of this type on human subjects, has required a rigorous screening process for the first trial recipients. First and foremost, the recipient must volunteer for and understand the risks associated with xenotransplantation.

Xenotransplantation is on the cutting edge of medical science and is therefore dealing with a lot of unknown risks and consequences for those who first undergo the procedure. The idea of possibly pursuing more than one path simultaneously, tailoring each to the unique needs of the individuals involved and/or different end goals, could be a beneficial practice when we begin to upload people. Having multiple teams could combat the tunnel vision that would result from going about the process in one way with one goal.

While "life"-long monitoring of the resulting emulation is a requirement of this type of research, we also need to be prepared to take care of the mind donor for the duration of their life. This person or persons will be in a situation like no one before them. Their privacy will be nonexistent, their deepest secrets, their most precious memories will be made available to another entity, and at the very least the staff that helped to develop that entity if not the public in general. We need to have the resources to assist individuals to cope with that new reality. It will be a wholly unique experience and no one can be truly prepared for what it will be like to be that exposed. We must also keep in mind that this total transparency will not be limited to just the individual to whom the mind belongs. Any person with whom that individual has come in contact with will experience the same transparency in so far as their interactions with the donor. Therefore, we must consider extending informed consent and post procedural care to the donors close relations and family.

With the long list of side effects in store for anyone who decides to donate their mind for uploading, we must ask, what are the benefits? What would a person gain from being uploaded? The obvious answer is that they will be the first person emulated. More than this, they will be the first person to achieve a form of immortality. A goal we have been chasing since we became aware of our mortality.

Selection Criteria

Taking into consideration the importance of choosing our first candidate(s) for uploading and referencing what we can learn from processes of selection used in other fields. Let us now take a look at what our selection criteria could look like.

Diversity

It is our hope that the search for the first person emulation will be a global endeavor, making a diverse pool of volunteers an inevitability. However, it is more likely that the task will be undertaken by a group of individuals that are much less diverse. Whomever is conducting the research should not be tethered to just their countryman when casting their net for volunteers; rather, this net should be cast globally! Hopefully we will have the means to upload multiple individuals in the first round of person emulations. Choosing a manageable number of individuals from a diverse assortment of ethnic and cultural backgrounds will have a number of benefits. First being, the benefits for human and person mind emulation interactions, a person is going to be much more likely to accept an artificial person if it "resembles" them. If the emulation speaks like them, knows their traditions, and cultural nuances, the technology will become quite relatable and less unnerving. Finally, creating multiple uploads of different individuals would be beneficial to the donors themselves. Rather, then being alone in this process, they would have a network of colleagues and friends who are dealing with the same unique situation.

Disposition

The mind donor's disposition will also play a role in the selection process. It would be best for the selected person(s) to have a predominantly positive view of themselves, humanity in general, and the future. They should be friendly and have shown a propensity to be charitable and helpful toward others. If these traits manifest in the emulation, we would create a "likeable" entity, one that would be more inclined to interact positively with the humans it comes in contact with. There is also the potential that the emulation will act in a more benevolent fashion toward its fellows. If the mind donor was compassionate toward those he or she came in contact with, it could only stand to increase the probability that the emulation would be more likely to act this way as well.

Intelligence

Let us consider Howard Gardener's Theory of Multiple intelligences, in which he proposed that intelligence is basically plural. Gardener proposed seven types of intelligence, but was not married to these particular seven or even the notion that there shouldn't be a greater or lesser number. Intelligence, he theorized, "… is an ability to solve a problem or to fashion a product which is valued in one or more cultural settings" (Gardner, 1987). This definition allowed him to quantify abilities that were valued by a community, but could not be quantified by the intelligence tests of his day.

In selecting a mind donor for our first emulation, it would be wise to choose someone who possesses a type of intelligence that we find desirable, and is difficult to learn. For an emulation, which at its heart is a computer program, spatial intelligence and the ability to problem solve should be relatively easy to "teach." There already exits programs to solve complicated mathematical equations and it is conceivable that we would be able to incorporate this type of program into the emulation. What about other desirable traits, that are more difficult to predict, quantify, and therefore code? Gardner points out the distinction between a person who is good at problem solving, and a person who is good at problem finding. Gardner made the point that coming up with a strong scientific theory is showing a propensity for problem finding, rather than solving and requires a wholly different skill set, a skill set that would be very difficult to code (Gardner, 1987). Therefore let us move this type skill, this type of intelligence to a higher priority when screening our pool of volunteers. Similarly we should prioritize a high level of interpersonal and intrapersonal intelligence, over high levels of, for example, spatial intelligence.

Ethics

It is important that all care is taken to treat all volunteers in an ethically sound fashion, which revolves around honesty, and transparency. Every aspect of the process (before, during, and after the procedure) must be laid out within a comprehensive and informed consent form, in compliance with the Declaration of Helsinki (or similar relevant document of the time). Each volunteer must prove that they understand every aspect of the informed consent and must prove that they are of sound mind, capable of making an informed decision as well as volunteering of their own free will and under no coercion. All steps must be taken to have lifelong support set up for those that are selected for the procedure, as they will be in a position unlike any person has ever been. They will have, quite literally no privacy, no secrets from their life up to the point of uploading. The well-being and experience for the first persons uploaded will set the tone of public opinion and the ease with which future research will be performed.

Selection Process

The process we use for selecting our first uploadees should be a multistep experience. Initially we should cast a wide net, as wide a net as possible. It is important that the media we use to advertise for applicants is highly accessible, so as not to inadvertently screen out persons who can't afford the media we use. Therefore it would be wise to use a variety of media platforms, certainly social media (or its equivalent), but also the newspaper's equivalent, billboards, etc. whatever the project can afford. In this way, we will hopefully generate positive excitement for the project, and get a deep and diverse pool of applicants. In this first step, we will gather general data about each individual, such as age, ethnic background, general mental health, medical conditions that would affect their brain function, and perhaps a short essay in which the applicant explains why they are interested in being uploaded. This application should contain a detailed description of what uploading is and what the potential risks are for any person who is uploaded (including nonphysical risks). Each applicant should be required to read this material.

Using the information gathered from the above applicants we should screen out those who do not meet age requirements, have suffered brain trauma, or do not meet requirements in some other, very obvious way. The remaining applicants will be asked to complete a number of tests, to determine their disposition and personality type. This second step in the process could be made somewhat long and tedious, to screen out those who are not interested enough in the process to complete it in its entirety. At the same time, this should not screen out those applicants who are unable to read, therefore a help network should be set up to allow those applicants who need it to call in and complete surveys with the aid of a staff member (taking whatever means necessary to keep that staff administrator as nonbiased as possible). This process should be used to find applicants that fit the personality, internal values, and intelligence profile desirable for our first upload.

The final stage of selection is the most involved. Using the information gathered in the two previous surveys, a manageable number of applicants should be selected to come live with each other and the research team. In this time, the applicants should be observed in their interactions with each other and researchers. In this time, applicants should be taught any skills they do not yet possess that would enhance the upload and a significant amount of time should be spent making sure that each applicant understands what it is they are doing and understands the consequences as we understand them at that time. This step in the selection process will allow the researchers to observe the applicants as they are naturally, allowing the applicants time to fully come to terms with the repercussions of being the first person(s) uploaded, and if need be, remove themselves from consideration. Therefore this step should not be short, and should be as long as fiscally possible for the project. At the end of this time, from the candidates that remain, and have been deemed to fit all criteria for uploading, the first person(s) to be uploaded should be selected.

Whom Not to Upload

As important as it is to determine who would make a good candidate for uploading, we must also consider who would not. We should not upload any person who has suffered significant brain injury or deviates significantly from "normal" brain function. This would exclude persons who have suffered from stroke or are presently suffering from dementia or other degenerative brain disorders. Persons diagnosed with certain psychological disorders should also be excluded from consideration. This should include those diagnosed with antisocial personality disorder, narcissistic personality disorder, schizophrenia, bipolar disorder, borderline personality disorder, etc. Individuals convicted of any violent crimes should also be excluded.

Additionally, no individuals from the research team or immediate relations should be considered. As discussed above within the section on the HGP, the inclusion of these individuals could result in feelings of obligation to apply for consideration, along with a compromised level of performance/judgment by the research staff members themselves if they are too closely related to or involved with the mind donor.

Conclusions

With regard to deciding which brain to upload first, there are several concerns to take into consideration. The first concern is what we want to accomplish with this first brain emulation. Do we just want to see if it is possible, or is there a hierarchy of important tasks that we believe a faster brain is more suited for? What is at the top of the hierarchy? A successfully uploaded and emulated brain can have many copies, all thinking about the same problem and at much faster speeds with perfect recall of past thoughts and a perfect record of past experiments. This would be a very large team of scientists working without any need for lunch breaks or naps. These copies can help with a myriad of problems, but which should be first?

The next thing to consider is whether or not we will have control and accountability over the emulation. In the case that the emulation has unlimited power, we need to ask ourselves if the risks are worth the benefit of accomplishing our task. Since this is not (yet) artificial general intelligence, many scientists feel that we can understand and limit the power of a Whole Brain Emulation, giving it goals that the original human brain identified with and also valued. Nonetheless structures would need to be in place to ensure that the emulation can be held accountable for its deliverables and safe for humanity. Having thought about accountability, it is also important to consider what kind of rights and autonomy will be given to the emulation and to the human it came from—if that human is still alive. It can be argued that ethical robotic engineering should not include emotions for robots; however, in the case of an emulated human brain it is difficult to imagine that the emotions of the human brain are not present. If the emulation chooses to stop working on the project because it no longer sees the value, is it ethical to terminate the emulation? If the premise is a contract between the original human and the researchers in charge of the emulation, is the emulation legally responsible to fulfill the contract that it had no part in signing? Answering these questions will guide the understanding of who should be uploaded first, and who should be uploaded next.

Given the possibility that whole brain emulation becomes a reality and considering the lack of any controls in place, the most important accomplishment would be the development of safeguards for humanity. Along with the attributes of individuals chosen as the first astronaut, the person chosen as the first upload will have to be well versed and experienced in AI research and understand the importance and the high risk impact of a technological singularity. If possible, it would be valuable to include a team of AI safety researchers to mitigate the possibility of a rogue emulation behaving unexpectedly and poorly. This research should be done as soon as possible, so as to have as much of a natural barrier to progress in the form of computing power, once human brains are successfully uploaded.

One final consideration is the issue of equality once safety has been achieved. Since a successfully emulated brain would suggest a path to immortality, the issue of accessibility should be thought through as well. This may be a major issue if our planet becomes uninhabitable for biological humans. As brain uploading moves from an issue of safety to simply an activity for the wealthy, and then a necessity for the masses, the protection of our physical environment may lose its purpose. At this point, brain uploading may become the only form of survival and it may not be available to all. But should this be the case?

We feel we have made a strong case for a thorough process, in determining who will make the best first candidate(s) for whole brain emulation. These individuals should first and foremost be volunteers, informed of the risks and benefits of the procedure to the best of our knowledge at the time. The person(s) chosen for the first emulation(s) should be of an appropriate age, free of physical trauma to the brain, and they should be without mental disorders. These persons should be found to be compassionate and able to empathize with others. They should already possess a strong ability to interact with and relate to their community, as well as an awareness of and ability to communicate how they are feeling internally. Depending on what the end use of the emulation will be, screeners should also add a propensity for skill sets that pertain to that end use. Finally, as already mentioned, this excludes persons too closely related to the research, to avoid unintended feelings of obligation.

There are still many unknowns when it comes to achieving a human emulation. Not least among these being that we don't know definitively how much of our *self* will be captured by a one-to-one structural replica of our brain. There is a notion of self that many of us believe exists apart from the physical structure that makes us who we are. It is exciting to think that the successful emulation of a person will bring us closer to understanding this dynamic. This uncertainty should not lessen the importance of whom we choose to upload first, for there are equal measures of possibility that our *self* will be uploaded with the more base brain functions, than not. The consequence of not developing thorough systems for selecting our first mind donor and arriving at an undesirable result outweighs the toil required to engage in a rigorous selection process.

References

Age of Majority. Retrieved May 6, 2016 from https://en.wikipedia.org/wiki/Age_of_majority.
Carlson, R. V., Boyd, K. M., & Webb, D. J. (2004). The revision of the Declaration of Helsinki: Past, present and future. *British Journal of Clinical Pharmacology, 57*(6), 695–713.
Collins, F. S., & Patrinos, A. N. (1996). NCHGR-DOE guidance on human subjects issues in large-scale DNA sequencing: Executive summary executive summary of joint NIH-DOE human subjects guidelines (issued 8/19/96).
Diener, E., Oishi, S., & Lucas, R. E. (2003). Personality, culture, and subjective well-being: Emotional and cognitive evaluations of life. *Annual Review of Psychology, 54*, 403–425.
Dorsen, N. (2006). The selection of US supreme court justices. *International Journal of Constitutional Law, 4*(4), 652–663.
Gardner, H. (1987). The theory of multiple intelligences. *Annals of Dyslexia, 37*, 19–35.
Hanson, R. (1994). If uploads come first. *Extropy, 6*(2).
Lilach Sagiv, S. H. S. (2000). Value priorities and subjective well-being: Direct relations and congruity effects. *European Journal of Social Psychology, 30*, 177–198.
North, W. J. (1965). Astronaut selection and training. *Annals of the New York Academy of Sciences, 134*(1), 366–375.
Project Mercury. (1956). Retrieved from https://www.nasa.gov/mission_pages/mercury/missions/program-toc.html
Sagiv, L., & Schwartz, S. H. (2000). Value priorities and subjective well-being: Direct relations and congruity effects. *European Journal of Social Psychology, 30*(2), 177–198.
Sandberg, A., & Bostrom, N. (2008). *Whole brain emulation: A roadmap*. Oxford: Future of Humanity Institute, Oxford University.
Schwartz, S. H., & Bardi, A. (2001). Value hierarchies across cultures: Taking a similarities perspective. *Journal of Cross-Cultural Psychology, 32*(3), 268–290.
Siegel, J. P. (2002). Human cells or Tissues Intended for Transplant into a Human Recipient that Have Ex-vivo Contact with Live Non-human Animal Cells, Tissues or Organs Letter. Retrieved from http://www.fda.gov/BiologicsBloodVaccines/SafetyAvailability/ucm136703.htm

Sotala, K., & Yampolskiy, R. V. (2015). Responses to catastrophic AGI risk: A survey. *Physica Scripta, 90*(1), 018001.

UN Preparatory Commission Report. (December 23, 1945).

World Medical Association Declaration of Helsinki. Ethical principles for medical research involving human subjects. (2001). *Bulletin of the World Health Organization, 79*(4), 373.

Yampolskiy, R. V. (2012). Leakproofing singularity—artificial intelligence confinement problem. *Journal of Consciousness Studies (JCS), 19*(1–2), 194–214.

Yampolskiy, R. V. (2015). *Artificial superintelligence: A futuristic approach.* Boca Raton, FL: Chapman and Hall/CRC.

Yampolskiy, R. V. (February 12–13th, 2016). *Taxonomy of pathways to dangerous AI.* Paper presented at the 30th AAAI Conference on Artificial Intelligence (AAAI-2016). 2nd International Workshop on AI, Ethics and Society (AIEthicsSociety2016), Phoenix, Arizona, USA.

CHAPTER SIX

The Intersection of the Human Senses and Exponential Technologies

Exploring Relevant Trends and the Future of the Senses

JOVAN D. REBOLLEDO-MENDEZ

Introduction

"Je pense, donc je suis; I think, therefore I am." In his famous statement, Rene Descartes (Cottingham, 2013) evokes the idea of human consciousness, a strong characteristic of the human species, rooted in the stimulus formed from the input of electrochemical signals in the brain. This stimulus is a result of our senses, which channel outside information and data that is processed so that the brain can interpret information and find patterns. These patterns ensure that individuals not only survive, but thrive within their environment. The evolution of each human sensory system is the result of thousands of years of environmental adaptation.

These experiences could be rapidly increased and augmented by current technologies like Oculus Rift (Oculus) and VIVE (HTC Vive), which are capable of creating completely new surroundings for us to experience with the use of our visual capabilities through augmented reality (AR) technologies. One example, HoloSens,[1] superimposes visual data and object simulation matching the dimensionality of the environment where those objects are seen.

Another set of possibilities include the manipulation of our senses, like the electric "salt-flavored fork" (Demetriou, 2016), trick on our taste buds so the user can reduce salt consumption. The development of haptic surfaces and embedded haptic devices that incorporate wind-elements (wixels) from Tactile Analogics (Demetriou, 2016) can be used to approximate visual information conveyed by pixels, or even to characterize unseen information or data onto tactile feeling.[2] Other examples are (1) a device that can use the tongue as a sensor to characterize visual information,[3] and (2) the well-established cochlear implant, which does the work of damaged parts of the inner ear (cochlea) to provide sound signals to the brain by receptors that transform the sounds into electrical signals.

Those technologies, among many others, fall under Moore's Law, which suggests that the design of silicon-based chips can be improved in efficiency, doubling processing power, every eighteen months. In 2006, Ray Kurzweil presents in his book *The Singularity is Near* (Kurzweil, 2006) the "law of accelerating returns" indicating that technologies that are based on silicon follow an exponential growth function. Accordingly, these technologies (e.g., artificial intelligence (AI) and Robotics, Digital Biology, Nanotechnology and 3D Printing, and Networks and Computer Systems) evolve exponentially.

The purpose of this chapter is to focus on one of my primary interests: the intersection between humanity's natural senses and exponential technologies, and how this intersection can facilitate a path for our senses to adapt to technologies based on information. I will begin with the introduction to and explanation of both exponential technologies and human and other animal senses, differentiating between traditional and nontraditional senses. I will explore the very powerful senses found in certain animals, and the neuroplasticity of human brains. This will lead me to consider empirical research regarding their trends in speaking about the senses, and about the inventors who have patented innovations related to the senses and inspired by our senses.

Exponential Technologies

From a broad inclusive technology view, exponential technologies should be divided into the following four groups: AI and Robotics, Digital Biology, Nanotechnology, and Networks and Computer Systems.

AI and Robotics

AI and Robotics are closely interrelated. Where the first is the mathematical approximation of how a mind (or certain brain functions) is replicated through a programming algorithm, the second is the applicability of these algorithms into the mechanical three-dimensionality of a mass that executes actuators according to the programmed functions, and potentially the inputs of its own sensing capabilities. AI is more concentrated on algorithms inspired by nature, that is, the simulated activity of the brain, whereas Robotics is the execution of certain algorithms in a real mechanical environment, using actuators and sensors.

Digital Biology

Digital Biology includes a wide range of techniques through which information from DNA can serve to not only understand but also improve biological systems, and where the manufacturing of DNA can enhance certain features of organisms, or even create new ones. This relatively scientific and technological area has recently made rapid advances with major drivers such as the CRISPR/Cas9 technique, allowing unprecedented specificity of targeted alterations to genomes and has extremely broad potential applications. One area of interest in Digital Biology is related to the microbiome, with many implications for our future diet and lifestyle. In relation with human senses, an example of applications in this area is a company which developed bacteria that, when applied to our bodies, eliminates body odors, that could potentially alter some health and hygiene habits based on the minimization of unpleasant smells (Waugh).

Nanotechnology

Nanotechnology is the manipulation of atoms as building blocks of all physical forms. A major driver of nanotechnology is 3D printing, which is the manufacturing and design of 3D structures. This "additive manufacturing" has been developed for use with a wide range of materials, including metal, plastic, glass, and organic tissue, and its application is rapidly expanding (with simple 3D printers available at the hobbyist level). Many other technologies are also included within the scope of nanotechnology, including high-powered instruments for analyzing structures at the atomic scale, as well as tools for producing novel, "designer" materials with desired properties. Such materials have been created for applications in diverse areas, from biomedical sensors and targeted drug delivery systems to improved efficiencies in the field of renewable energy. Some startups like Nauga Needles (Needles) are creating and commercializing new types of nanostructures, and current research projects like OIST's recent "Ukidama" discovery are also creating new techniques for a variety of applications (OIST, 2016). This field holds potential for many new breakthroughs, and novel applications of new materials.

Networks and Computer Systems

Finally, Networks and Computer Systems have enabled the rapid growth of the Internet, including its connectivity and reach, and the rise of many new social and economic systems and platforms that rely on (or sometimes even exist only inside of) the Internet's capabilities. This technological area is driving such fundamental changes as "dematerialization" and digitization of vast amounts of information and data. Consider, for example, the rapid increase in online retail, the absolute transformation of the music industry, and the changes in the consumption of newspapers and magazines from hard-copy sales to online platforms.

Senses, from Traditional Human Senses to Exotic Natural Ones

There are five basic (or traditional) human senses: sight, hearing, touch, olfaction and taste.

Sight

Sight, or visual perception, is by far the most advanced sensory system within human beings. Its complexity and its fast and direct access to the brain demonstrate it to be the most evolved, or at least the best understood. In animals, it allows the assimilation of reflected light information from their environment. The process of seeing initializes when the cornea and the lens of the eye focus an image from the environment onto a light-sensitive membrane, the retina. The retina then converts patterns of light into neural signals by using some regions of the brain. This mechanism relies on rods and cones that detect the photons of light and actuate by producing neural impulses. Those currents then travel through a very structured series of cells in the eye and brain into the central ganglia, producing our experience of sight.

Hearing

Hearing is the sense created by transforming physical vibrations from [typically] airwaves, via the intricate mechanisms of the ear.

Touch

Touch or tactile sensing is controlled by the somatosensory nervous system or SNS, which is composed of many series of nerve cells which actuate to the contact of surface or internal state of the body, and the produced signals that travel along a series of nerve cells to the spinal cord to be processed and finally transmitted to the brain. There are a variety of receptors associated with a diverse array of stimuli, including chemicals, temperature, movement, and others.

Olfaction

Olfaction functions via specialized sensory cells of the nasal cavity (for humans), where floating molecules bind to specific points of the olfactory receptors (the ones that indicate the presence of smell), which then transmit signals to the olfactory bulb, located above the nasal cavity and below the frontal lobe.

Taste

Taste, which is closely related to olfaction, is the sensation when chemicals in foods or drinks stimulate receptors in the mouth, particularly on the tongue, and send signals to the brain.

Each of the "traditional senses" in humans relies on the detection of stimuli, followed by the transmission of signals from each sensory system and interpretation of the signals by the brain. There are also other nontraditional human senses, like balance or equilibrium, thermoception, kinesthetic sense (proprioception), pain sense (nociception), and several others (Wikipedia). There seems even to be some evidence of usage of "echolocation," a sense that is found in some animals like dolphins, by human.[4] These nontraditional senses also follow similar patterns of detection, transmission, and interpretation for producing our perceptions.

Beyond human beings, there are senses in nature that we do not possess. For example, ants communicate, work, and survive thanks to the chemical signals that they transmit and sense among themselves in a well-balanced and distributed community. In the animal kingdom there are also other types of sensors that exist in only a few species; next are two types of sensing mechanism found in nature that are of relatively high specialization:

1. The *star-nosed mole*, defined as "a gold mine for discoveries about brains and behavior in general" (Wikipedia) by neuroscientist Kenneth Catania, contains more than twenty thousand receptors for tactile sensory mechanisms, and the sum of all those receptors is similar to the human visual sensory system. Each receptor is formed by a complex set of cells that translate information from the environment to signals via physical touch.
2. The *mantis shrimp*, or *stomatopod*, is a type of marine crustacean that has the amazing capacity to carry 16 types of color eye receptors (compared with only three types in humans). It is suggested that this gives the crustacean the ability to recognize light wavelengths that are unimaginable by

other species [13]. Of these receptor types, twelve are used for analysis of colors in "different" wavelengths (nontraditional wavelengths from a human perspective), including ultraviolet light (Corwin, 2001).

The evolutionary capabilities of these sensing systems give many animals advantages to survive and adapt to their environments. In summary and in general, for every sensory system, whether traditional or nontraditional, there are receptors that channel signals to a part of the brain where those signals are processed. The brain is always playing a critical role in transforming the received signals into perceived features of the reality that is in the environment that surrounds each individual. It is certain that there are many more sensing systems to be discovered and explored among the diverse range of living organisms on Earth.

Neuroplasticity, Biology, and Exponential Technologies Convergence

One important feature of our brains is neuroplasticity: the capacity to readapt, rewire, redistribute, and relearn functions among the different sections that form the brain. For instance, since humans began to make use of cochlear implants, the brain has shown the amazing capability to make sense of signals that come into the cochlear nerve and to characterize such electric signals into perceived sounds. This amazing readaptation of the brain and its strong capacity for pattern recognition, makes our brains an extraordinarily sophisticated biological computing system.

Indeed, it is at the intersection of technology and the biology of our senses that we find some type of readaptation can occur. This begs the question: is it possible for the human species to adapt to new information from new types of information sources? In fact, according to research done by David Eagleman, humans can adapt to new patterns of information via new ways of perceiving (e.g., using tactile sensations of movements on the back, which are produced by a vest, to interpret information from the stock market or weather conditions) (Novich & Eagleman, 2015). Engleman's laboratory is pursuing a variety of projects to push the boundaries of our sensory systems, like understanding the limits of our tactile perception (Novich, 2015), color classification (Witthoft & Eagleman, 2015), synesthesia (triggering one sense from the stimulus of another) (Zamm, Schlaug, & Loui, 2013), etc.

Another innovation related to tactile sensing which is being pursued by multiple teams using a variety of approaches is to create a "tactile display" which translates visual information into tactile information. Companies like Tactus Technology (Technology) (which uses bubbles that make it possible to feel the display), Freedom Scientific (Scientific) and Kurzweil Educational Systems (Systems) (which offer technologies for visually impaired people like Braille readers and text-to-speech technologies). Disney Research is pushing for interactive graphics with projects like Aireal (AIREAL) (vortexes of haptic air) and Surround Haptics (immersive tactile experiences/ illusions via tactile mechanical actuators that can be simulated in any area). In addition to this, Tactile Analogics (Rebolledo-Mendez, 2016) is creating arrays of hundreds and thousands of micro-pneumatic actuators that can be independently controlled in terms of pressure, frequency, and temperature of air bursts. These "wixels" or wind-elements (equivalent to pixels for visual information) are expected to be embedded in different surfaces for a variety of novel applications.

The current push in micro- and nanotechnologies for use as actuators and sensors will permit the embedding of such micro/nano devices into many if not most materials, including biological human skin, organs, etc. Embedding thousands of micro-pneumatic actuators that are self-controlled on a new type of smartphone display to create haptic information to the user is one of the long-terms goals of Tactile Analogics and many other startup companies. Building on a related approach, for example, Emerge (a startup from Singularity University) uses Tactile Analogics' concept of tactile characterization via ultrasonic/parametric speakers.

Relying on the exponentiality of some technologies, many coming products and services may rely on the plasticity of the brain for their functions. Getting access to new visual information, for example, could include not only virtual reality/AR but also extensions of our natural capabilities such as hyperspectral images, where the brain will be able to understand very quickly, once semi-trained, to classify as quickly as the different electromagnetic spectra are presented to the brain.

Finally, a subset of AI helps enormously to allow the rapid sorting and intelligent searching/classification of information by automating the access and identification of visual data. An example is another company born from Singularity University, AIPoly, a startup dedicated to transforming the capabilities of smartphone cameras to allow the direct-voice communication to the user, specifically targeting blind people. Another approach of utilizing the same resource, via crowdsourcing, is BeMyEyes (2018). This startup has a strong social approach, but relies on technology to help blind people understand their surroundings via the participation of volunteers.

Much as Steven Kotler (2014) suggests, where athletes now use all kinds of biosensors and quantified-self devices in order to perform better, many people believe that the widening of the capabilities of the senses represents a step toward maximizing human output. Ultimately, from simple technologies such as eyeglasses, to implantable pacemakers, or sound-to-electrical signals for the ear in a cochlear implant, technology continually evolves to improve and augment human sensing. In this sense, we are entering an age when exponential technologies will push the boundaries even further beyond what *aid* means toward what *human expansion* could become.

Foreseeing Senses in 2045

By looking at and analyzing information from two sources of innovation, namely research papers and patent applications, it is possible to glimpse how society has been working to create or recreate sensors via different technologies over several years. Indeed, we might project forward and have a reasonable expectation of what technologies will exist in the future to augment human senses. Researching both Google Patents (Google) and Google Scholar (Google), I have collected data that reflects a tremendous and rapid creation of innovations related to the human senses.

Patenting Innovations of Senses

By looking at the yearly growth of the patents related to the senses, one has a better understanding of the ways in which people have invested in creating technologies and patenting these technologies. Figure 6.1 shows a set of plots where one can see that the growth of innovation related to the senses is very significant.

Based on the results of this research into intellectual property (IP) related to the senses (see Figure 6.1), it seems that although research and innovation related to nontraditional senses (hereafter NTS IP) have traditionally lagged behind research and innovation related to the traditional senses (hereafter TS IP), there is a shift underway. Trend lines show that NTS IP is increasing rapidly, and could possibly catch up with or even surpass TS IP. One possible explanation for this is that traditional senses are more straightforward and accessible, and thus research began earlier, but more and more researchers are realizing the potential impacts of creating new technologies related to nontraditional senses. It should also be noted that the total number of patent applications is rising, with total applications increasing each year from 2009 to 2014, with a total of 2.7 million patent applications in 2014 (WIPO, 2015). This is an exciting area full of possibility, and we can expect many more innovations and applications in the future. Breaking down the data by the total number of patent applications by decade (b) clarifies the trend, in which both TS IP and NTS IP seem to be growing exponentially.

Just the five traditional senses are plotted in (c), showing the relative emphasis in technologies related to each sense. Initially, the greatest emphasis by far has been

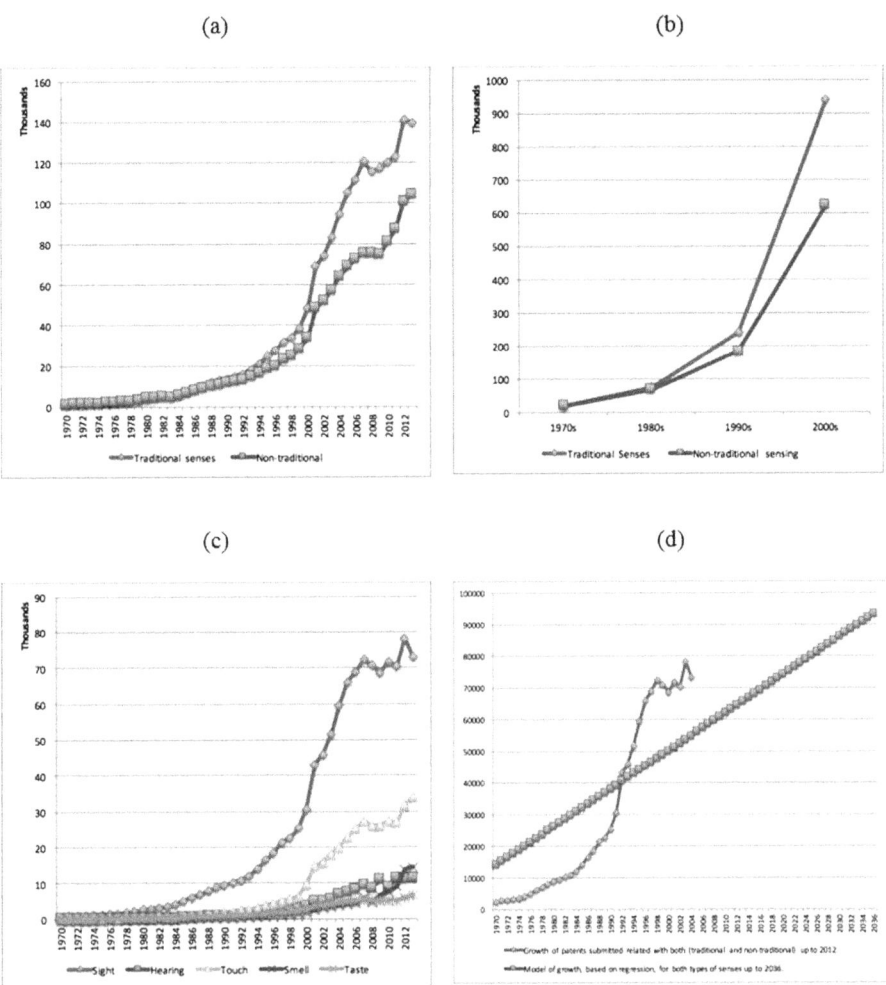

Figure 6.1: Behavior of patent submissions per year: (a) shows the growth in patents related to traditional and nontraditional senses, (b) growth of submitted patents related to traditional senses; (c) total growth by decade of both traditional and nontraditional senses; (d) regression model of the total growth of patents submitted that relate to both (traditional and nontraditional senses) up to the 2000s.

on technologies related to augmenting vision. Certain forces, such as motivation to create solutions targeting the visually impaired population, have contributed to the development of many of these technologies. It is interesting to note that the tactile sense is also gaining rapidly in importance. Since around the year 2000, IP in areas related to all 5 traditional senses has increased more rapidly than ever before, but visual and tactile research areas are especially pronounced.

Cumulative numbers of all patents (both TS IP and NTS IP) are plotted in (d), a regression model of the growth of patent applications. Even in a regression model it is expected that growth is pronounced, but this shows particularly high growth. In order to attempt to foresee future trends, the regression is stretched to 2045.

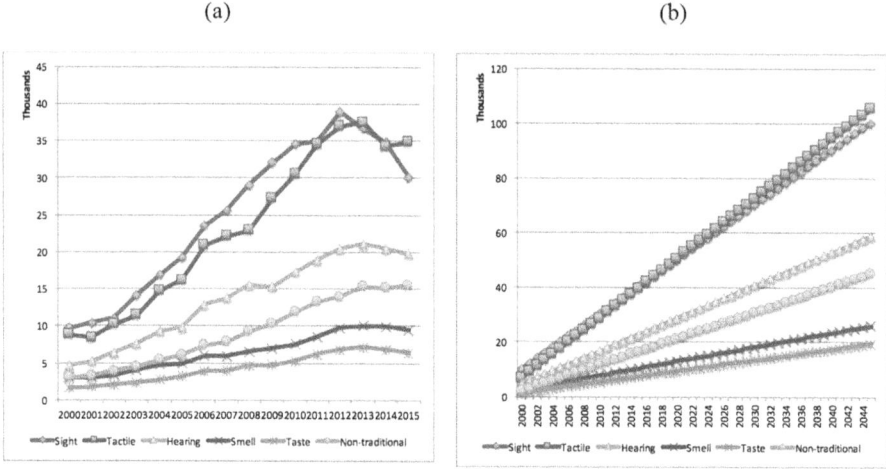

Figure 6.2: Plotting of number of publications in journals based on Google Scholar from 2000 to 2015 (a), and projection of to 2045 with regression model (b). Note that tactile research might be expected to overpass the visual research by 2040 already.

Another important aspect of innovation is publications in peer-reviewed journals. Using data from Google Scholar, trends were analyzed for publications related to each of the traditional senses, as well as nontraditional senses. Figure 6.2 shows plots of each of these categories. As with IP, all areas show growth since 2000, but the strongest growth has been in the areas of visual and tactile senses. Interestingly, in 2014, tactile research surpassed visual research for the first time. Based on this data point, as well as the regression model, it appears that we are currently in the middle of a transition in which tactile research overtakes visual research. It will be interesting to see how this trend impacts future trends in IP applications and innovation.

In addition to researching data on trends, a survey was also conducted among over twenty experts in exponential technologies. Results are shown in Figure 6.3. The y-axis shows the number of these experts who expect each sense to be used frequently in conjunction with new technologies by 2045. They expect that the most used human sense by 2045 will be sight, followed by touch. Two traditional senses, smell and taste, as well as two nontraditional senses, pain and temperature sensing, were not considered strongly. Based on their predictions, we can expect to

THE INTERSECTION OF THE HUMAN SENSES AND EXPONENTIAL TECHNOLOGIES | 139

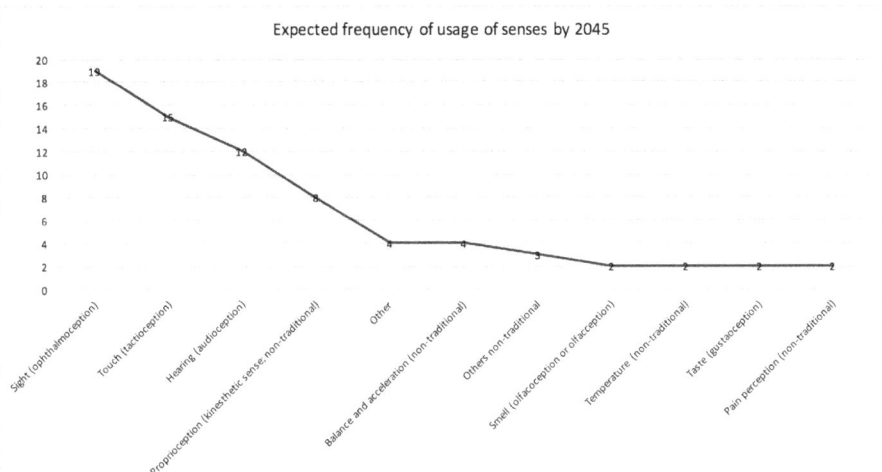

Figure 6.3: From survey to exponential technologies practitioners, the expected frequency of usage of sense augmentation by 2045 is plotted: sight is expected to continue being very well used, and tactile in second place, while taste and pain perception might not be very frequently used by 2045.

see the introduction of most new technologies related to sight and touch, followed by hearing and kinesthetic augmentation. These predictions line up well with the trends noted in the research above. Of course, there is always the possibility of disruptive research and innovation dramatically shifting trends in one of the currently less-emphasized research areas (Figure 6.4).

Interestingly, between 5 and 10% of the people interviewed showed transhumanist tendencies in some of their predictions. For instance, in a future evolved entity into which a human mind has been uploaded, senses such as taste, temperature, pain, and smell would be much less relevant than they are to our biological bodies. In fact, a large percentage of experts predict that we will enjoy an enhanced sense of taste. The largest overall predicted decreases in perception relate to temperature and pain, followed by smell and balance. Interestingly, more than 60% of experts surveyed predict that hearing, sight, and touch will be exponentially more used than they are now.

Predictions of Most Important Exponential Technology for Sensing Related Interfaces

Experts were also asked about their expectations regarding the future importance of each of the exponential technologies discussed above as they related to interfacing with our senses (Figure 6.5). They were asked which exponential technology they think will be the one that will be the most used to interface with our senses

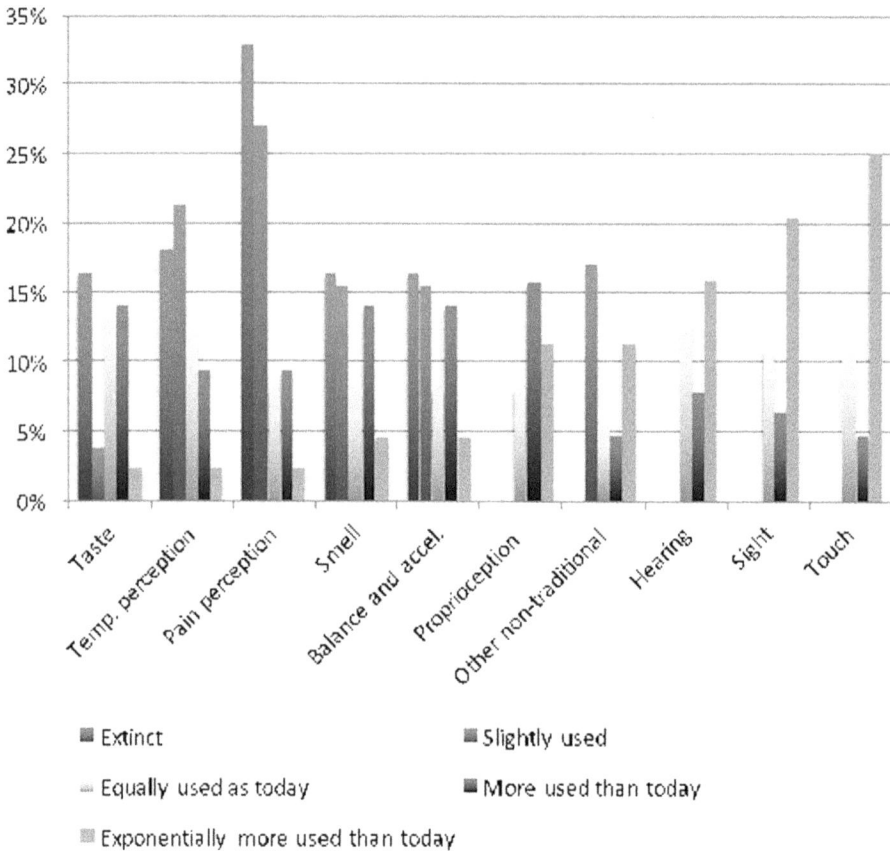

Figure 6.4: Difference of expectation of usage of different human senses by 2045, compared with usage in 2016.

in 2045. AI and Digital Biology were most highly ranked for their expected use in such future interfaces.

Expected frequency of usage of exponential technologies with our senses is plotted in Figure 6.6. Highest predictions of the highest usage frequency (every nanosecond) were in the areas of AI (nearly 60%), Nanotechnology (nearly 50%), Networks and Computer Systems and Biotech (around 40%).

The Rise of Artificial and Augmented Senses: Benefits and Risks

Another potential in human sense enhancement is deep brain stimulation and cyborg initiatives, for instance, the work made by Kevin Warwick which

THE INTERSECTION OF THE HUMAN SENSES AND EXPONENTIAL TECHNOLOGIES | 141

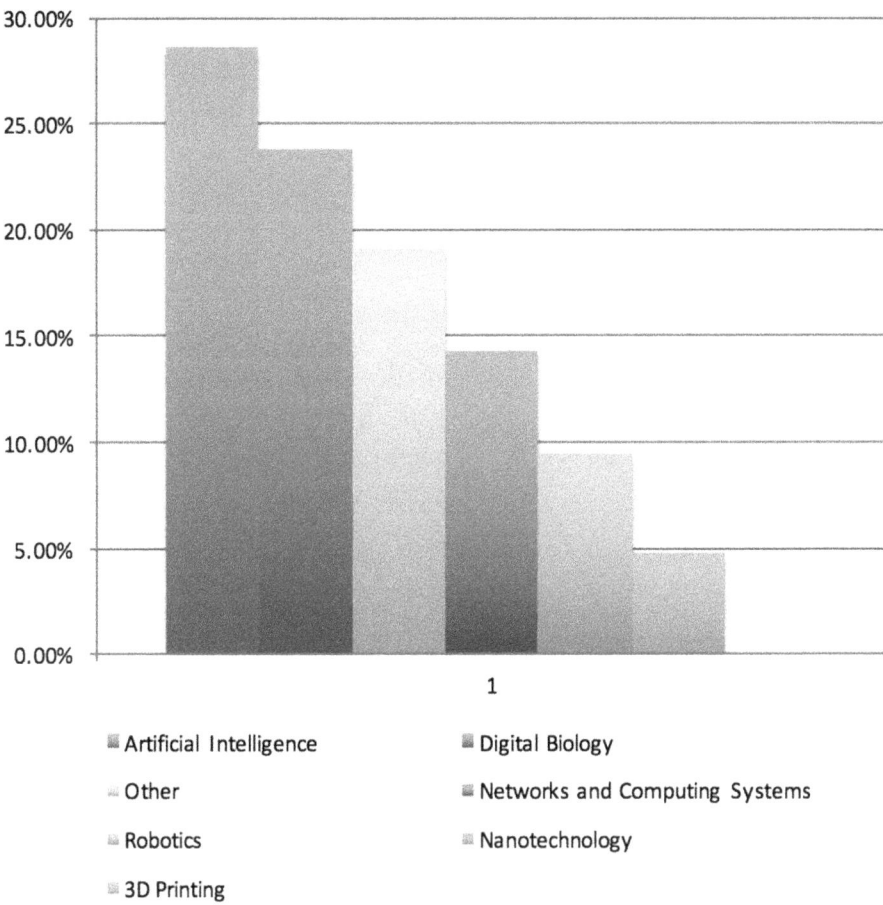

Figure 6.5: From exponential technologies experts, this plot shows the expectation of importance of exponential technologies by 2045.

demonstrated that not just Parkinson symptoms can be controlled. By inserting some chips into the body, specifically one hundred electrodes array interfacing his nervous system directly (Warwick et al., 2003), diverse range of possibilities of digital interactions have been enabled.

The time for intelligent electronic eyes, electronic noses, telepresence tactile capabilities, augmented smelling capabilities, taste-changing silverware and cutlery, synesthesia among two or more senses, combined with exponential technologies, such as AI, robotics, digital biology, nanotech, and computer and network systems is now on the horizon. To be sure, there are many benefits from these augmenting technologies that could lead to better health, better prevention of diseases, and "natural" telepresence communication, among many others.

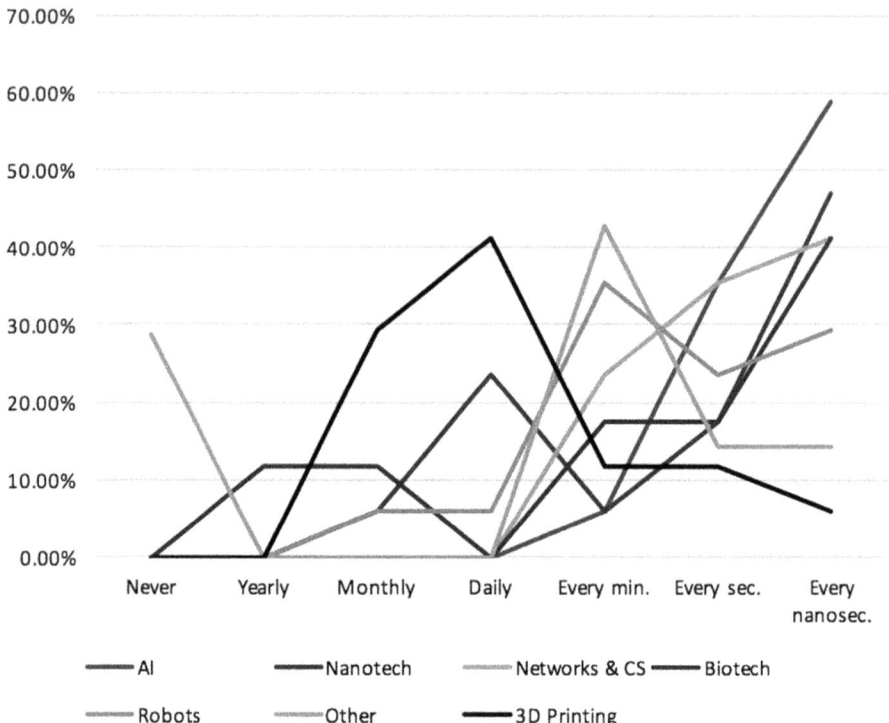

Figure 6.6: From exponential technology practitioners, this plot shows the expectation of exponential technology usage frequency in interaction with human senses.

Alongside these benefits, there are potential risks that should also be understood: among these risks are social problems, the likelihood of cyber hacking, and the risk of abuse that can come from such symbiotic relationships between biological matter and augmenting technologies. Furthermore, there is a risk of unexpected side-effects as natural systems are synthetically altered. As with the rise of any technology, the possibility of emergent problems is real and significant. As an evolving society, we should be prepared for these risks, and perhaps, better educated to make the most of our potential in the application of augmenting technologies to the senses, so that we might continue to push forward into a better world.

Acknowledgments

Thank you to my wife for her patience, encouragement, and suggestions to improve the draft. Also, my most sincere appreciation to Juan Monzon, and all those who helped me during the research with their support of this chapter, especially to all who participated in the survey, and for their comments and suggestions.

Notes

1. https://www.microsoft.com/en-us/hololens.
2. Full disclosure: the author is the inventor of wixel technology and part owner of Tactile Analogics.
3. http://www.wicab.com/
4. https://goo.gl/0cG67u

References

"Be My Eyes—Bringing sight to blind and people with low vision. (n.d.). Retrieved December 30, 2018, from https://www.bemyeyes.com/"
Sodhi, R., Poupyrev, I., Glisson, M., & Israr, A. (2013). Aireal. ACM Transactions on Graphics, 32(4), 1.
BeMyEyes (2018). Retrieved from http://www.bemyeyes.org/
Corwin, T. W. (2001). Sensory adaptation: Tunable colour vision in a mantis shrimp. *Nature, 411*(6837), 547–548.
Cottingham, J. (2013). *René descartes: Meditations on first philosophy: With selections from the objections and replies*: Cambridge: Cambridge University Press.
Demetriou, D. (2016). Japan invents electric 'salt-flavoured fork'. Retrieved from http://www.telegraph.co.uk/news/2016/03/30/japan-invents-electric-salt-flavoured-fork/
Diamandis, P. (2015). Plugging into your brain. *The Blog*. Retrieved from http://www.huffingtonpost.com/peter-diamandis/plugging-into-your-brain_b_8624288.html
Google. Google Patents. Retrieved from https://patents.google.com/
Google. Google Scholar. Retrieved from https://scholar.google.com/
HTC Vive. Retrieved from http://www.htcvive.com/
Kotler, S. (2014). *The rise of superman: Decoding the science of ultimate human performance*. Boston, MA: Houghton Mifflin Harcourt.
Kurzweil, R. (2006). *The singularity is near: When humans transcend biology*. London: Penguin (Non-Classics).
Needles, N. Retrieved from http://nauganeedles.com/

Novich, S. D., & Eagleman, D. M. (2015). Using space and time to encode vibrotactile information: Toward an estimate of the skin's achievable throughput. *Experimental Brain Research*, *233*(10), 2777–2788. doi:10.1007/s00221-015-4346-1

Oculus. Retrieved from https://www.oculus.com/

OIST. (2016). New 'Ukidama' nanoparticle structure revealed. Retrieved from https://www.oist.jp/news-center/news/2016/6/10/new-ukidama-nanoparticle-structure-revealed

Rebolledo-Mendez, J. D. (2016). Tactile analogics. Retrieved from http://www.tactileanalogics.com/

Scientific (Freedom Scientific). Retrieved from http://www.freedomscientific.com/

Systems (Kurzweil Educational Systems). Retrieved from https://www.kurzweiledu.com/default.html

Technology (Tactus Technology). Retrieved from http://tactustechnology.com/

Warwick, K., Gasson, M., Hutt, B., Goodhew I, Kyberd P, Andrews B, ... Shad A. (2003). The application of implant technology for cybernetic systems. *Archives of Neurology, 60*(10), 1369–1373. doi:10.1001/archneur.60.10.1369.

Waugh, R. Here's what happens when you use this 'miracle' bacteria spray instead of showering. Retrieved from http://metro.co.uk/2015/12/07/heres-what-happens-when-you-use-this-miracle-bacteria-spray-instead-of-showering-5548882/, 2015.12

Wikipedia. Sense. Retrieved from https://en.wikipedia.org/wiki/Sense-Non-traditional_senses

Wikipedia. Star-nosed mole. Retrieved from https://en.wikipedia.org/wiki/Star-nosed_mole

WIPO. (2015). Global patent filings rise in 2014 for fifth straight year; China driving growth. Retrieved from http://www.wipo.int/pressroom/en/articles/2015/article_0016.html

Witthoft, N, W. J., & Eagleman, D. M. (2015). Prevalence of learned grapheme-color pairings in a large online sample of synesthetes. *PLoS ONE, 10*(3), e0118996. doi:10.1371/journal.pone.0118996.

Zamm, A, E. D., Schlaug, G., & Loui, P. (2013). Pathways to seeing music: Enhanced structural connectivity in colored-music synesthesia. *NeuroImage, 74*, 359–366.

CHAPTER SEVEN

Augmented Intelligence Continues to Be Embodied Intelligence

STAN RUECKER AND SUSAN LIEPERT

Introduction

Sensory augmentations that can allow people to perceive more, focus better, and act more effectively are all strategies for augmenting, not just perception, but also intelligence. The senses are not always associated with intelligence, because the tendency for people when discussing intelligence is to think more or less in terms of the brain in the vat of early science fiction and philosophy. In discussing the connection between intelligence and the body, modern neurophysiologists (e.g., Paul M. Churchland, 2012) and philosophers (e.g., Searle, 2015) have argued that a body is a necessity for intelligence, since not only do all intelligences we know have bodies, but in fact they are inextricably connected: intelligence is an emergent property of having a body. With respect to how seeing better or hearing more can result in a person being more intelligent, Gardner (1983) points out that definitions of intelligence have historically been too constrained, and that there are in fact 9 kinds of intelligence: naturalist, musical, logical, existential, interpersonal, kinesthetic, linguistic, intrapersonal, and spatial. More generally, if we think of intelligence as belonging to a system rather than an organ, we can more easily recognize that we need input to our thinking processes, which are embodied, and that input comes from the senses, which require bodies to work. This chapter will draw on a range of recent experiments in bodily augmentation in the context of their relationships to intelligence of various kinds. It will also position the discussion of the embodied mind within an historical trajectory that has a number of significant implications for design in the future.

The Future of the Embodied Mind

"Embodiment" is a pretty simple concept. It means that there's a particular living organism in the world that people think of as *themselves*: as their body. In fact, for most practical purposes, that living organism *is* the person.

Embodiment matters to augmented intelligence because the body—that living, organic *self*—is a part of every interaction people have with their environment. No matter what kind of interaction or technology is involved, it's hard to rule embodiment out of the equation.

What this means in practical terms is that the technologies that augment our brains will work most effectively if they are also associated with technologies that augment our bodies, and in particular, our senses.

A Brief History of Embodiment and Technology

Until fairly recently, the standard history of embodiment and technology looked like this:

> Throughout recorded history, the human body has more or less stayed the same. During the same time period, technology has changed many times, and in some pretty drastic ways. In turn, this has changed the way we understand bodies and how they interact with objects and information.

But in the last thirty years or so, there's been a sudden surge of development in the theory and science of embodiment. We now know that a standard history of embodiment and technology should look *much* more like this.

> Throughout recorded history, the human body has changed many times, and in some pretty drastic ways. These changes have generally coincided with technological change, because the two strongly influence each other. And *both* are critical to understanding bodies and how they interact with objects and information.

This new and improved history may seem a little hard to swallow. It's easy to understand how ideas *about* the body or representations *of* the body might change.

But surely the biological *facts* always remain stable. Unfortunately, that's not the case. Here's an example of how that works.

Figure 7.1 shows two anatomical illustrations of the female reproductive system. Both were created by highly skilled scientific anatomists, based on meticulous, multiple dissections of actual human bodies.

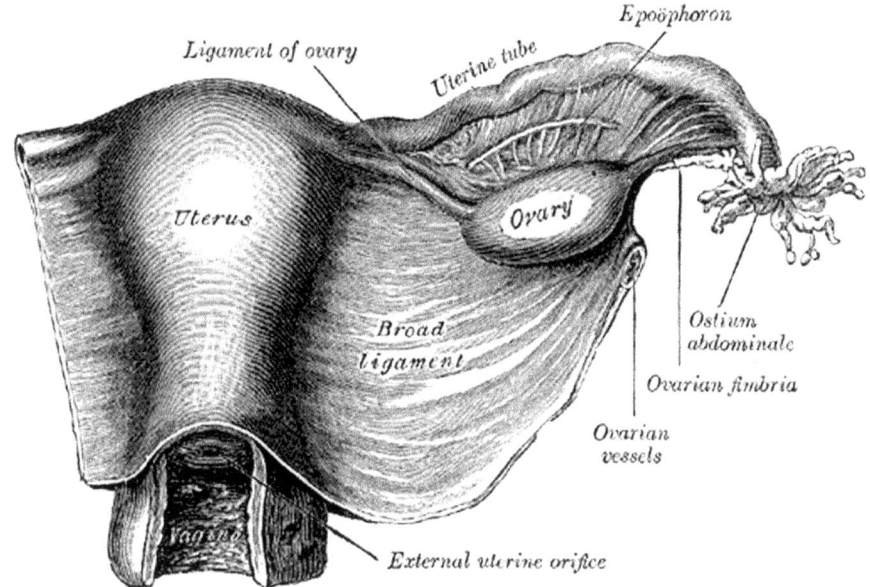

Figure 7.1: Anatomy of female reproductive system, contemporary.
Source: Grey's Anatomy.

Figure 7.1 is from *Grey's Anatomy*, a textbook first published in 1858 and still in print today. Figure 7.2 was hand-drawn in the late 1400s, and looks pretty similar. But there is one critical difference: the older image shows two tiny anatomical "pipelines" connecting the uterus to the breasts. This structure is called the vena kiveris. *Grey's Anatomy* doesn't show the vena kiveris at all. The reason is that the female body of the Renaissance absolutely had to have a structure that connected the uterus and the breasts. Our modern bodies don't.

In the late 1400s, bodies were basically containers for holding different kinds of fluid. And it was very clear that a particular kind of fluid process occurs when a woman is pregnant. The uterus *stops* producing a liquid that's dark, thick and kind of gross—menstrual blood. Then the breasts *start* producing a liquid that's light-colored, thin, and very, very good for feeding babies—breast milk. When breastfeeding stops, the white liquid vanishes and the dark liquid starts appearing

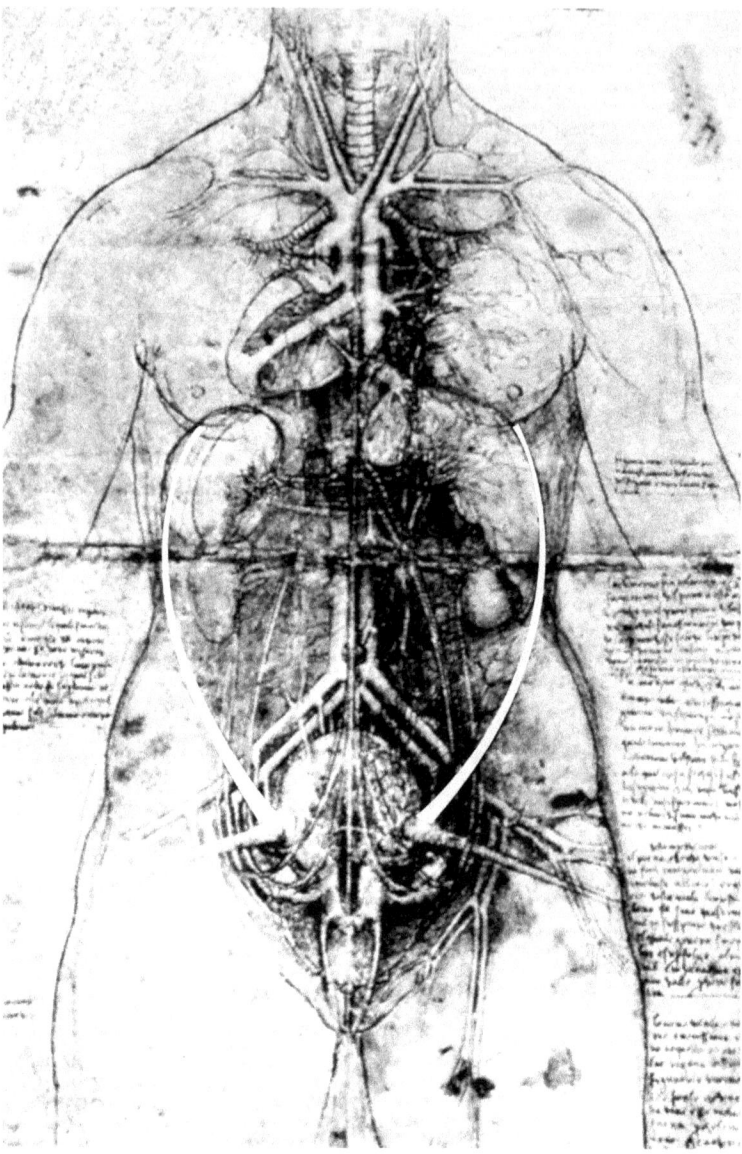

Figure 7.2: Anatomy of female reproductive system, late 1400s.
Source: Biblioteca Ambrosiana. Artist: Leonardo da Vinci.

again. So some sort of body structure must be transporting blood from the uterus, up to the breasts, where it's somehow transformed into milk.

And sure enough, there *is* a structure for this—the vena kiveris, as highlighted in Figure 7.2. In the late 1400s, its existence was just as real, and just as much a scientifically proven fact, as its *non*existence is today.

There's another way to look at this, of course, which is to say that the anatomist who drew the image made a mistake. He was too ignorant or too careless or too prejudiced to understand what he was looking at, and he just drew things wrong.

Here's the problem with that view of things. The Renaissance image is by Leonardo da Vinci. If one of the world's most historic geniuses could make that so-called "mistake," then it's absurd to suppose that today's scientists could have done any better given the same set of circumstances. If they were working from the story that Leonardo Da Vinci was working from, they'd find a vena kiveris, too.

So, for most practical purposes, it *is* reasonable to say there was a different body back in Da Vinci's day. And that's the body that interacted with Renaissance technology, and had an impact on how it developed.

A Brief History of Bodies

So, how many bodies have we had in the Western world, anyway? The answer is 6, with a 7th recently emerging. Here's a very loose and general summary of where the research on that stands.

Medieval Bodies Were Containers for Souls

The medieval body was a container for holding a soul. Because souls don't have a sex, bodies didn't either—females were basically men who hadn't finished developing properly. During this time, embodiment meant interacting with the environment in an amazing range of ways. If the soul was the strongest part of a person, then it gave the body a fundamental connection to God, the spirit world, the zodiac, the four elements, the phases of the moon, and so on. As a result, bodies might be able to see divine visions, or become impervious to pain, or become all-powerful against their enemies. If someone had an exceptionally strong soul, his or her body could even keep having these kinds of strengths after it was dead.

On the other hand, embodiment made the soul vulnerable to the physical environment. The body's openings were particularly dangerous, and had to be actively guarded. The soul might use them to escape. That is why people say Gesundheit when someone sneezes: if there isn't a blessing, something important might get out. Or even worse, something might get *in*. Remember how Hamlet's father died? Someone poured poison in his ear. So all interactions needed to be extremely cautious.

Renaissance Bodies Were Bags of Fluids

The Renaissance body is the one we've already talked about: the bag of fluids. This body's interactions had to be managed *constantly*, to prevent its fluids (or "humors") from getting out of balance. Being out of balance wasn't just a matter of getting sick. It could change you completely. Soldiers eating a diet of "cold" foods (like lentils) became weak and cowardly. Women who exercised too much eventually became male from the increased body heat. Every interaction with the environment had to be evaluated for its potential impact, and counteracted where necessary.

One of the most famous medical treatments intended to balance the humors involved taking away excess blood, either through bloodletting with a scalpel or through the judicious application of leeches. Some people are surprised to learn that we still employ leeches in modern medicine, although the purpose is different, because we are not attempting to balance the humors, but instead to take advantage of the anticoagulant in the leech's spit, as well as draw excess blood away from reattached body parts while we wait for the veins to grow back (Hirshon, 2016).

Enlightenment Bodies Were Solids

In the 18th century, solid structures, not fluids, were the body's main elements. In a normal body, these all worked together like parts in a complicated machine. The heart was a pump, the eyes were lenses, and bones, muscles and tendons acted as levers, supports, hinges, and so on. Two distinct *sexes* emerged for the first time, structurally specialized for two different functions. Embodied interactions became exciting opportunities for observation and discovery, which technology could heighten and extend.

Romantic Bodies Were Harps

For a brief period, around the time of the French Revolution, a very unusual body appeared, then disappeared almost as quickly. Medical theory at the time described it as the sympathetic body. It capitalized on the features of embodiment that were clearly *un*machine like. Amputated arms could itch. A nail puncture in your foot could lock your jaw muscles. Just reading about something unhappy could make your tear ducts drip. What kind of physics or chemistry could explain *that*?

The sympathetic body was filled with an invisible life-force, vibrating like a sound wave. In fact, the most famous metaphor for the body in this period was the Aeolian Harp, which responds to the wind. However, as pointed out by the poet

Coleridge, it will also respond to another harp being played nearby by vibrating its own strings, in effect playing along (Figure 7.3).

Figure 7.3: The Aeolian Harp provided an image for how sympathetic vibrations worked in people.
Source: Concord Museum, Concord, Massachusetts, USA. Artist: Henry David Thoreau.

This vibration helped the parts of the body communicate with each other, and if it was powerful enough could even transmit itself between bodies. A whole new range of interactions opened up, not just with the environment, but also with other people. The sympathetic body was very popular with political radicals, but it vanished almost entirely when the revolutionary movement was stamped out.

Victorian Bodies Were Steam Engines

The Victorian body was all about Health. This powerful force could be created by keeping the body's chaotic energies under tight control. Restrictive clothing, dieting, and daily medications became common. Exercise was invented. Sexual urges were restrained ruthlessly, and, for the very first time, bodily privacy was enforced. Health could be the foundation of vast personal, social and political good, but it could only be enjoyed when the body was constantly disciplined, and tightly contained.

This way of thinking about the body is inscribed in some of the metaphors that we continue to use without really considering them. For instance, "everyone is under a lot of pressure lately," "she was steaming mad," or "he blew his top." The Victorian body has also long been a favorite of cartoonists, since it can produce some dramatic imagery: think, for example, of some cartoon character with a steam whistle blowing while the steam blasts out of each ear. If this model of the body made our actual experience of interaction difficult, unpleasant, or even dangerous—well, that's just the nature of the machine.

Modern Bodies Aspired to Disappear, Leaving Only Brains Behind

The body of the 20th century was almost entirely the creation of medical science. In earlier eras, doctors had relied on roughly the same information that their patients did: how bodies looked on the outside, how they behaved in certain cases. In the modern age, the types and amounts of information available increased dramatically—but only experts had access to it. As more and more of the body's invisible structures became known, scientists believed that the structure of things like intelligence, decision-making, and moral character could be determined as well. The 20th-century body was as much a certain quantity of information as a material thing.

In addition, the 20th-century body's interactions with the environment were increasingly mediated by artificial objects and systems. A wholly mediated life, independent from embodiment, wasn't just an element in philosophical debate—the "brain in a vat" was a goal that technology could eventually achieve, and we still find it in science fiction stories where a person is "uploaded" to the internet (although, of course the internet also relies for its existence on physical media, as theorists like Kirschenbaum (2008) have elaborated).

A Quiet Revolution

Now we get to the part that's interesting. Not everybody has noticed yet, but our bodies underwent another major shift in the 1980s and 1990s. Two drastic things have happened to embodiment.

First, we have ended our long, long struggle to keep our bodies separate from—and, if possible, subordinate to—all the other parts of ourselves. There's no soul-body division any more. There's no mind-body division any more. There's not even a real barrier separating our bodies from our environment. We have accepted that existing as a brain in a vat is simply an impossibility. We can imagine the experience through immersive gaming, perhaps—the same way that Medieval people imagined life as a spirit through music and art—but scientific consensus now says the thing can't happen.

Second, we abolished the distinction between Self and Other. For all practical purposes, person A is experiencing person B, and person B is experiencing person A. It's the closest thing to the sympathetic body of the Enlightenment that the West has experienced in 200 years, and in many ways, it's more radical. As *organisms*, we automatically detect and respond to each other's states and behaviors.

We haven't provided all the tedious scientific and medical details about how most of the other Western bodies developed, and what kinds of theories and evidence grounded them, so we are going to skip that explanation here, too. But for everyone who hasn't yet done some reading on the topics "embodied cognition," and "mirror neuron," it's time to get on the bus. Here's a good place to start: a very provocative and readable online article by a practicing neurologist called V. S. Ramachandran (2000).

Perceptive Computing

We have already started integrating our technology physically, and we're going to continue doing this until the boundary between the two disappears. Instead of wearables, we'll have implantables, and we'll think about them pretty much the same way we think about of the rest of our physical selves. Ubiquitous computing won't stop where our skin starts.

Our interactions with the internet of things, for example, will be like a kind of proprioception or interoception, two of the senses we have already. Our bodies don't send us texts to let us know what our limbs are up to, or email us a report that analyzes how we're feeling today. We just perceive it, like we perceive the color red or the smell of a hot cinnamon bun. And soon, we're going to perceive many of our digital interactions the same way (e.g., TED Talk by David Eagleman).

This "perceptive computing" is substantially different from the "calm technologies" that Palo Alto scientists started predicting in the mid-1990s, when they developed the concept of ubiquitous computing. One of the defining characteristics of a calm technology is that it can function both at the center of user attention and at its periphery, moving easily between the two. Users will be able to access information, without having all of it competing for space at the center of their attention. In a seamless interaction, users will be able to stare *or* glance *or* shift their focus as they choose.

This is a picture of the future that still understands technology and information as external things that demand to be let in. We have to defend our openings against them, and carefully manage their amount and flow, because otherwise, bad things could happen. Sound familiar?

But we're *already* information *ourselves*. Technology shouldn't be our window: it should be our eyesight. It should be a *constitutional* element of attention. This is already happening with the technologies we have. When a 20-year-old woman can't get cellphone service, she doesn't just *feel* like she's gone blind, or deaf—for all practical purposes, she has genuinely lost a big part of her ability to see and hear. This is eventually how we're going to think about not being able to know what's in the fridge at home, just by the way we're feeling at the moment.

Here are some of the indications that perceptive computing is beginning to develop.

The specific systems that make up embodied cognition are just hitting the horizon of what neurologists and computer scientists can understand through research. Researchers working with brain-controlled interaction (BCI) are mapping exactly how our bodies communicate with these interfaces. One discovery is that good proprioception makes us better at BCI—and *vice versa*. People with good proprioception find BCIs easier to use. And people who develop good BCI skills improve their proprioception at the same time. The way our bodies perceive themselves seems fairly well-adapted to perceiving computer interactions, as well.

Interoception looks similarly promising. Even a relatively small amount of mindfulness training, for example, improves BCI performance, which means that a better sense of what our bodies are doing helps us to interface more effectively with computers. The most ancient and effective tools for grounding us in our bodies *also* work for grounding us in BCI-controlled devices.

Perceptive computing may not just turn out to be possible—it may turn out to be something that our bodies are naturally well-adapted to accommodate, which is more than can be said for many of the digital technologies we're using now. Why our proprioceptive and interoceptive systems have this developmental potential is a matter for speculation. Perhaps there is sufficient redundancy built in that we can co-opt some of it when necessary. Perhaps it is not so much a matter of untapped potential as a fluidity in the human system that allows us to adapt individually in order to accommodate changes in the environment.

How soon can we expect perceptive computing to arrive at the local Apple store? Almost certainly within our lifetimes. DARPA is on the case already, and in their opinion, there are two main roadblocks right now, beyond the eternal difficulty of developing robust interface modeling and hardware for a new class of technology.

The first is the lack of a good method for imaging the activity of individual neurons in real time. We have already dramatically improved on the speed of capture and image resolution of the original MRIs, but significant advances still need to be made to even get close to the speed of neuronal activity. With that in mind, DARPA have just instituted a new program aimed at solving the problem: Neuro-FAST—the Neuro Function, Activity, Structure, and Technology program.

The second roadblock is the lack of a truly noninvasive, subcutaneous neural interface. To crack this one, DARPA isn't just instituting a new program. They're doing something almost unprecedented: opening up the work! This doesn't just mean collaborating with people—that's nothing new at DARPA. For BCI research, they're going to make data dissemination one of their highest-priority selection criteria for funding projects. And not just dissemination between DARPA teams—between DARPA teams and the global scientific community. Talk about removing the barrier between self and other. This new model will be a primary factor in speeding the arrival of a useable perceptive computing system.

One caution: we have made it sound as though every era produces *one* well-defined kind of embodiment. This has never been true. There's always a set of alternative bodies available—from history or from counterculture or from some new way of thinking that's going to make the next body possible. So embodiment isn't a law. It's a set of opportunities and relationships. It's just not a closed set.

Augmented Intelligence

The preceding discussion of the changing phenomenological status of the human body is really a precursor to the larger thesis that augmented intelligence is necessarily associated with embodiment, and that taking this fact into account might lead us in useful directions.

To begin with, *artificially supplementing* our existing senses might help us to make and maintain more effective contact with the environment. Granted that much of our existing perceptual apparatus exists to filter information as much as to deliver it to further cognitive processing, we might consider futures where an enhanced intelligence could support more input.

Speed is an example. Pigeons spend less time in imminent danger of being run over than we think they do, partly because they see three times as fast and have reactions that can accommodate the additional information. We can fool people into seeing motion with as little as 24 frames per second, which for a pigeon is a fairly slow slide show (Neatorama, 2007).

There is also range to consider: our senses operate only within a narrow band of conditions that more or less correspond to the operating constraints of the body. But we have already devised ways to survive in more severe environments; what if our senses were also augmented to accommodate those locations? Could we learn how to taste liquid nitrogen without killing ourselves? Could we smell various scents of plasma, and listen to the many variations of the solar wind?

We have plenty of precedent for artificially supplementing our senses, from telescopes to microscopes to radar systems and MRIs. However, for the most part these supplements have not yet been implanted. We come closer with contact lenses and hearing aids, but we have begun to cross a boundary with the biohackers, who, among other things, have embedded tiny neodymium magnets in their fingertips, so that they have, for instance, a tugging sensation around electromagnetic fields (Dvorsky, 2013).

This experiment represents one of the possibilities for *adapting our existing senses* for new kinds of input, like David Eagleman's vest for internet vibrations, or the augmented reality devices that superimpose 3D digital information on our visual perception of the 3D analog world. In this case, it is the input that has changed, while the senses have remained the same. We are still dealing with various forms of vision and touch and feeling, except they have been repurposed so that what we are seeing, touching, or feeling are inputs that extend beyond previous inputs of the systems.

Finally, we have *the creation of new senses* altogether. There is some debate about how many senses we already have. Traditional wisdom since Aristotle gives us five (sight, hearing, taste, smell, and touch). We can make good arguments for adding proprioception and interoception to the list, giving us seven. If these are subdivided into their components, the numbers go up quickly: there are, for example, two different kinds of light receptors in the eyes: rods for intensity and cones for color. Touch can similarly be nuanced into individual types of systems for pressure, hot, cold, pain, and itching. Looking at it this way, we may have as many as 21 (HowStuffWorks, 2000).

In this case, however, the goal would be to create a new one. For candidates, we might think of any phenomenon that we can't currently directly sense, then imagine a system that would inform us about it. For example, we can imagine advantages in being able to directly perceive radioactive materials (geigeroception, maybe?) or poisonous gases that are colorless and odorless (chemoreception). In fact, earthworms and catfish already have chemoreceptors on their skin (Loomis, 2014), which suggests that another strategy would be to start by looking at senses that various animals have that we do not.

It is fairly well known that bees respond to magnetic fields (Lord, 2013) using rings of magnetic particles in their abdomens that swell or shrink, and red wood ants reportedly use their sense of the magnetic to predict earthquakes, in order to be able to evacuate their nests in time (Loomis, 2014). Magnets embedded in the fingertips might simulate this kind of awareness, but it is being done through the system that responds to touch. To be a truly new sense, we would need a new system, involving perhaps a new sensory organ and new neuronal pathways.

The human body, however, does not consist entirely of sensory input and cognitive processing. We are aware, consciously or subconsciously, of abstractions that might be inspired, derived, or triggered by our senses, but are in themselves much more than simple awareness. These forms of conceptual understanding inevitably occur within a physical medium, just as virtual information must inevitably reside somewhere on a hardware layer. Without hardware, no databases; without bodies, no idea of the database.

Conclusion

The human body has been understood in different ways down through the centuries, and each way of understanding it has influenced the technologies developed around it. The model from the early 20th century, of the body as a support system for the brain, is more recently being replaced by a body that is difficult to disassociate from its environment. We therefore need to exercise some critical judgment in attempting to augment intelligence by working with a somewhat outmoded model of what human beings are. Success more likely lies in the direction of accommodating the latest research on embodiment, resulting in technologies that artificially supplement our senses, adapt them for new kinds of input, or even provide new senses altogether.

References

Churchland, P. M. (2012). *Plato's camera: How the physical brain captures a landscape of abstract universals*. Cambridge, MA: MIT Press.

Dvorsky, G. (2013). What you need to know about getting magnetic finger implants. Retrieved from http://io9.gizmodo.com/what-you-need-to-know-about-getting-magnetic-finger-imp-813537993

Gardner, H. (1983). Frames of mind: The theory of multiple intelligences. New York, NY: Basic Books.

Hirshon, B. (2016). "Modern leaching." Science netlinks. American Association for the Advancement of Science. Retrieved from http://sciencenetlinks.com/science-news/science-updates/modern-leeching/

HowStuffWorks.com. (April 2000). How many senses does a human being have? Retrieved from http://science.howstuffworks.com/life/question242.htm

Kirschenbaum, M. (2008). *Mechanisms: New media and the forensic imagination*. Cambridge, MA and London, UK: MIT University Press.

Loomis, M. (April 2014). 20 things you didn't know about animal senses. Discover: Science for the Curious. Retrieved from http://discovermagazine.com/2014/may/26-20-things-animal-senses

Lord, Z. B. (April 2013). 10 unusual animal senses. Listverse. Retrieved from http://listverse.com/2013/04/13/10-unusual-animal-senses/

Neatorama. (2007). Retrieved from http://www.neatorama.com/2007/09/22/fun-pigeon-facts-super-vision/

Ramachandran, V. S. (2000). Mirror neurons and imitation learning as the driving force behind the great leap forward in human evolution. Edge 69. Retrieved from https://www.edge.org/conversation/mirror-neurons-and-imitation-learning-as-the-driving-force-behind-the-great-leap-forward-in-human-evolution

Searle, J. (2015). *Seeing things as they are: A theory of perception*. Oxford: Oxford University Press.

CHAPTER EIGHT

Augmenting the Posthuman

The Return of Humanist Discourse in Posthumanist Environments

ALIX RÜBSAAM

The Future of Humans and Technology?

The design and development of Artificial Intelligence (AI) could be considered the pinnacle of human intelligence. In this sense, AI is the ultimate augmentation of human thinking translated onto a technological platform. Alongside progress in human innovation, however, we also find growing anxiety related to technology's potential threat. This chapter aims to combine the theoretical underpinnings of critical posthumanism with a discussion on the development of AI in order to appreciate the future convergence of technology and human society.

As I will suggest, the future of humanity is in coevolution with technology. Increasingly, various technologies are coming to play an important role in augmenting how and where human activities such as working and learning take place. It is important, then, to explore the ways we might articulate developments in technology that affect human activity in a manner that is creative and productive in order to appreciate the potential outcomes. Critical posthumanism offers a perspective on this process that might contextualize technological advancement in accord with a broader discussion on human social development.

Critical Posthumanism, Fluid Demarcations, and Distributed Subjects

Critical posthumanism is a set of theories that, in many different ways, respond to 19th-century humanism by problematizing and decentering the humanist subject of the Enlightenment. The aim of critical posthumanism is to transcend cultural demarcations that differentiate the human from the nonhuman, including the boundary between the human and its environment. As such, posthumanism also challenges the perceived demarcation between humans and the technologies that they translate their activities through. Posthuman theories can, thus, significantly contribute to any discussion around human augmentation through technology, and how such developments should be contextualized. Additionally, they can aid in avoiding pitfalls that would root a human(ist)-centered discourse at the heart of technological development. Posthumanism benefits our understanding of emergent technologies such as AI in connection with questions of the human and the nonhuman, and the increasingly porous boundary between the two, because it seeks to problematize culturally constructed demarcations of difference. This is relevant in any discussion on the ways in which human augmentation may shape our being if we are to think of the future of human learning and about how such an activity may become augmented through technology. In this sense, critical posthumanism can assist us to maximize our potential rather than limit it by demarcating and alienating parts of that future.

Judith Halberstam and Ira Livingston (1995) describe how humanist thinking operates differently from posthumanist thinking. According to these thinkers, the human "functions to domesticate and hierarchize difference within the human (whether according to race, class, gender) and to absolutize difference between the human and the nonhuman," whereas the posthuman "does not reduce difference-from-others to difference-from-self, but rather emerges in the pattern of resonance and interference between the two" (Halberstam & Livingston, 1995, p. 10). Put simply, posthumanism offers a way in which identity can be articulated that does not depend on marking a list of things as not-Self, or Other, so as to construct the Self. This sentiment is similar to what Donna Haraway (1991) describes in her "Cyborg Manifesto" where she identifies three "leaky distinctions" or "crucial boundary breakdowns" that are transgressed by what she calls the cyborg. These are the animal and the human, the animal–human and the machine, and the physical and the nonphysical (Haraway, 1991, pp. 151–153). Importantly, Haraway's cyborg comes into existence by transcending a social reality in which these "leaky distinctions" are perceived as and function as definitive, "natural," markers of difference and moves into a vision where these boundaries are cultural and constructed, and thus transgressable. Thus, she proposes "a way out of the maze of dualisms in which we have explained our bodies and our tools to ourselves" (Haraway, 1991, p. 181). Obviously, within this maze of dualisms we should expect to find the perceived dualism that so often appears to exist between humans and technology. As Eugene Thacker (2003) explains, Haraway's cyborg challenges "our conceptions of the sharp division between active subjects and passive objects" (p. 80). Posthumanism paves the way for an explanation of technology that is not so distantly and definitively removed from our selves.

Furthermore, because the humanist subject becomes decentralized in posthumanism, it becomes possible to think of the subject as more distributed among different locations. As Theresa Heffernan (2003) argues, posthumanism offers an "alternative to the conception of the self as fixed, autonomous, authentic, coherent, and universal" (p. 118). A not-exactly-fixed subject can support a conception of human-ness that is augmented through various technologies.

And so, posthumanism is a mode of thought that challenges cultural boundaries and demarcations of difference as a source of (dis)identification, and attempts to overcome these demarcations. The challenge that posthumanism poses to these boundaries calls for a reevaluation of the human as a discrete and clearly demarcated entity. What, then, are we to make of a posthuman figure that is both human and machine, that problematizes the boundary that we tend to place between those two and between our selves and our technology? And how can a decentralized, nonhierarchical view on the human and the nonhuman and thus, by extension, on the human and its technology, aid in understanding how we relate to AI or the augmentation of human intelligence in general?

Posthuman theories tend to reflect on AI because it is the ultimate extension of human activity onto a technological platform. The process of the evolution of technology and changing perceptions of the human go hand in hand. As Cary Wolfe (2010) argues, "posthumanism names a historical moment in which the decentering of the human by its imbrication in technical, medical, informatic, and economic networks is increasingly impossible to ignore, a historical development that points toward the necessity of new theoretical paradigms" (p. xv). Because AI, by the suggestion of its very existence, challenges the privileged hierarchy wherein the human is the most intelligent thing on the planet, it already decenters the human subject from this unprovoked location into a place that is less certain, less secure, and increasingly in need of a reformulation of its status in relation to its environment. Posthumanism offers a similar departure: "a new theoretical model for biological, mechanical, and computational processes that removed the human and *Homo Sapiens* from any particularly privileged position in relation to matters of meaning, information and cognition" (Wolfe, 2010,

p. xii). That is not to say that critical posthumanism is necessarily only relevant (or co-occurrent) when human activity expands to AI or even to technology in general. Wolfe (2010) explains that even before any "historical onset of cyborg technologies that now so obviously inject the post- into the posthuman (...) functional differentiation itself determines the posthumanist *form* of meaning, reason, and communication by untethering it from its moorings in the individual, subjectivity and consciousness" (p. xx). Nonetheless, discussing how humans relate to AI, as an extension of their thinking, a threat to their existence, or both, must be contextualized in a manner that is theoretically grounded. Posthumanism offers this foundation.

Posthuman Artificial Intelligence

The objective is, then, to avoid nightmare visions sketched as worst-case outcomes in the development of AI, to avoid pitfalls prospected by posthumanism, to learn to think of AI in a posthuman context, and to produce a constructive perspective for the future of human cognition. Robert Pepperell (2003), whose work I will discuss in greater detail below, underwrites the relevance of thinking about AI from a posthumanist frame of reference, saying that "much of the disputed territory between the supporters of strong AI and its antagonists rests on assumptions about humans and machines which, in themselves, are subject to revision in the posthuman era" (p. 149). Indeed, not all assumptions need to be rejected, but being cognizant of their tentative status is imperative to the furthering of constructive conversations about AI. Already, AI's default status as strictly nonhuman seems problematic, but it is worthwhile to trace the etiology of this persistent confusion. It is important to establish why AI might be perceived as such a perilous entity rather than an augmentation of human agency and whether the grounds on which this perception takes place are properly argued for.

Artificial Intelligence as Existential Threat, Nonhuman Other, or Neither?

Nick Bostrom (2014) has written extensively on what he identifies as the risks associated with the development or emergence of AI in his book *Superintelligence*. He claims:

> The first superintelligence may shape the future of Earth-originating life, could easily have non-anthropomorphic final goals, and would likely have instrumental reasons to pursue open-ended resource acquisition. If we now reflect that human beings consist of useful resources (such as conveniently located atoms) and that we depend for our

survival and flourishing on many more local resources, we can see that the outcome could easily be one in which humanity quickly becomes extinct. (p. 116)

In short, Bostrom is afraid AI will outsmart, outlive, or even destroy "us." To Bostrom, AI is a wholly demarcated life-form that is utterly Other. One of the closing remarks in his book is that "the challenge we face is, in part, to hold on to our humanity: to maintain our groundedness, common sense, and good-humored decency even in the teeth of this most unnatural and inhuman problem" (Bostrom, 2014, p. 260). In his view, AI is not only nonhuman, but also a threat to the human itself. I will present two instances where Bostrom's interpretation of humans and AI as clearly demarcated from one another, and the problems he associates with this demarcation, become less tenable. It is in these examples that it will become obvious that the border that Bostrom attempts to uphold between organic and machine life is itself, for lack of a better word, quite artificial.

Bostrom discusses what he marks as a difference between humans and AI in a passage where he speaks on what he calls the first and second principal-agent problems. "The first principal-agent problem," he explains, "arises whenever some human entity ('the principal') appoints another ('the agent') to act in the former's interest" and the agent, for whatever reason, does not fulfill the assignment (Bostrom, 2014, p. 128). Bostrom recognizes that "principal-agent problems of this sort are ubiquitous in human economic and political interactions" (p. 128). However, he then poses what he calls the second principal-agent problem. Now, the agent is a "superintelligent system," which "poses an unprecedented challenge" (p. 128). Because what if such a system does not behave in the manner in which it is instructed by the principal? What if this agent does something else entirely? However, in differentiating the "first" from the "second" principal-agent problem, Bostrom suggests that a difference in agents (human or machine) marks for a significant difference about the problem itself. He claims that because the problem with AI arises in the "operational phase," it is different than a human instructing another human to develop something. But the latter, of course, is as much an operational phase as the first and as such should not require anything but the "standard management techniques" that Bostrom claims are sufficient in the first principal-agent problem (p. 128). What he seeks is to control AI in a way that we cannot even control other humans. The two agency problems are the very same. Instructing a human to do an assignment is as much a leap of faith that that human will actually do your bidding as instructing an AI to do an assignment. Unless properly motivated and properly instructed, either may not follow instructions. Presuming, as a human, that one knows all the intricate ways in which another human will respond (both internally and externally) to a command is as dangerous as presuming a computer will. Divorcing these two control problems from each other only demarcates human from nonhuman actors when, in practice, there is, no difference for a human subject or "principal" between trying to control another human or a nonhuman, as long as the potential for autonomous agency of those two entities is recognized. This control problem does not need to be solved for AIs any more than it needs to be for humans. What Bostrom refers to as a "control problem" here is similar to claiming that not being able to control all humans on earth is a "problem."

Bostrom demonstrates another example of this nonhuman-demarcation-fallacy later on in his book. He asks,

> suppose that we had solved the control problem so that we were able to load any value we chose into the motivation system of a superintelligence, making it pursue that value as its final goal. Which value should we install? (…) How could we realistically hope to achieve errorlessness in a matter like this? We might be wrong about morality; wrong about what is good for us; wrong even about what we truly want. (Bostrom, 2014, p. 209)

The scenario he proposes here is not that the technology malfunctions or does something wrong but rather that it operates perfectly and that the humans who control it make a mistake in using it. It becomes increasingly clear that Bostrom is not afraid of this technology inasmuch as he is afraid of humans and the flawed decisions they might make. The problem he sketches is not a technology problem, it is a people problem of the kind that philosophers, people who question democracy as a system or governmental structures as a whole, and those who doubt the wisdom of human beings to govern themselves since long before AI began to be developed.

This is not the only, and definitely not the most entertaining, example of discourse on this specific AI problem. Several iterations of AI have dominated popular culture and scientific discourse for decades, both as developmental goals and as characters in Science Fiction and other fictional contexts. Such fictional AI characters hold several, sometimes competing, categorical positions that evoke existential questions about the human as well as the nonhuman and about where to claim failed responsibility when things go wrong, similar to the ones Bostrom struggles with. One of the most hilarious examples is from Dan Harmon's (2013) animated show *Rick and Morty* in the episode "The Ricks Must Be Crazy" (2015) which closely resembles the arguments proposed by Bostrom. In the episode, Rick's car, outfitted with an AI that is instructed to "keep Summer safe" (that is the exact command given by Rick, in an attempt to protect Summer, his niece), which continuously misinterprets the preferred outcome of fulfilling its programmed function. It kills the first person that walks up to the car, paralyzes the second, emotionally blackmails the third, et cetera. Summer, all the while sitting in the car, attempts to modify the AI methods to keep it from doing more catastrophic damage by reactively requesting it not kill people, then not physically hurt people, then not use emotional extortion, et cetera. Eventually, the AI, responding to Summer's requests, says "My function is to 'Keep Summer safe,' not 'keep Summer being, like, totally stoked about, like, the general vibe and stuff'." Their exchange is a perfect example of both the principal-agent problem (though, in fact, the car's AI does exactly as it is instructed) and the possibility that the principal fails to instruct or communicate what is actually the good or desired outcome.

As said, these examples demonstrate the artificiality of what Bostrom sees as a clear demarcation between the human-ness of the human and the nonhuman-ness of AI. Explained differently, the problem he sketches with AI is the same as the problem that people have with each other because they ultimately cannot trust each other to do what they want and they cannot have access to the inside of other people's perceptions and motivations. Bostrom deems this technology nonhuman on terms that, when examined closely, do not hold. But what is more, these examples show how negotiated and constructed these boundaries are and how they can come into being. In order to better understand the underlying structures of Bostrom's argument and the etiology of the boundaries that he builds upon, it is necessary to dive deeper into the theoretical foundations of posthumanism.

From Body-Less Information and Uploaded Minds to Embodied Human Consciousness

N. Katherine Hayles (1999) wrote in her *How We Became Posthuman* that "a defining characteristic of the present cultural moment is the belief that information can circulate unchanged among different material substrates" (p. 1). This is an important observation that subscribes the idea that it is possible for human intelligence, consciousness, or cognition to occur outside the human body. Additionally, a

> posthuman view configures the human being so that it can be seamlessly articulated with intelligent machines. In the posthuman, there are no essential differences or absolute demarcations between bodily existence and computer simulation, cybernetic mechanism and biological organism, robot teleology and human goals. (Hayles, 1999, p. 3)

But Hayles warns that thinking about a human as "seamlessly articulated" with its environment can turn sour when such a vision is contingent on thinking of information as body-less. She sketches two scenarios:

If my nightmare is a culture inhabited by posthumans who regard their bodies as fashion accessories rather than the ground of being, my dream is a version of the posthuman that embraces the possibilities of information technologies without being seduced by fantasies of unlimited power and disembodied immortality, that recognizes and celebrates finitude as a condition of being human and that understands that human life is embedded in a material world of great complexity, one on which we depend for our continued survival. (Hayles, 1999, p. 5)

What she warns of, then, is thinking of posthumanism as a way to escape the body, and failing to recognize its importance in shaping human cognition and intelligence. Furthermore, she recognizes that the existence of information technologies themselves make that "whether or not interventions have been made on the body; new models of subjectivity emerging from such fields as cognitive science and artificial life imply that even a biologically unaltered Homo Sapiens counts as posthuman" (Hayles, 1999, p. 4). Indeed, the fact that human intelligence has been extrapolated onto nonhuman platforms in and of itself alters the way human intelligence and cognition are viewed. Thus, she calls for a recognition of the importance of embodiment, precisely in the face of emergent technologies such as the AI that Bostrom talks about, that propose to radically augment the human experience that she so firmly places within the body.

An interesting example of how prescient Hayles was in presenting her arguments in *How We Became Posthuman* no less than fifteen years before Bostrom wrote *Superintelligence* is her foreshadowing the pitfalls of reducing human being to informational processing and nothing else. The "great dream and promise of information is that it can be free from the material constraints that govern the mortal world," she writes (Hayles, 1999, p. 13). This dream, which she considers a gross oversight of the importance of embodied experience and a reduction of human consciousness to only information, suggests "it will soon be possible to extract human memories from the brain and import them intact and unchanged, to computer disks" (Hayles, 1999, p. 13). The passage where Bostrom describes "whole brain emulation" exhibits that he thinks of human brain function as nothing more than information processing and that he considers the brain to be not much more than a complex computer. The process he describes, where "raw data from [brain]scanners is fed to a computer for automated image processing to reconstruct the three-dimensional neuronal network that implemented cognition in the original brain" (Bostrom, 2014, p. 30), reduces human cognition to not just information, but to a 3D image. Tellingly, he proposes that whole brain emulation "does not require that we figure out how human cognition works or how to program an AI. It requires only that we understand the low-level functional characteristics of the *basic computational elements of the brain*" (Bostrom, 2014, p. 30, emphasis mine). Clearly, he proposes that if someone manages to capture these "basic computational elements" and store them properly in a computer, that they have effectively reproduced human consciousness in a machine, foregoing the possibility that human consciousness is made up of more than information processing. Bostrom does refer to other processes that may be going on in the brain later on. He calls it "the messy biological detail of a real brain" (Bostrom, 2014, p. 33). Hayles, of course, would respond that it is precisely these messy details that inform a crucial part of human being. She emphasizes this when she describes that

> if the name of the game is processing information, it is only a matter of time until intelligent machines replace us as our evolutionary heirs. Whether we decide to fight them or join them by becoming computers ourselves, the days of the human race are numbered. The problem here does not lie in the choice between these options; rather, it lies in the framework constructed so as to make these options the only two available. The computational universe becomes dangerous when it goes from being a useful heuristic to an ideology that privileges information over everything else. (Hayles, 1999, p. 243)

Using Hayles' argument, it becomes possible to subvert Bostrom's. AI poses a threat to humanity and what it means to be human only if we use too narrow a definition of what the "human" is. We must think of that entity as being more than just information that has, by coincidence, been trapped in a biological body. From Bostrom's tendency to think of the "basic computational elements" of the brain as the only relevant ones, it is obvious that to him human cognition is not much more than meat-based information processing. Approached from a more embodied venture point, it becomes possible to look at the development of AI as less threatening because while it may become a force that is better at information processing than we are; it still cannot outdo us at being human.

Hayles warns about the effects of gradually reducing how we think of ourselves to just that, information computing meat-machines. Now it is clear that a productive way to underpin discourse on AI must be a model that avoids the nightmares of both Bostrom and Hayles. In other words, we should not think of AI as a radical other that threatens to snuff out our existence, nor should we think of human existence as seamlessly articulated into a technological, informational, platform, with no grounds in human embodiment. How can we articulate this precarious balance?

The Posthuman and Technological Environment of the Human and Artificial Intelligence

Urgently relevant to this question is the manner in which Robert Pepperell (2003), in *The Posthuman Condition*, outlines the difference between a humanist and a posthumanist view. "Where humanists saw themselves as distinct beings in an antagonistic relationship with their surroundings," he suggests, "posthumans tend to regard their own being as embodied in an extended technological world" (Pepperell, 2003, p. 152). This is important for the location in which technology is supposed to find itself and how that location ties to the location of the human. Pepperell's view on this posthuman, embodied, but extended technological world unifies a solution to the anxiety of Hayles that humans stand to lose their bodies and Bostrom's fear that humans are at risk of losing themselves in the face of overwhelming information technologies such as AI. "The debate between supporters of strong AI and its antagonists," Pepperell notes, "rests on a further assumption: that humans and machines are distinct entities," which underpin a "methodological fallacy known as 'technological determinism,' in which technologies generally are seen as having specific determining influence on the course of human events, while forgetting of course, that humans develop technology in the first place" (Pepperell, 2003, p. 152). Contrary to this assumption, the information that informs technology is not detached from the human that it emerges from. So while "finding algorithms that encapsulate human thought is what strong AI claims as its goal," it should not be forgotten that "although algorithms can be used to describe aspects of reality (…) they are nevertheless constructions of the human mind" (Pepperell, 2003, p. 142). Thus, any worldview that is generated or held by an AI is nothing but a human worldview, however augmented. Such a view of AI as augmented human cognition facilitates a posthuman interpretation wherein there is no struggle between the human and its technology, but rather an embodied, extended relation between the two.

Posthumanism, for Pepperell, is exactly that set of theories that aims to transcend cultural demarcations that have held reign over how we view ourselves. The boundary that he is interested in is that which is provoked by technologies that "blur the distinction between organic and mechanical" (Pepperell, 2003, p. 9). He sees such technologies as "the background to what I call here posthumanism, and it leads us to ask—how will we distinguish between the real and the artificial, the original and the simulated, the organic and the mechanical" (Pepperell, 2003, p. 11). It is precisely this question that provokes posthumanism to suggest that there is less of a need for an answer because the question itself is becoming outdated. Consider Pepperell's (2003) suggestion:

> If it is the case that the long-held separation between brain and body, or between the mental and the physical, is being eroded as the tide of contemporary ideas run against it, then we might be gradually drawn to the conclusion that our minds, our bodies, and the world are continuous. (…) The apparent separation between the human and the environment is invalid in the posthuman era and, therefore, needs revision. (p. 20)

Following this view, "the human is a 'fuzzy edged' entity that is profoundly dependent on its surroundings, much as the brain is dependent on the body" and because of a "perpetual exchange between the living human organism and its surroundings, there can be no fixed state of a living human" (Pepperell, 2003, p. 20). While avoiding the pitfalls that make Hayles nervous, Pepperell finds a way to "seamlessly articulate" the human and technology. He does not erode the body but rather highlights its importance. Furthermore, he opposes Cartesian dualism and proposes

> if we accept that the mind and body cannot be absolutely distinguished and that the body and the environment cannot be absolutely distinguished then we are left with an apparently absurd, yet logically consistent conclusion: that consciousness and the environment cannot be absolutely distinguished. (…) The general implication is that we can never determine the absolute boundary of the human, either physically or mentally. (Pepperell, 2003, p. 22)

There are two conclusions that can be drawn from posthuman theories like Pepperell's that firmly embed the human mind as contingent on the human body and its environment. Either it means that AI (if it is to match human intelligence or surpass it on the same linear scale, rather than be a wholly different form of intelligence, or just one aspect of it) cannot be created unless it has as human a body as we do. Or, it is untenable to think of such an AI as anything but the extension of human intelligence and cognition, human activity bled into the environment it was already inseparable from. From the latter conclusion it follows that humans and AI are not in "perpetual antagonism" with one another, but rather that either the one (AI) is an externalization, an augmentation, of a process of the other (the human) that seeps into its environment or that they (AI and human) are already inseparable from one another. These two possibilities depend on whether we view AI as a creation, a tool made by humans and nothing else, or whether we think of it as a nonhuman entity with agency of its own that exists in the environment of the human as much as the human exists in its environment. Note that this last distinction does not matter much either way because both views approach AI as part of the environment that the human is entangled with. The point here is to think from the human to its environment and in both cases we find AI within that environment.

What is more, the theoretical context in which AI can be thought of may itself depend on a posthuman explanation of human cognition:

> the continuous view of human existence not only rejects the idea that humans are in opposition to nature, it also rejects the long-cherished belief that human thought is a

unique case amongst natural phenomena—something that can never be replicated in any other medium. (Pepperell, 2003, p. 77)

Only rejecting this view would even allow for the idea that a human kind of intelligence could occur in the environment that it is so deeply entangled with. So, as Pepperell (2003) argues, "in posthuman terms, the process of thought is distributed, not only through the brain but through the whole body, and even into the environment" (p. 96). If that process becomes augmented, and expressed in other contexts, such as AI, we can see how AI is an augmentation of human activity.

Perhaps most convinced about the possibilities of the extensions of the human brain is Andy Clark. Clark (2003), the title of whose book *Natural Born Cyborgs* reveals what he thinks about the prospects of human coevolving with our technology "not in the merely superficial sense of combining flesh and wires but in the more profound sense of being human-technology symbionts—thinking and reasoning systems whose minds and selves are spread across biological brain and nonbiological circuitry" (p. 3). However, he asserts, this is not some novelty in the history of the human as "cognitive hybridization (…) is an aspect of our humanity, which is as basic and ancient as the use of speech and which has been extending its territory ever since" (Clark, 2003, p. 4). This follows from Clark's observation that the human brain is inherently plastic. In his view, human cognition can adapt to any change in embodiment, but, importantly, it can only do so as long as it is, in fact, embodied. He talks about the distribution of human cognition in that he recognizes that "what is special about human brains, and what best explains the distinctive features of human intelligence is precisely their ability to enter into deep and complex relationships with nonbiological constructs, props, and aids" (Clark, 2003, p. 5). The human and its environment are fluid as "many of our tools are not just external props and aids, but they are deep and integral parts of the problem-solving systems we now identify as human intelligence" (Clark, 2003, p. 5).

Interestingly, although Clark does appear to subscribe to a brain-as-computer-vision here, he does not exclude the embodiment of said brain (be it a computer or not) from being a crucial and even defining factor. Because the brain is essentially plastic, malleable, and adaptable to virtually anything, it does not matter to his argument what the metaphorical workings of it are, because it displays such plasticity that it can adapt to any environment. In fact, this plasticity subscribes the importance of the environment because it is that which the brain "adapts" to, what shapes it, and what it is shaped by. In other words, the brain is contingent on its environment for its behavior and existence and Clark's notion of cognitive plasticity argues for embodiment being one of the most important characteristics of human cognition. A defining human quality is thus "our capacity to continually restructure and rebuild our own mental circuitry, courtesy of an empowering web of culture, education, technology and artifacts" (Clark, 2003, p. 10). The question of where this "mental circuitry" takes place, or what locations it might be limited to is less relevant than the fact that it is continuously being reconfigured. Following his research and the tests Clark (2003) has conducted, he concludes that "despite the probable presence of some present genetic components in our body-images (…) our brains depend on *perceived correlations* to continuously construct a model of—and hence a sense of—our bodily bounds and locations" (p. 61). Hayles (1999) appears to think of embodiment as quite stable or constant when she warns against viewing the body as a vessel for form-less information or "the original prosthesis we all learn to manipulate, so that extending or replacing the body with other prostheses becomes a continuation of a process that began before we were born" (p. 31). But Clark (2003) sees our body-image as much more fluid. He exemplifies the brain's dependency on perceived correlation: "one reason that this makes sense, of course, is that our bodies *do* change during our lifetimes" (p. 61). The physical process of aging already requires a cognitive flexibility that might be put to use in the extrapolation of human cognition in nonhuman environments. He calls the brain

> in many ways special, but it is not special in the sense of providing a privileged arena such that certain operations must occur *inside* that arena, or in directly wired contact with it, on pain of not counting as part of our mental machinery at all. (Clark, 2003, pp. 26–27)

Rather, he thinks there is "a complex matrix of brain, body and technology [that] can actually constitute the problem-solving machine that we should properly identify as *ourselves*" (Clark, 2003, p. 27). The question Clark (2003) raises—"do I merely *use* my hands, my hippocampus, my ventral cochlear nucleus, or are they part of the system—the 'me'—that does the using?" (p. 29)—This underpins the notion that what he calls "the system," "cognitive machinery," or the "problem-solving machine" not only includes but are constituted by the human body. As such, adding tools to the body to augment its agency, extends the possibilities, without undermining the embodiment of the mind. Who we are then is "as much informed by the specific sociotechnological matrix in which the biological organism exists as by those various conscious and unconscious neural events that happen to occur inside the good-old biological skin-bag" (i.e., Clark's (2003) affectionate term for the body, p. 33).

Conclusion

The future of AI is contingent on a technology problem, not a human problem, namely on how fluidly it can be interwoven into our experience. As Clark (2003) observes,

> the difference between links forged by nerves and tendons, by fiber-optic cables, and by radio waves are relevant *only insofar* as they affect the timing, flow, and density of informational exchange (…) because they affect the nature of our relationship with the various kinds of tools, equipment and subsystems. (p. 103)

Only when these links function as well as our bodies do will "the interface between the conscious user and the tool [be] liable to become transparent, allowing the tool to function more like a proper part of the user" (Clark, 2003, p. 103). That is to say, if using AI becomes as unnoticeable as when we "use" our legs, will it have grown into its potential. Clark (2003) offers an example of how used we have become to writing things down: "to see the contribution of tools such as pen and paper is thus in terms of a deep *complementarity* between what is the biological brain is naturally good at, and what the tool provides" (p. 74). He shares Bostrom's view that language has been a crucial first step in becoming conscious, and sees this as our first coupling with technology: "With speech, text, and the tradition of using them as critical tools under our belts, humankind entered the first phase of its cyborg existence" (Clark, 2003, p. 81). So if we consider the acquisition of language (as a tool) to be the historical point at which humans became humans, then, as Hayles (1999) asserts, "we have always been posthuman" (p. 279). Becoming posthuman is, thus, not a biological, evolutionary, or historical rupture, but a shift in perception with regard to how we think about what it means to be human.

With Clark's vision then, the solution is complete, the loop is closed. Bostrom's view on AI as distinct from the human is unsustainable, Hayles' nightmare of disembodied information is avoided. Pepperell's proposition that the human consciousness, the human body, and its environment are in a continuously contingent relationship with each other, and, finally, the plasticity with which Clark views the human brain, human intelligence, and cognition as able to be distributed in an ever-changing, ever-adapting manner into multiple technological environments, including AI. Thus, thinking of AI as wholly nonhuman is untenable. Any threat that exudes from it, then, is a threat we pose to ourselves. Furthermore, it does not hold to think of the human as demarcated from its environment. When that environment is our technology, the boundary between human and machine must be assessed as equally porous. If human intelligence is embodied, then any technology that flows from that is too. In the development of AI, it is easy to think of whatever comes out of it as equal and similar to all that humans are or have to offer in terms of cognition. But thinking of AI that way actually reduces the human to an information processing meat-machine. Posthumanism offers a way to think of ourselves as embodied because it challenges the binary divide of human/nonhuman in technology. As such, augmenting ourselves with AI no longer poses the risk for us to lose our bodies or our selves.

References

Bostrom, N. (2014). *Superintelligence: Paths, dangers, strategies.* Oxford: Oxford University Press.
Clark, A. (2003). *Natural-born cyborgs: Minds, technologies, and the future of human intelligence.* Oxford: Oxford University Press.
Halberstam, J., & Livingston, I. (Eds.). (1995) *Posthuman bodies.* Bloomington, IN: Indiana University Press.
Haraway, D. J. (1991). *Simians, cyborgs, and women: The reinvention of nature.* London: Free Association Books.
Hayles, N. K. (1999). *How we became posthuman: Virtual bodies in cybernetics, literature, and informatics.* Chicago: University of Chicago Press.
Heffernan, T. (2003). Bovine anxieties, virgin births, and the secret of life. *Cultural Critique, 53*(1), 116–133.
Pepperell, R. (2003). *The posthuman condition: Consciousness beyond the brain.* Bristol: Intellect Books.
Roiland, J., & Harmon, D. (Writers), & Polcino D., & Michels P. (Directors). (2013). The Ricks must be crazy [Television series episode]. In J. Roiland & D. Harmon (Producers), *Rick and Morty.* Atlanta, GA: Adult Swim.
Thacker, E. (2003). Data made flesh: Biotechnology and the discourse of the posthuman. *Cultural Critique, 53*(1), 72–97.
Wolfe, C. (2010). *What is posthumanism?* Minneapolis, MN: University of Minnesota Press.

CHAPTER NINE

What Augmented Intelligence?

Power and Control in the Era of Open Networked Learning

RITA KOP

Introduction: What Intelligence?

In 1977, Heidegger proposed that the contemporary world was in transition from the modern to the technological way-of-being. In this environment, humans and objects act upon one another in ways that mutually transform their characteristics and activity. He wrote this at a time when technologies were relatively simple and could be classified as tools. Today, however, emerging technologies are quite different. They are complicated assemblages of data and artifacts with which humans interact, and their availability to humans involves multiple algorithms produced by computer scientists. This complicates scrutiny of the tools and the assessment of their value to augment the human/technological way-of-being.

This chapter highlights the challenges and opportunities for working with algorithms and machine learning technologies to augment intelligence in networked learning environments. Before discussing intelligence augmentation (IA), however, it would be useful to define what is meant by the word "intelligence." Intelligence is a contested concept that tries to clarify how individuals differ from one another in their ability to "understand complex ideas, to adapt effectively to the environment, to learn from experience, to engage in various forms of reasoning, to overcome obstacles by taking thought" (Neisser et al., 1996, p. 77).

The relationship between the idea of intelligence and the concept of "intelligent quotient" (IQ) remains strong. Intelligent quotient refers to the psychological test used during schooling for cohorts of children to measure general intelligence related to the acquisition of knowledge. However, there are many critiques of this narrow interpretation of intelligence. Shaviro (2016), for example, establishes that the concept of intelligence is a lot more complicated because of the complexity of the functions of the brain and mind:

> We don't even understand our own intelligence and mental activity. We live in a golden age of neuroscience; every year, we learn more and more about the functioning of the brain. And yet, despite this accumulation of knowledge, nobody really knows what consciousness is, or how it works. Philosophers and scientists disagree on even the most basic issues. We have no idea how to get from the brain to the mind: from electrochemical processes in our neurons to things like feelings and thoughts and experiences. (Shaviro, 2016)

This uncertainty regarding how the mind really works has for many years led to a discussion about the narrow interpretation of the concept of intelligence as cognitive processes related to the verbal-linguistic, logical-mathematical, and bodily-kinesthetic. It also problematizes the notion of basing technologies on such narrow assumptions of how the mind works and how intelligence is defined. This is especially obvious with regard to Gardner's work on multiple intelligences (Gardner, 2003; Hanafin, 2014; Jackson, 2009, Kincheloe, 2004; Vennema, 1997; Vieira, 2014). Gardner believed that the work on intelligence should be interpreted not only on the basis of test performance by school children, but also by exceptions to these rules; exceptional performers not in schools. He suggested that this would lead to the need for a much wider spectrum of criteria to base intelligence on and Gardner proposed eight characteristics as a commonality with regard to how human beings carry out tasks in relation to goals set. As a complement to the three characteristics used in most intelligence tests of verbal-linguistic, logical-mathematical, and visual-spatial intelligence, also bodily-kinesthetic, musical, he introduced the interpersonal (the capacity to understand what other people's intentions and motivations are), the intrapersonal (the capacity for reflexivity, to understand oneself, including emotions and motivations), and the naturalist. Gardner initially received much criticism from psychologists as he was not interested in testing these perceived characteristics in the traditional way. However, educationalists had an instinctive affinity with his theory as their practice showed on a daily basis that learner performance and experiences are greatly influenced by the additional intelligences suggested by Gardner. This position also agrees with the situated view of mind that has become increasingly popular (Bredo, 1999;

Lave & Wenger, 2002; Meyes, 2002, Picard et al., 2004). My experience as an educationalist, developer, designer, and researcher of education has also suggested that intelligence should be perceived as a wider spectrum of abilities and competencies related to how people learn in the context of everyday activities (Kincheloe, 2004; Kop & Carroll, 2016). If we were to accept this perspective it means that created learning opportunities should be related to day-to-day activities and should appeal to a wide spectrum of participants. Moreover, it suggests that education itself should be accessible to all and equitable, while outcomes should not be related solely to a narrow set of test criteria.

Why did I go to this depth in explaining the concept of intelligence? If intelligence does not exclusively entail a cognitive ability narrowly based on language and mathematical ability in an artificial school setting, but includes other states and characteristics of the human mind in day-to-day experiences also, then this complicates the choice of technologies used to augment these states and characteristics. Moreover, if it acknowledges that learning is a complex process, this will also influence which technologies will be used and their suitability to augment intelligence. Furthermore, it might mean that "augmented intelligence turns data into valuable knowledge that is actionable for the user—effectively shifting information from passive intelligence to results-driven intelligence" as suggested by Lucini (2014, p. S4). This suggests that knowledge, instead of being passively transferred, is situated in the context in which it was created. For the purposes of this chapter, my premise is that the mind and learning involve more than cognitive ability and development and that intelligence is a complex dimension in the human learning process. If emerging assemblages of technologies are being used to "augment" learning, then these technologies need to be scrutinized to determine whether or not they are based on "wide" ideas of intelligence. Clearly, this will give researchers food for thought when developing algorithms for educational purposes. It requires the close scrutiny of the architecture of the Web and an analysis of emerging technologies to provide transparency and clarity with regard to the problems and challenges ahead.

The Complexity of Information and Data on the Web

We humans live in an era in which the availability of information and artifacts has shifted from scarcity to a large and abundant stream that requires filtering to bring it back to a manageable level for learning. This information stream consists not only of knowledge verified by experts, but also of communications and artifacts produced by you and me. We have seen substantial growth and development of the Web over the past several years. The Web only fifteen years ago mainly consisted of fairly static content and basic sharing opportunities. This has now changed with the addition of social media, the Cloud, the use of Web semantics and mobile and wireless technologies. Content is increasingly produced by users and there has been an exponential growth in the use of social media such as blogs and video-sharing sites.

The Web has grown exponentially (Internet World Stats, n.d.) and is increasingly distributed via personal presence sites such as Facebook and YouTube in addition to micro blogging sites such a Twitter. All this data is stored, used, and reused in different ways and mashed up into new information.

People's information habits have "deeply ingrained habitual patterns" (Fisher & Naumer, 2006, p. 2). It seems that people will first and foremost obtain information from people with whom they have a strong relationship; those whom they trust. These are usually found in their circle of family, close friends, and their local communities. The Web is supplementing these "information grounds" and is also creating new structures for obtaining information. People start to use multiple tools and trusted people, information filters, online to deal with the vast amounts of information that need to be processed. In networked learning, information brokers have started to appear. They might be hubs on networks, who recommend information, and to whom people are attracted because of their reputation. Studies using social network analysis show that people's opinions and beliefs are influenced by these conduits (Granovetter, 1978; Xie et al., 2011, p. 1).

A further complexity on the evolving Web is that data and data storage have also evolved under the influence of emerging technologies. Instead of capturing data and storing them in a database, the large data-streams that users need to deal with might be stored in the Cloud and could be represented and visualized through the use of algorithms and machine learning. However, once we start analyzing the available tools and strategies for filtering and managing the information and data streams it becomes clear that software and algorithms are not simply some lines of code, but are shaped by a number of different social, political, and economic interests that might influence their value for the augmentation of human intelligence. Moreover, as Fenwick (2015) suggests, when discussing changes big data force onto professional practice, this is happening without much discussion by stakeholders involved and is

> the reduction of knowledge and terms of decision-making. Data analytics software works from simplistic premises: that problems are technical, comprised of knowable, measurable parameters, and can be solved through technical calculation. Complexities of ethics and values, ambiguities and tensions, culture and politics and even the context in which data is collected are not accounted for. (Fenwick, 2015, p. 70)

Perhaps it is time that some questions be asked, such as: Who decides what data and information is important; what knowledge is valuable? The computer scientist who produces the algorithm, or governments? One of the problems highlighted in the development of algorithms is the introduction of researcher and developer biases in the tool, which could affect the quality and the value of the recommendation or search result (Hardt, 2014). I will come back to this later.

Another major challenge for learning is that the availability of any piece of knowledge and information to anyone is called into question, as was the initial suggestion when the Web was developed. Even though it seems on the surface that people have access to any piece of information and resource they would like on the Web, in reality this access is restricted by the structure of the Web and by the ranking of information by search engines (Barabasi, 2003; Goldman, 2010; Grimmelmann, 2010). Search engines are driven by algorithms. Gillespie (2014) suggests that these algorithms play a role not only in ranking and finding information, but also in producing and endorsing knowledge. He contests that "the algorithmic assessment of information represents a particular knowledge logic, one built on specific presumptions about what knowledge is and how one should identify its most relevant components" (p. 2). Mager (2014) even suggests that there is an algorithmic ideology based on Silicon Valley capitalist principles that determines search results.

In the field of education it is now possible for human beings to connect with "knowledgeable others," creating and exchanging information and digital artifacts, and developing knowledge on an unprecedented scale within an open environment. In this sense, there is an alternative to both algorithms and the professor. Human beings can take control of shaping their learning experiences and making their own learning decisions Clearly, transparency of the tools and technologies used will be required to allow learners to effectively make choices about technologies to augment their intelligence. It would be a major step in an educational context for instance to move from the validation of knowledge and information by professors to the validation of knowledge by the algorithm. Algorithms are assemblages composed of data and in an open environment of big data. The first step in clarifying algorithms and their use is to analyze what they consist of.

Working with Big Data

The term "big data" is relatively new; the hype really started in 2013, and several people have shown an interest in the concept, because big data might have the potential to open up access to ideas, vast amounts of quantitative data related to what humans do and how they do it. At the same time, critical questions have been fielded about its usefulness, if the analytics following from "crunching" the large numbers would not lead to understandable analytics (Boyd, 2010; Chomsky, 2013). In the words of Chomsky: "our problems are not lack of access to data, but understanding them. [Big data] is very useful if I want to find out something without going to the library, but I have to understand it, and that's the problem." This sentiment was also expressed by Boyd: "Unfortunately, what gets lost in this excitement is a critical analysis of what this data is and what it means" (Boyd, 2010, p. 2). In dealing with so much data and information, technologists, researchers, and developers need to envisage the optimal processes and techniques for analyzing the data and translating them into understandable, consumable, or actionable modes of representation for results to be useful and accessible for users to digest. The ability to effectively communicate complex ideas is critical in producing something of value, which translates research and development findings into practice.

But Boyd and Crawford (2012) suggest that Big Data work does not only force a change in scale and effectiveness in analysis, but also a "profound change at the levels of epistemology and ethics" (p. 665). They highlight that we should be mindful that if we change the essence of the information used, or the methods that we use to collect information or interpret it, we also alter the essence of the created knowledge and the theories they are build upon. This suggests that we need to go a little deeper in our analysis of the heart of algorithms, the building blocks and assemblages most commonly used to analyze and parse data to make the resulting information usable and accessible for people.

Power and Control of Algorithms

> We should interrogate the architecture of cyberspace as we interrogate the code of Congress.
> —Lawrence Lessig (2000)

Software and its inherent technologies have slowly but surely become more and more powerful and are now at the heart of society's digital activities. "It has become a universal language, the interface to our imagination and the world. What electricity and the combustion engine were for the early 20th Century, software is to the early 21st Century" (Manovitch, 2013, p. 2). Scholars have scrutinized digital and cultural technologies, but only recently have they started to scrutinize their underlying systems. Diakopoulos (2013), Kitchin (2014), and Danaher (2015) suggest that the Web's architecture, and in particular algorithms, are not only in control, but that they are really out of control as algorithms are increasingly becoming powerful in the decisions people make. As algorithms are the basis for much development on the Web, which is increasingly our superhighway to usable and accessible information, it is necessary for scientists to scrutinize the architecture, the underlying structure of the information we access, and to determine its value to society, not just its effectiveness for information retrieval, but also to pay heed to how algorithms are developed and what their influence is on our information, knowledge, and learning.

Who Influences the Content of Data-Driven Systems?

If we consider the ethics of moving from an environment characterized by human communication to one that is data-driven and includes technical elements, over which the people who use them have little or no control, and that have over the past few years grown exponentially in delivering and recommending information, it is clear that new challenges have been introduced to the environment that will affect augmenting intelligence, education, and learning. For instance, one of the problems suggested in the development of algorithms is the introduction of researcher biases in the technology itself, which could affect the quality of the recommendation or search result (Hardt, 2014). Moreover, Fenwick points out the lack of training in work with big data by educationalists (Fenwick, 2015), which was also emphasized by Boyd and Crawford (2012). Currently, the majority of "data-workers" are computer scientists and mathematicians, who do not necessarily have a background in the social sciences. Boyd and Crawford (2012) suggest that

> When computational skills are positioned as the most valuable, questions emerge over who is advantaged and who is disadvantaged in such a context. This, in its own way, sets up new hierarchies around "who can read the numbers", rather than recognizing that computer scientists and social scientists both have valuable perspectives to offer. Significantly, this is also a gendered division. Most researchers who have computational skills at the present moment are male and, as feminist historians and philosophers of science have demonstrated, who is asking the questions determines which questions are asked. (p. 674)

What their quote suggests is that computer scientists and social scientists should work together at developing bias-free high-quality (predictive) analytics tools, and that team-working of people in different fields for the mining and analysis of big data would also be desirable. Of course, as data is widely available and abundant, it is tempting to make use of them, but as Fenwick (2015) suggests new techniques used might change our own practices that have evolved on a premise of trust as in the past human beings used to discuss and communicate to reach a level of agreement, rather than that technologies would make decisions for them.

These practices are relational experiences based on human engagement with technologies and will be forced to change as we increasingly rely on technologies. The binary way through which technologies make judgment calls will undoubtedly increase with a reliance on comparison and prediction that "can be self-reinforcing and reproductive, augmenting path dependency and entrenching existing inequities" (Fenwick, 2015, p. 71). Humans, the materials and technologies they use, morph into one action, and educationalists need to be aware what effect the ever evolving technologies have on their practice. This will especially be the case if the people producing the algorithms are not aware of their own influence on the reinforcement of stereotypes when using big data for advanced developments if this is not counterbalanced by expertise from social scientists. Clearly, also the development of automated algorithm development has inherent management problems, as there will be a moment that things go wrong, and it will be difficult to determine who is responsible. Furthermore, as most current algorithm-based search results are produced by large powerful corporations, Mager (2014) suggests that these corporations should be counter balanced by the development of a noncorporate web index. Such counterbalance safeguards data and information, and makes accessible all information to people, rather than to rely on recommendations by commercial search engines. This is especially important in an education sense, when learning is the goal and when attempting to augment intelligence as search corporations' customers are their advertisers, not necessarily learners who might like to be able to find valuable information for their learning projects that involves not necessarily monetary profit for the search engine involved.

Government Control Over Data and Algorithms

There have been calls for a public search engine, owned by government. The problem with this stance, however, is which government should own it and what should governments own? It is clear from current "data and publicity-wars" online that governments are increasingly trying to create and own as much data as possible as these can be used for defense, but also in wars, and are already used in wars (Owen, 2015). It would be too much for this chapter to go into this too much, but as all algorithm systems contain inherent biases (as they were designed by human beings), this is a frightening prospect. In the words of Owen:

> If algorithms represent a new ungoverned space, a hidden and potentially ever-evolving unknowable public good, then they are an affront to our democratic system, one that requires transparency and accountability in order to function. A node of power that exists outside of these bounds is a threat to the notion of collective governance itself. This, at its core, is a profoundly undemocratic notion—one that states

will have to engage with seriously if they are going to remain relevant and legitimate to their digital citizenry who give them their power. (Owen, 2015, p. 5)

Clearly, there are major challenges related to the neutrality of the Web and who is in charge that might influence the structure and democracy of the Web.

Harnessing the Power of Algorithms for Learning and Augmenting Intelligence

Throughout the ages, and also in online education and connectivist learning communication dialogue between participants has been seen to be at the heart of a quality learning experience (Bates, 2015; Jones, Dirckinck-Holmfeld, & Lindstom, 2006). It is even suggested that this human touch is a necessary component in learning and needs to be incorporated into the design and development of learning systems and learning environments (Bates, 2015). The presence and engagement of knowledgeable others is seen to be vital in extending the ideas, critical analysis and thinking of participants in any learning setting (Jones et al., 2006).

This means that when developing data-driven technologies for learning, it is important to somehow harness this human element for the good of the learning process. However, this also means that the filtering of information, or the asking of Socratic questions, the aggregation of information, should be mediated through human beings (Kop, 2012; Qoussini & Jusoh, 2014). Social microblogging sites, such as Twitter, have been shown to do this successfully, as the followers, who provide information and links to resources, have been chosen by the user and are seen to provide serendipitous information; they are valuable as people who are "followed" have the trust of the user.

In using algorithm-based searches this level of trust is much more problematic to achieve. However, if algorithm-based platform developers can raise the levels of "serendipity" in the information stream this might also enhance thinking and critical analysis levels in users as this seems to be the closest an automated learning environment can come to a critical knowledgeable other (Saadatmand & Kumpulainen, 2013). If a combination of "social" searching and "serendipity" can be incorporated in technology-based learning ecosystems it might be possible to enhance people's learning. The challenge, if we also want to augment multiple intelligences, is that it will be necessary to provide a variety of information and multimedia that are connected to human actions (Lucini, 2014), but that also involve the "entanglement" of nonhuman active algorithms with human intentions to create worthwhile experiences (Knox, 2015, p. 75).

Clearly, these developments are only in their infancy. Shedroff suggests that,

> most technological experiences—including digital and especially, online experiences—have paled in comparison to real-world experiences and have been relatively unsuccessful as a result. What these solutions require first and foremost is an understanding by their developers of what makes a good experience; then to translate these principles, as well as possible, into the desired media without the technology dictating the form of the experience. (Shedroff, 2009, p. 3)

It is imperative to not let the technology dictate the development. Interactive learning ecosystems are currently under development by several research groups worldwide (Fournier & Kop, 2015). Researchers are experimenting with a combination of the use of algorithms to provide recommendations for information and media, with human communication and interaction to create worthwhile learning experiences. Their aim is to support users in the management of their lifelong learning, for instance by providing recommendations of information, or visualization of progress along the learning journey. Research in these fields has made clear that there are still major challenges in using technology to analyze learning and to use predictive analytics and visualizations to advance learning, not in the least ethical concerns related to privacy and ownership of data (Qoussini & Jusoh, 2014) and concerns related to biases in the technologies developed.

These concerns force researchers working on the development of data-driven learning systems to reflect on what they are replacing human interaction with, and what might be the value, the strengths and weaknesses, of the replacement to education and learning.

Conclusions

When discussing IA, it is clear that there are challenges to the complicated concept of intelligence itself, particularly if one agrees that intelligence is not solely composed of cognitive, language, and logical components in an artificial school environment, but that it also involves the messier aspects related to the affective, active, and intuitive human experiences in a particular situation. Enhancing these through technology is problematic. If we further acknowledge that learning is a complex process, it becomes clear that the choice of technologies used and the suitability of chosen technologies to augment learning complicates this even further. We might believe that technologies such as video, audio, and their application in a learning management system (in addition to asynchronous discussion forums) are fairly simple to implement. However, more intrusive and less transparent technologies, such as the personalization of the learning environment and the use of data-driven technologies including visualizations and recommendations of information—which are based on algorithms, are more problematic. These assemblages, produced by people, might contain biases depending on who produced them.

This leads me to a possible role of social scientists in these developments. They could contribute to the integrity of the developed systems through an involvement from the start in ensuring avoidance of biases in the architecture and designs, and also in ensuring high ethical standards in data use. In addition, it would help to situate the human in equitable communicative action in knowledge and information projects that consist of more than effectiveness in retrieving or recommending information. It suggests the need for thought not only at the technology development level but also at government levels on power and control issues related to the future world that we are creating.

References

Barabasi, A. (2003). *Linked: How everything is connected to everything else and what it means*. New York, NY: Penguin Books.

Bates, A. W. (2015) Teaching in a digital age: Guidelines for designing teaching and learning. Retrieved from http://opentextbc.ca/teachinginadigitalage/

Boyd, D. (2010). Streams of content, limited attention: The flow of information through social media. *EDUCAUSE Review*, 45(5), pp. 26–36. Boyd, D., & Crawford, K. (2012). Critical questions for Big Data, in Information. *Communication & Society*, 15(5), 662–679.

Bredo, E. (1999). Reconstructing educational psychology. In P. Murphy (Ed.), *Learners, learning and assessment* (pp. 23–45). London, Thousand Oaks, CA, and New Delhi, India: Paul Chapman Publishing and Sage Publications.

Chomsky, N. (2013). Panel discussion at MIT's Engaging Data 2013 Conference. Retrieved from http://news.idg.no/cw/art.cfm?id=B1428B45-F71E-347F-694D9B225EA5D663

Diakopoulos, N. (2013). Algorithmic accountability reporting: On the investigation of black boxes. A tow/knight brief. Tow Center for Digital Journalism, Columbia Journalism School. Retrieved from https://towcenter.org/research/algorithmic-accountability-on-the-investigation-of-black-boxes-2/

Danaher, J. (2015). How to study algorithms: Challenges and methods, *H+ Magazine*, retrieved from http://hplusmagazine.com/2015/07/28/how-to-study-algorithms-challenges-and-methods/

Fenwick, T. (2015). Professional responsibility in a future of data analytics. In B. Williamson (Ed.), *Coding/learning, software and digital data in education*. Stirling: University of Stirling.

Fisher, K., & Naumer, C. (2006). Information grounds: Theoretical basis and empirical findings on information flow in social settings. In A. Spink & C. Cole (Eds.), *New directions in human information behaviour* (pp. 93–111). Amsterdam: Kluwer.

Fournier, H., & Kop, R. (2015). MOOC learning experience design: Issues and challenges. *International Journal on E-Learning*, *14*(3), pp. 289–304. Chesapeake, VA: Association for the Advancement of Computing in Education (AACE).

Gardner, H. (2003). *Multiple intelligences after 20 years*. Paper presented at the American Educational Research Association, April 21, 2003. Retrieved July 4, 2007 from http://ocw.metu.edu.tr/pluginfile.php/9274/mod_resource/content/1/Gardner_multiple_intelligent.pdf

Gillespie, T. (2014) The relevance of algorithms. forthcoming, in *Media Technologies*,(Eds). T. Gillespie, P Boczkowski and Kirsten Foot. Cambridge, MA: MIT Press.

Goldman, E. (2010). Search engine bias & the demise of search engine utopianism. In B. Szoka & A. Marcus (Eds.), *The next digital decade: Essays on the future of the Internet* (pp. 461–474). Washington, DC: TechFreedom.

Granovetter, M. (1978). Threshold models of collective behavior. *American Journal of Sociology*, *83*(6), pp. 1420–1443.

Grimmelmann, J. (2010). Some skepticism about search neutrality. In B. Szoka & A. Marcus (Eds.), *The next digital decade: Essays on the future of the Internet* (pp. 435–460). Washington, DC: TechFreedom.

Hanafin, J. (2014), Multiple intelligences theory, action research, and teacher professional development: The Irish MI project, *Australian Journal of Teacher Education*, Vol 39(4), pp. 126-142.

Hardt, M. (2014). How big data is unfair: Understanding sources of unfairness in data driven decision making. Retrieved from https://medium.com/@mrtz/how-big-data-is-unfair-9aa544d739de

Jackson, A., Gaudet, L., McDaniel, L. and Brammer, D. (2009), Curriculum integration: The use of technology to support learning, *Journal of College Teaching and Learning*, Vol 6(7), pp. 71–78.

Jones, C., Dirckinck-Holmfeld, L., & Lindstom, B. (2006). A relational, indirect, meso-level approach to CSCL design in the next decade. *International Journal of Computer Supported Collaborative Learning*, *1*(1), pp. 35–56.

Kincheloe. J.L. (2004) (ed.) *Multiple intelligences reconsidered*. New York: Peter Lang, pp. 261.

Kitchin, R. (2014). Thinking critically about and researching algorithms. The Programmable City Working Paper 5, National University of Ireland Maynooth, Ireland. Retrieved from http://papers.ssrn.com/sol3/papers.cfm?abstract_id=2515786

Knox, J. (2015, January). The 'Tweeting Book' and the question of 'non-human data'. *TechTrends*, *59*(1), pp. 72–75.

Kop, R. (2012). The unexpected connection: Serendipity and human mediation in networked learning. *Educational Technology & Society*, *15*(2), 2–11.

Kop, R., & Carroll, F. (2016, January-March). Colouring the gaps in Technology Enhanced Learning: Aesthetics and the visual in learning and analytics. *International Journal of Distance Education Technologies*, *14*(1), pp. 92–103.

Lave, J., & Wenger, E. (2002). Legitimate peripheral participation in communities of practice. In R. Harrison et al. (Eds.), *Supporting lifelong learning, volume 1, perspectives on learning* (pp. 111–126). London, Routledge Falmer.

Lessig, L. (2000). Code is law: On liberty in cyberspace. *Harvard Magazine Feature.* Retrieved from http://harvardmagazine.com/2000/01/code-is-law-html

Lucini, F. (2014), Augmented intelligence in a new era of search, *KMWorld Web Magazine*, Retrieved from http://www.kmworld.com/Authors/Fernando-Lucini-6476.aspx

Manovich, L. (2013) The algorithms of our lives, The Chronicle of Higher Education, December 16th, 2013, The Chronicle Review, Retrieved from https://www.chronicle.com/article/The-Algorithms-of-Our-Lives-/143557

Mager, A. (2014), Defining algorithmic ideology: Using ideology critique to scrutinize corporate search engines, *tripleC* 12(1), pp. 28–39

Mayes, T. (2002). The tTechnology of lLearning in a sSocial Wworld,. Iin R Harrison et al. (Eeds.), *Supporting Lifelong Learning, volume 1, pPerspectives on learning* (pp. 163–175)., London: Routledge Falmer, pp. 163–175.

Neisser, U (1996), Intelligence: Knowns and unknowns, Chair Task Force APA, Board of *American Psychologist*, Vol. 51, No. 2, pp. 77–101

Owen, T. (2015). The violence of algorithms: Why big data is only as smart as those who generate it. The Council on Foreign Relations, Foreign Affairs, 25th May 2015. Retrieved from https://www.foreignaffairs.com/articles/2015-05-25/violence-algorithms

Picard, R., Papert, S., Bender, W., Blumberg, B., Breazeal, C., Cavallo, D., ... Strohecker, C. (2004). Affective learning—a manifesto. *BT Technology Journal, 22*(4), pp. 253–269.

Qoussini, A. E. M., & Jusoh, Y. Y. B. (2014). *A review on personalization and agents technology in mobile learning.* International Conference on Intelligent Environments, pp. 260–264.

Saadatmand, M., & Kumpulainen, K. (2013). Content aggregation and knowledge sharing in a Personal Learning Environment: Serendipity in open online networks. International Journal of Educational Technology, v. 8 Special issue 1, pp. 70–77.

Shaviro, S. (2016) Discognition. Repeater Book, London, UK.

Shedroff, N. (2009). Experience Design 1.1: A manifesto for the design of experiences. Experience Design Books. Retrieved from http://nathan.com/experience-design-1-1-book-design-writing-and-production/

Vennema, S, Hetland, L. and Chalfen, K. (Eds., 2007). Multiple intelligences: The research perspective, a brief overview of the theory. *The project zero classroom: approaches to thinking and understanding*, Harvard Graduate School of Education and Project Zero. Vieira, L. M. M., Ferasso, M., and da Silva Schroeder, C. (2014), connecting multiple intelligences through open and distance learning: Going towards a collective intelligence? *European Journal of Open, Distance and e-Learning*, Vol 17(1), pp. 108–117.

World Stats. (n.d.) *Internet growth statistics: Today's road to e-commerce and global trade internet technology reports, And the "Global Village" became a Reality,* Retrieved from https://www.internetworldstats.com/emarketing.htm

Xie, J., Sreenivasan, S., Korniss, G., Zhang, W., Lim, C., & Szymanski, B. (2011). Social consensus through the influence of committed minorities. *Physical Review E, 84*(1), 011130.

CHAPTER TEN

Augmented Intelligence with Human–Machine Integrity

Future-Oriented Hybrid Governance Integrating Holistic Analytics, True Cost Economics, and Open Source Everything Engineering (OSEE)

ROBERT DAVID STEELE

Introduction

Stepping back from the many unsubstantiated claims of the Artificial Intelligence (AI) community, I humbly suggest that Intelligence Augmentation (IA) is also making many of the very same mistakes common to an oversold and underperforming computer "ubber alles" mindset—a mindset that currently dominates thinking within the Singularity/AI domain. And with a troubling creep into the IA world.

The potential of machine intelligence in and of itself is not only severely overstated, but misses the fundamentally important role that humans have played in the past and will play in the future with regard to technology. Given the fact that we collect less than 1% of the information available today and process less than 1% of what we collect, it is obvious that the infinite potential of human intelligence and imagination has been denigrated—whether intentionally or not—to the point that the AI value proposition is simply not credible when tested against reality (Steele, 2016a).

Consider the fact that the National Security Agency (NSA) in the United States has spent at least a half trillion dollars on "advanced" computers, including

AI but not IA, and yet has shown little or no return on investment to the taxpayer. Illuminating this point, James Bamford, the single most published observer of the NSA, ends his book *Body of Secrets* with the following (Bamford, 2002):

> Eventually NSA may secretly achieve the ultimate in quickness, compatibility, and efficiency—a computer with petaflop and higher speeds shrunk into a container about a liter in size, and powered by only about ten watts of power: the human brain.

This chapter puts forward a concept for achieving a human-centric World Brain conceptualization in which Applied Collective (Human) Intelligence comprises 80% of the whole, while augmented (machine) intelligence provides no more than 20% of the whole (Steele, 2014a, 2015a). Focusing on the human (and especially the now-marginalized five billion poor at the bottom of the pyramid) and the potential of aggregated orchestrated human intelligence in every clime and place, this chapter focuses in general terms on the severe shortfalls in the current approach to computing, which fails at every level when evaluated in relation to the needs of human beings and a sustainable Earth. I argue against short-term corporate profit taking and government control needs and conclude with an argument for the unlimited wealth that is possible if we get serious about taking Data and IT to the next level.

We can do better. For example, for $500 per person, a one-time cost, I can relocate one million Somalis from UN displacement camps in Ethiopia, Kenya, and Uganda, to the uncontested northeast portion of Somalia that has three things in abundance: dirt, seawater, and sunlight. $500 million dollars will buy them the Global Village Construction Set (GVCS) inclusive of pressed-brick shelters, free energy, unlimited desalinated water, in-home compost sewage, free cellular and Internet services, and an aquaponics industry (fish and plants) free of pesticides (Steele, 2013a).

Unrecognized by most other authors in the IA and AI spaces, is the true cost of computing as practiced today; this true cost includes the opportunity cost of failing to empower humans to learn, connect, and decide at every level of scale from local to global, and the tangible cost of an economic model that is 50% waste across the board, drawing down on natural capital (including human capital) at an unsustainable rate, and toxifying the air, land, and sea toward a definitive "sixth extinction" (Kolbert, 2014).

From Class A carcinogenics only legal in China—a central element of "smartphones" that puts hundreds of thousands of Chinese into leukemia wards and early graves (Suleman, 2014)—to the opportunity costs of using technology to perpetuate the financial perversion of the economy known as "flash trading" (Lewis, 2014) computers are "costly" at all levels. The problem, in my view, is that *computing today does the wrong things righter* at greater and greater expense, rather than doing the right things to enable true IA (Ackoff, 2014). From massifying a retarded industrial-era educational system—Massive Open Online Courses have a completion rate of 4% to 15% (Jordan, 2015; McKendrick, 2013), to perpetuating a Western development model that glorifies scientific reductionism and a military-police-intelligence-industrial complex, it has become clear that our current society is simply not at all focused on creating a prosperous world at peace.

The existing corporate media system is corrupt to the bone—truths are repressed and official narratives perpetuated, with money displacing integrity on every topic of public import (Dubose & Bernstein, 2006; Lewis, 2014; Rampton & Stauber, 2003; Risen, 2014). The existing modern Western political system is a mix of *faux* democracy often bordering on outright fascism—corporate control of political puppets (Amato, 2009; Steele, 2013b). Consider that 40 of 42 dictators (Palmer, 2005) are embraced by Western democracies for the convenience that a semblance of control offers, despite the cost of repressed publics, 25% unemployment (Donovan, 2015; Williams, undated), and the millions of illegal immigrants (Steele, 2002a, 2002b) driven by desperation toward Australia, Europe, and the United States.

This chapter is a manifesto on behalf of authentic human intelligence combined with human integrity that outlines very specific steps for empowering humanity toward human-centric computing so as to create a prosperous world at peace. That is, a world that works for all.

The 80–20 rule applies. Although machines could indeed run amok, I worry far more about Artificial Stupidity (not to be confused with but very similar to the Singularity threat). Indeed, the bottom line is that machines require authentic, comprehensive, persistent data to be effective. That means a required capacity to process data in near-real-time at exascale speeds across a broad geospatial and temporal spectrum. Neither of these are likely to happen in our lifetime absent an across-the-board commitment to Open Source Everything Engineering (OSEE).

What *could* happen in our lifetime is the creation of a World Brain in which all humans are linked to all information in all languages all the time, and augmented by machine processing and machine tools. This is to say, an open (decentralized, mesh) cloud augmented by open source processing and open source tools including in line machine translation that understands slang and detects "fake news."

To be blunt, the data and computing industries as now trained, equipped, and organized, are there to serve the narrow self-interest of wealthy elites—retarded for the rest of us, by design. Major and minor companies are doing interesting things on the margins. All of them without exception are failing to leverage the center of gravity for the creation of infinite wealth with the only source of infinite innovation on Earth: the Human Factor.

Fundamentals of Intelligence

Intelligence—whether human or machine—is an isolated irrelevant capability in the absence of the fundamentals against which it can become Applied (Collective) Intelligence (ACI). Below are three of the fundamentals that can help us appreciate the potential of both IA and AI going forward. (1) Holistic Analytics, (2) True Cost Economics, and (3) Open Source Everything Engineering (OSEE). I will explain each of these concepts in detail.

Holistic Analytics

Holistic analytics includes universal data access and a comprehensive analytic model that allows for free and open consideration of all possible causes and effects across all domains. This is not what occurs today from any of the eight information "tribes" that largely avoid the sharing of information—or insights.

Universal Data Access

Below I discuss the data paucity that characterizes our analytic pretense today. Suffice it to say here that collecting 1% (formally published) of 1% (written) of 1% (known)—and processing only 1% of what we collect in the way of "Big Data," is pitiful (Arnold, 2014; Meeker, 2014). Data may be the "new oil" but our entire modern society is posturing over one "oil spot" and failing to recognize the potential value of liberating all data in all languages and mediums. … that is to say, making available to all humans "all information in all languages all the time." Neither governments nor vendors are helpful to this end. From rigged war games to rigged demonstrations, fractional data sets are used to make grandiose claims that are borderline criminal.

A Comprehensive Analytical Model

The Earth is a closed system and natural capital is not renewable. Those are facts ignored by all existing analytical models (Linebaugh, 2014). Changes to the Earth that used to take 10,000 years now take three years (Linden, 2006). Indeed, humanity is on the verge of a sixth extinction. These are facts that a few acknowledge, but these facts also are "shut out" by all governments and vendors eager to use fiction as bridge to the future, because fiction allows for short-term profit by the few without accountability to the many for long-term sustainability. A comprehensive analytic model for decision-making would at a minimum be effective at four levels of decision-making (strategic, operational, tactical, and technical) and it would provide for the simultaneous integrated appraisal of the ten threats to humanity, the top twelve core policies from agriculture to water, and the top eight demographics defining the future irrespective of any decision we make. I explain this below.

Here are two simple models for multidisciplinary, multilingual analytics: (1) demand "teamwork" across all boundaries, and (2) develop a massive new approach to how we collect, process, and analyze data—not just within a single government, but across all eight information "tribes" and across all governments and *their* eight information "tribes."

The eight information "tribes" I have been speaking and writing about for the past quarter century are listed below (Table 10.1):

Table 10.1: Eight information "tribes".

Academic
Civil society (Labor, Religion)
Commerce (especially Small)
Government (especially Local)
Law enforcement
Media (including Bloggers
Military
Nongovernment/Nonprofit

As I have noted on more than one occasion, there are iron curtains between these tribes, wooden walls between organizations within each tribe, and plastic curtains between individuals within each organization. If we are to achieve peace and prosperity, empowering these "tribes" to share information and make sense *together* on behalf of humanity is a first step.

The dysfunctional nature of our current data universe cannot be overstated. Add to that the failure of education and the paucity of IA tools for collaborative information-sharing and multidisciplinary sense-making across time and space as well as all forms of cultural and political boundaries, and you have the proverbial Tower of Babel—a very *expensive* as well as dysfunctional tower of babbling pundits, scribblers, and dilettantes.

The graphic below is an idealized depiction of what a "standard" academic organization should be able to do in the aggregate. Instead we have disciplinary stove-pipes with no cross-fertilization to speak of. The current "fad" of multidisciplinary research and interdisciplinary teaching is a fraud, in my view—lip service at best. Students need to understand both the data sources and data gaps for each of the disciplines, and the analytical models—their strengths and weaknesses—for each of the disciplines, and how to "do" comprehensive or "holistic" analytics (Figure 10.1).

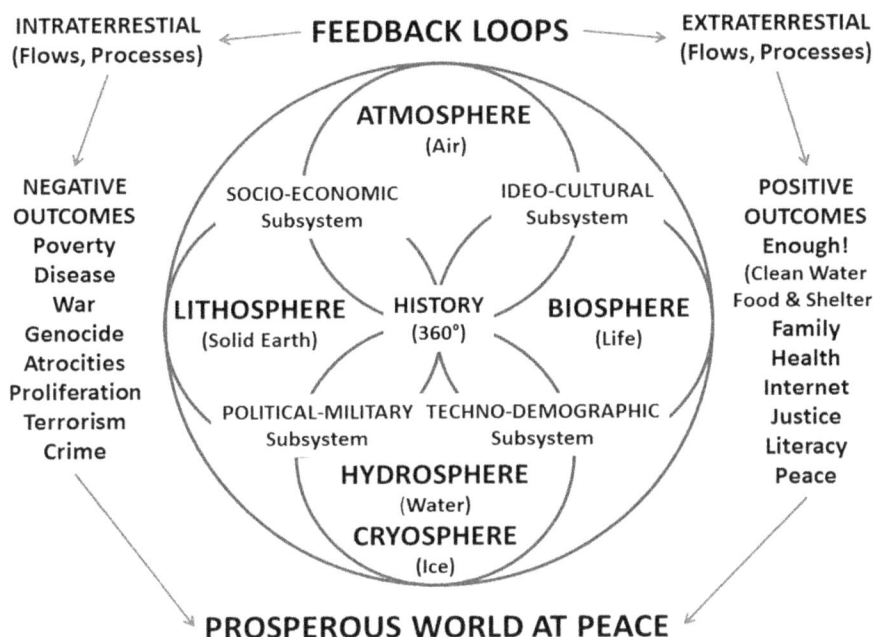

Figure 10.1: Whole earth analytic model. Overview of most of the elements that must be considered to do holistic analytics.

The ten high-level threats (some but not all listed above—all listed below in priority order) are as identified by Lieutenant General Dr. Brent Scowcroft, U.S. Air Force (Ret) and the other members of the United Nations High-Level Panel on Threats, Challenges, and Change (2004). The twelve core policy domains shown below are as extracted by the Earth Intelligence Network (EIN) team from a review of presidential "Mandate for Change" transition books across four different election cycles. The eight demographics are comprised of the five most populous countries plus Iran and Venezuela, with an open-ended Wild Cards slot for countries such as Turkey.

In Table 10.2, note that the U.S. Government (USG) and the U.S. secret intelligence community (IC) focus on war and terrorism to the exclusion of all else. In my view, no one in the USG or U.S. IC is serious about holistic intelligence in the public interest.

Table 10.2: Operational analytic model in three dimensions.

Threat dimension	Policy dimension	Competitor dimension
01 Poverty	01 Agriculture	01 Brazil
02 Infectious disease	02 Diplomacy	02 China
03 Environmental degradation	03 Economy	03 India
04 Interstate conflict	04 Education	04 Indonesia
05 Civil war	05 Energy	05 Iran
06 Genocide	06 Family	06 Russia
07 Other atrocities	07 Health	07 Turkey
08 Proliferation	08 Immigration	08 Venezuela
09 Terrorism	09 Justice	09 Europe/UK
10 Transnational crime	10 Security	10 Wild Cards
	11 Society	
	12 Water	

True Cost Economics

I will itemize just three of the many more reasons why I believe that modern Western civilization is collapsing today:

First, scientific reductionism and specialized (stove-pipe) learning has led to multiple generations of PhD/DBA "graduates" who know everything about nothing and nothing about everything.

Second, in the absence of informed and honest oversight from governments and the public, Western industry has been based on chlorine, oil-based plastics, and corn sugar. All three are toxic beyond the comprehension of most citizens (Thorton, 2001). While "true cost" economics has a niche following, in my own direct experience, 99% of all organizations refuse to recognize this as a foundation for their decision-making. The system is "rigged" toward short-term profits favoring the few over long-term sustainability favoring the many. Until the 99% "get a grip" in all that can be known, they will continue to be "farm animals" to be exploited as ignorant consumers.

Third, government corruption and the deliberate dumbing down of the public have led to an artificial reality in which lies define public understanding, rather than the truth. The USG, for example, lies about unemployment—the real rate is 23%, with 40% characteristic of people of color, single moms, new college graduates, and old guys like me (Williams, 2017); inflation—it is as much as 72% in some easily manipulated product categories (Durden, 2015), and justice—there is one legal system for the very rich who can manipulate foreign exchange and interest rates with impunity, and another for the rest of us (Taibbi, 2014), putting more African-Americans in prison than there were slaves at the beginning of the Civil War (Alexander, 2011, 2012). A total of 935 now-documented lies led the West into Iraq, Afghanistan, and other countries, at a cost of over 4 trillion dollars and millions of lives lost or displaced (Bilmes & Stiglitz, 2008; Lewis, 2014).

Rather than maintain this trajectory of occlusion and deception, our objective should be to achieve a renaissance of the data and IT industries—and a resurrection of holistic education, intelligence, and research—such that citizens in the aggregate no longer suffer the many atrocities that represent "business as usual" for the West that is imposed on the rest of the world.

At a strategic level, TCE considers both the ecological and social costs of any product, service, policy, or behavior, and the full cradle to grave life-cycle costs of every artifact. Landfills and the toxins emitted from landfills, for example, are a cost not now considered. At the tactical level—and in the aggregate at the strategic level, TCE demands that we accurately calculate across the entire extraction, production, transport, utilization, and disposal cycle, the virtual water, total fuel, toxin emitted, child labor, regulatory violations, and tax avoidance. To be sure, more nuanced studies can detail other factors as well.

Open Source Everything Engineering (OSEE)

In the 1980s I founded and led the Open Source Intelligence (OSINT) movement at the same time that Richard Stallman and others pioneered the Free/Libre/Open Source Software (FLOSS) movement.

Together we watched the concept expand, first to Open Source Hardware and OpenBTS (Base Transceiver Station) along with Open Spectrum, and then to other areas.

My latest book, *The Open Source Everything Manifesto: Transparency, Truth, and Trust* (Steele, 2012a) itemizes over sixty "opens." I have since collaborated with Marcin Jacubowski of Open Source Ecology (OSE) and Michel Bauwens, founder of the Peer to Peer (P2P) Foundation, to define nine major open source domains (Table 10.3), with three subsets for each (Peer to Peer Foundation, 2015).

Table 10.3: Open Source Everything Engineering (OSEE) baseline.

01 Open data • Open geospatial • Open history • Open language	04 Open health • Open cures • Open drugs • Open procedures	07 Open provisioning • Open energy • Open food • Open water
02 Open decision-support • Open access • Open document • Open research	05 Open infrastructure • Open API* • Open BTS** • Open spectrum	08 Open software • Free software • Libre software • Open code
03 Open governance • Open money • Open politics • Open standards	06 Open manufacturing • Open circuits • Open hardware • Open materials	09 Open space • Open cities • Open design • Open innovation

* Application Program Interfaces; ** Base Transceiver Station

This matters hugely because it has been reliably established that OSEE approaches cost as little as ten percent (10%) of the full life-cycle of industrial-era proprietary "solutions" and are especially helpful in eliminating training, licensing, maintenance, and mandatory spare parts sourcing from the original vendor (Jacubowski, 2016). OSEE also provides for liberal interchangeability of parts, as pioneered by the GVCS team, and offers a sustainability aspect that is perhaps one hundred times (100X) that of proprietary "solutions" that are designed to fail and fail often.

The admirable and necessary seventeen Sustainable Development Goals (SDG) of the United Nations (UN)—listed below (Table 10.4) cannot be achieved by today's industrial-donor paradigm where roughly 20% of the promised donations materialize (Annan, 2005) and only a fraction of the funds—from 1% to 20% of the 20% of the sought funding that is actually received all promises to the contrary—reach the village level (Slemrod, 2015; Ortel, 2016). The hard reality is that industrial-era "solutions" are too costly, take too long, are not interoperable, and generally collapse within a few years.

IA—and a new mindset about how we integrate holistic analytics, TCE, and OSEE—is essential if we are to achieve these seventeen goals that will both restore the viability of Earth as a long-term habitat for all species, and avoid the sixth extinction focused on humans specifically (Steele, 2016b; United Nations, 2016).

A prosperous world at peace is possible, only if we embrace HA, TCE, and OSEE, now.

Table 10.4: UN sustainable development goals.

01 End poverty	07 Energy for all	13 End climate change
02 End hunger	08 Inclusive economy	14 Save oceans
03 Health	09 Infrastructure	15 Save ecosystems
04 Education	10 Global economy	16 Justice for all
05 Gender equality	11 Safe smart cities	17 Unify humanity
06 Water for all	12 Sustainable economy	

Where Have We Gone Wrong?

Bankers and technologists as well as the politicians that serve them have one major flaw in common: a complete disregard for reality at the grassroots level.

There are two breaking points for the globalized economy: the first is the Earth and the limitations of the natural capital that we are not only consuming, but also destroying (geoengineering and fracking are especially pernicious even treasonous endeavors), and the second is the Human Factor—at some point, after the 99% has been screwed 99% of the time, no combination of "wedge issues," no efforts to revive race wars, no number of lies from the government about unemployment or health or concocted threats, will stop a revolution. I predicted the illegal immigrant break-out that is now afflicting Australia, Europe, and the United States (Steele, 2002b)—this tsunami of destitute humanity is going to swamp the West and we have only ourselves to blame.

Computers against the Earth

In the 1970s, the alleged academic discipline of Political Science (previously known as Current History) took a terrible turn away from ethnographic qualitative field work that required a grasp of foreign culture, foreign history, foreign language, and foreign nuances, and turned instead toward "Comparative Studies." Comparative Studies in this context is code for never having to learn a foreign language or meet a foreign person or walk a foreign path—it substitutes "data analytics" that can be done from the same air-conditioned cubicle one has always inhabited. Rather than arousing the scorn it merited, this wrong turn was embraced by peers, each recognizing that as long as no one was held accountable for actually understanding anything or producing useful new knowledge, the "bubble" of pretense could see them through a full academic or "think tank" career.

At the national level, the U.S. IC is a manifestation of all that is wrong with excessive reliance on computers over humans. Despite spending over $1.2 trillion dollars (an average of $40 billion a year over each of 25 years, with $100 billion a year at the high point), the U.S. IC is abjectly incapable of producing "decision-support" for the President, Cabinet officers, and major commanders and ambassadors—it produces "at best" 4% of what a major commander needs, and nothing for everyone else (Zinni, as cited in Steele, 2007, 2009). Unlimited money borrowed and printed in our name, combined with secrecy that is nothing more than a "get out of jail free" card—dismissive of Congressional oversight, media investigation, and accountability to the public—have enabled the spending of hundreds of billions of dollars across three major technical domains: imagery computing, signals computing, and death by drone. Neglected has been the Human Factor—the fifteen slices of Human Intelligence (HUMINT) inclusive of all that can be known from indigenous sources via Open Source Intelligence (OSINT), is illustrated below in Figure 10.2 (Steele, 2010).

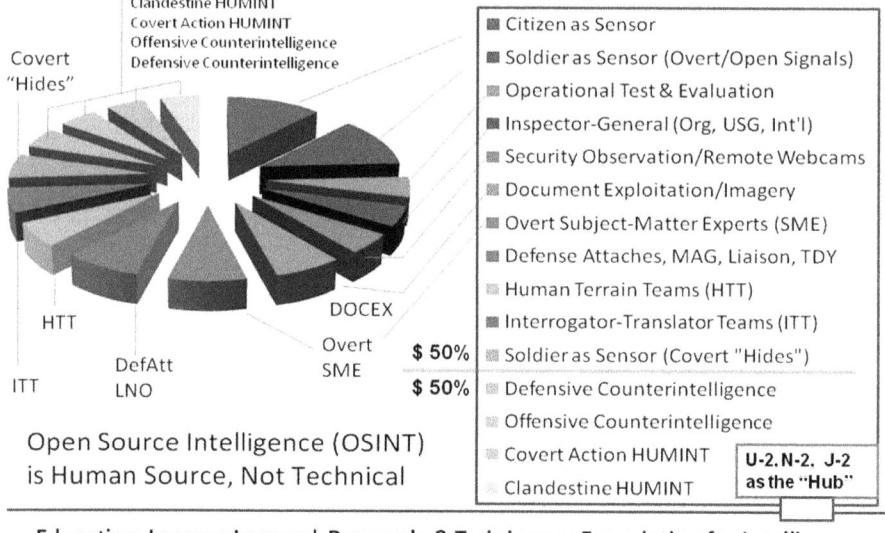

Figure 10.2: Full-spectrum human intelligence (HUMINT). All types of human intelligence must be managed and integrated as a whole.

In the aggregate, the loss of integrity across the "tribes" of information—academia, civil society, commerce, government, law enforcement, media, military, and nongovernment/nonprofit organizations—has been radically compounded and perpetuated by a global computing industry focused on sales and public relations instead of long-term outcomes and engineering.

> Information technology only makes bad management worse (Paul Strassmann, 1992)

> The militarization of the U.S. economy compounded the debilities imposed by the financialization of the economy. Government specification cost-plus "engineering" displaced competitive and innovative engineering able to do more with less. Franklin (Chuck) Spinney (2014, 1985)

My own applicable quote is "Technology is not a substitute for thinking" (Steele, 2006, 2013c, 2013d). The failure of computers is a human failure. As with any artifact, the responsibility for design, for manufacturing, for utilization, and for harmonization within the larger construct of civilization is a human responsibility.

As this chapter concludes, intelligence with integrity is rooted in human intelligence and human integrity. AI and IA are only as good as the humans that develop and utilize these tools. It is those humans—and the weak arguments dismissive of holistic analytics, true cost economics, and OSEE—that are at the root of our failure to properly augment human intelligence with machine intelligence, while establishing and maintaining integrity across the whole rather than within the parts alone.

Computers against Humanity

Howard Rheingold is the original modern prognosticator on the importance of tools for thought (2000), and Kevin Kelly is the original visionary who understood "hive mind" as well as the potential (but still unrealized) benefits of networked economies that empower individuals over corporations (1995, 1999). Both have been ignored by the computer industry—and especially by the U.S. IC—because of the inherent corruption of the Western governance paradigm that concentrates wealth and power among the 1%.

> It is the lack of intelligence with integrity—human intelligence and human integrity—that permits such gross destabilizing distortions to develop. Machines can assist humans in collecting, processing, and analyzing all information in all languages all the time, but ethics is the root human operating system and machines are not the source of ethical depth and breadth. Ethics is the ultimate operating system. Without human ethics, all machine systems lack root integrity. (Danalylov & Steele, 2016)

More recently Micah Sifry (2014) has written a superb book entitled, *The Big Disconnect: Why the Internet Hasn't Transformed Politics (Yet)*. His book is so relevant to this chapter that I offer four brief quotes below:

QUOTE (34): "... has not made participation in decision-making or group coordination substantially easier."

QUOTE (49): "We can save the body politic, but to do so we must remember that the purpose of democracy isn't only for each of us to have our say, but to blend individual opinions into common agreements. ... We need a real digital public square, not one hosted by Facebook, shaped by Google, and monitored by the National Security Agency."

QUOTE (159): "Many weak causes do not add up to a stronger movement."

QUOTE (161): "First, we need to insist on tools and platforms that genuinely empower users to be full citizens. And second, we have to take back our own digital agency."

In the next table I provide a relatively comprehensive depiction of all of the preconditions for revolution, most of which exist today in every industrialized country and most but not all other countries. The two greatest preconditions for revolution are the concentration of wealth and the loss of legitimacy of the government, in the larger context of a loss of balance across all the domains for any given society. For a revolution to occur, a precipitant is needed (e.g., a Tunesian fruit seller) and, as Chris Hedges (2016) has pointed out in his most recent book, the military and police must abandon the 1% and align themselves with the protesting public. Below (Table 10.5) is my original view of the preconditions of revolution (Steele, 1976).

Table 10.5: Preconditions of revolution.

	Political-legal	Socioeconomic	Ideocultural	Technode-mographic	Natural-geographic
Perception	Isolation of elites; inadequate intelligence	Concentration of wealth; lack of public disclosure	Conflict myths; inadequate socialization	Acceptance of media distortions; inadequate education	Reliance on single sector or product; concentrated land holdings

	Political-legal	Socioeconomic	Ideocultural	Technode-mographic	Natural-geographic
Identity	Lack of elite consensus; failure to define priorities	Loss of economic initiative; failure to do balanced growth	Loss of authority; failure to provide and honor national myth system	Failure to accept and exploit new technologies or new groups	Failure to integrate outlying territories into national system
Competence	Weak or inefficient government; too much or too little bureaucracy	Breakdown of fiscal, monetary, development, or welfare policies	Humiliation of leaders; loss of confidence by population	Failure to enforce priorities, with resulting loss of momentum	Failure to prepare for or cope with major national disasters
Investment	Egocentric or parochial government	Excessive or insufficient mobility; lack of public sector	Cynicism; opportunism; corruption	Failure to nurture entrepreneurship or franchise all groups	Failure to preserve or properly exploit natural resources
Risk	Elite intransigence; repression; failure to adapt	Failure to deal with crime, especially white collar crime	Failure to deal with prejudice, desertion of the intellectuals	Failure to develop national research & development program	Failure to honor human rights; failure to protect animal species
Extroversion	Ineffective tension management; failure to examine false premises	Structural differentiation; lack of national transportation network	Elite absorption of foreign mores; failure to deal with alienation	Failure to develop communications infrastructure, shared images	Failure to explore advantages of regional integration
Transcendence	Foreign control of government; arbitrary or excessive government	Loss of key sectors to foreign providers; loss of quality control	Media censorship; suppression of intellectual discourse	Failure to control police, army, or terrorists; failure to employ *alphas*	Failure to respect natural constraints or support organic growth

(Continued)

Table 10.5: (*Continued*).

	Political-legal	Socioeconomic	Ideocultural	Technode-mographic	Natural-geographic
Synergy	Failure to assimilate all individuals or respond to all groups	Status discrepancies; lack of economic motivators	Absence of sublimating myths; failure of religion	Failure to provide program and technology assessment	Failure to distribute benefits between urban and rural areas
Complexity	Garrison, industrial, or welfare states	Unstable growth; excessive defense spending	Cultural predisposition toward violence	Excessive urbanization, pollution, or development	Lack of land for expansion; inefficient use of land

Humans, not machines, revolt when oppressed—these are the reasons why they revolt

What Is to Be Done?

There are some very specific capabilities that we need to build to manage the transition to effective human–machine integration, capabilities that the major industrial enterprises—old as well as new—have thus far refused to address. I will use the traditional intelligence cycle—collection, processing, analysis, dissemination—to present these, first at the strategic level and then at the end-user level.

Strategic Initiatives

Collection

Every discussion of human and machine intelligence must begin with recognition of the fact that we are collecting less than 1% of the relevant information in all languages and mediums. I cannot overstate this. Of all the scientific papers written, only 1% are published. All of those scientific papers that are written and mostly (99%) not published in turn represent a tiny fraction—perhaps 1% of all of the other publications from nonprofit think pieces to graduate student research papers to government studies to citizen advocate white papers and so on. Beyond that is all the knowledge that has not been published—that is resident in the minds of indigenous human beings and transient experts. My conclusion: the "formal" world of "published" information is at best 1% of 1% of what we know.

- We need to achieve, in increments, 20%, then 40%, then 60%, then 80%, eventually 100% of analog and digital information in all languages and mediums and 100% opt-in participation of all humans in all locations as "on call" sensors and "on call" thinkers. This requires, among other things, a universal open sparse matrix on top of a 1:5,000 geospatial plot, and not just Open Access and Open Document but Open Hypertextdocument System (OHS) as conceptualized by Doug Engelbart (1994).
- A World Brain Institute sponsoring World-Brain.net, World-Brain.edu, World-Brain.org, and World-Brain.com, together (Figure 10.3) with a United Nations Open-Source Decision-Support Information Network (UNODIN) (Steele, 2010, 2012b, 2014b) and an enabling Open Source (Technologies) Agency such as I recommended to Vice President Joe Biden (Steele, 2015b) and more recently to President Donald Trump (Steele, 2017a). Included in this universal open network would be a Global Game supportive of holistic analytics, true cost economics, and OSEE return on investment (RoI) calculations.

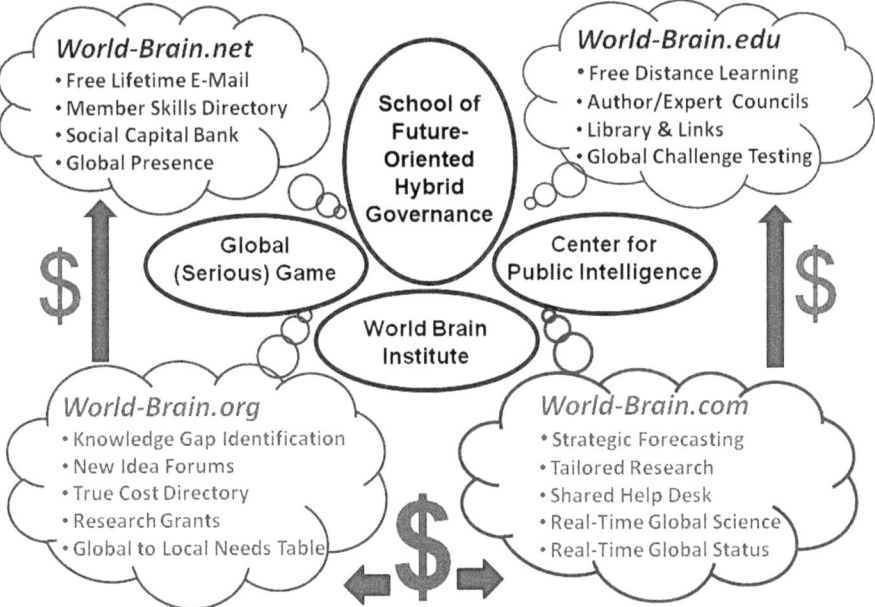

Figure 10.3: World brain concept. Four fully integrated information domains—together, all information accessible by all humans.

Processing

We process 1% of the "big data" that is in digital form. Bearing in mind that most data is either in analog form or unpublished in any form (human knowledge *in situ*), and that what we collect and process has been driven by industrial-era scientific reductionism, we must recognize that as with collection, processing is at the 1% of 1%, representing a severe level of dysfunction.

- We need to achieve the ability to process all data in all forms across all threat and policy and demographic domains, in time and space context (Figure 10.4).
- This requires something we do not have today and are not likely to achieve in our lifetime absent a global consensus on the need: a massive open sparse matrix on top of a 1:5,000 geospatial map of the world, and exascale processing as well as an end to all vendor-specific data processing barriers.

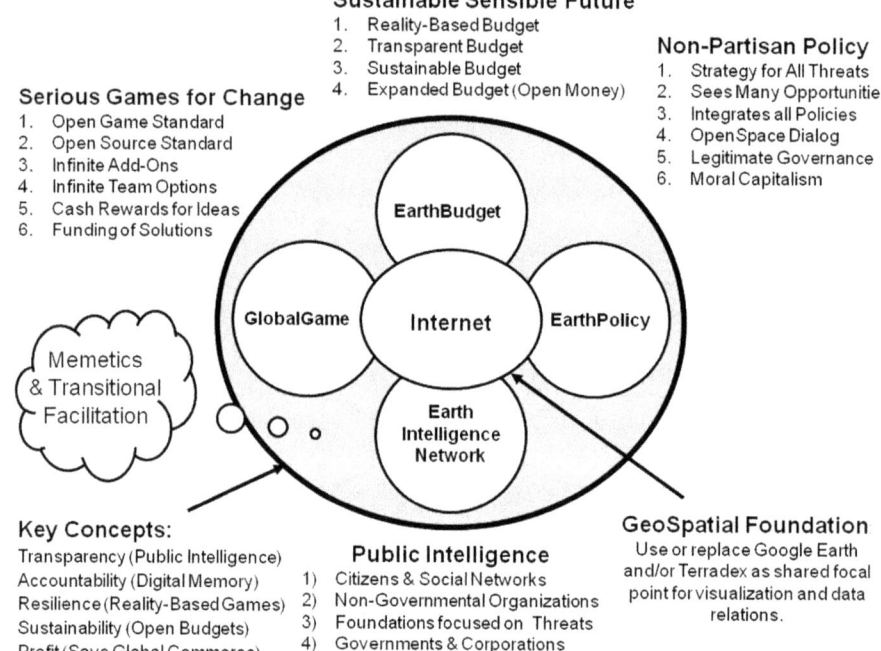

Figure 10.4: Earth intelligence concept. Applied intelligence demands budget and policy applications—open national conversations.

Analysis

Analysis in the West tends to be monolingual, stove-piped by topic, and devoid of depth while also lacking any semblance of true cost economics.

- We need to abandon the unilateral nationalist top-secret analysis paradigm, and shift instead to the multinational, multilingual open source paradigm (Figure 10.5). We also need to abandon the stove-pipe organizational approach to analysis in which each organization within each of the eight information "tribes" does its own analysis in its own way against single topics or issue areas. Governments must devise new means of orchestrating information-sharing and sense-making across all boundaries, both at home and abroad. Connecting humans to one another is 80% of the challenge—knowing who knows, knowing who cares, knowing who is open to collaborative engagement. At the strategic level, pattern analysis and anomaly detection across all domains, and the reliable tracking of true cost economic information for all products and services, all policies and behaviors, will be critical to the redesign of everything (all domains now suffer significant waste—as much as 50%!).

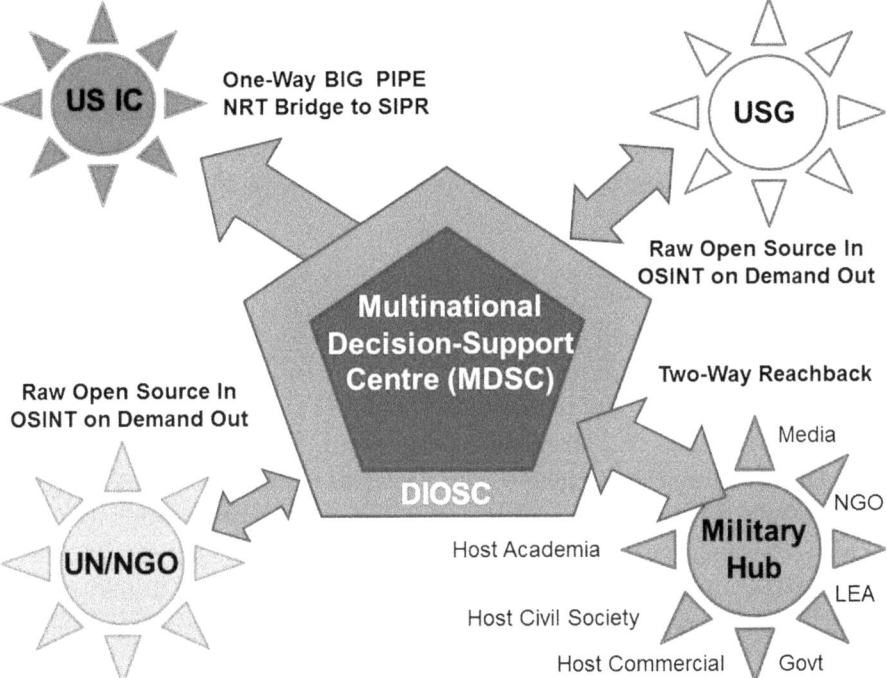

Figure 10.5: Local to global information-sharing concept. The military may be best suited to serve as a hub for open global sharing.

Dissemination

The death of Thomson Reuters and Elsevier is to be welcomed. They represent a refusal to adapt to the Open Science era, and now Sci-Hub is beginning to bury them both. Knowledge is air. Knowledge is life. Knowledge is an "absolute good." This fencing of the commons and its destruction of the tangible physical earth manifests itself in the intangible world as intellectual property law. Like diapers for babies, this law must be set aside in favor of open dissemination of knowledge and information.

- We need a distributed Internet along the lines of what Sir Tim Berners-Lee is seeking to devise. It must be one that is not only impervious to censorship and data manipulation and destruction, but that also makes possible a universal and complete two-way participation by any human mind desiring to opt-in. "One time data entry, universal access" was the objective for the digital innovators in the 1980s. However, this worthy objective has been systematically stymied by politicians in the service of greedy corporations that have sought to lock-in customers with information gulags, guarded by constantly mutating Application Program Interfaces (API). What we all require instead is an interactive network allowing any combination of humans to come together at any time on any topic and do so without censorship outside the boundaries of law such as Amazon, Facebook, Google, MeetUp, PayPal, Twitter, and YouTube, among others, among others, have sought to impose on dissident views. (Steele, 2017b, 2018).

End-User Initiatives

Collection

If collection is hosed at the strategic level (1% of 1%) it is worse at the tactical level, where end-users must put up with—to take just one example—a multiplicity of search engines that are largely dysfunctional. Some of them—Google for example—are positively dangerous with regard to the ways in which they skew search results for financial gain, in some instances, manipulating search results for political reasons (something that is tantamount to an undeclared campaign contribution and a violation of federal electoral laws). I appraise the availability of relevant information to the end-user as being 1% of the strategic 1% of 1%: 0.000001.

- We need a rapid migration from the current tolerance of Portable Document Format (PDF) artifacts that are not full-text indexable, and a vast acceleration in the ability of any end-user to migrate an analog document—including crumpled captured documents covered in mud (a requirement I articulated in 1988 and something we still cannot do)—at the same time that all audio and video must be instantly transcribed into full text online.

Processing

The state of processing at the end-user level is roughly equivalent to that of collection. It is simply not possible for the average end-user to make sense of even a modest amount of information—say 2,500 pages—from which all names, dates, locations, times, and subject matter tags must be extracted. As my colleague Stephen E. Arnold has documented so well over the years, and most recently in his new book *CyberOSINT: Next-Generation Information Access* (2015; Steele, 2015c), none of the current end-user processing systems—and I explicitly include i2 and Palantir—are worthy of consideration as foundations for moving forward.

- What we need is a completely integrated local to global processing system that enables all opted-in processing units to be part of one massive exascale-plus cloud with zero proprietary boundaries supporting anonymity, identity protection, privacy, rights, and security across individual, organizational, national, and multinational boundaries. We also need machine-speed translation across 33 priority languages and another 150 "local knowledge" languages.

Analysis

The analysis domain suffers from a corrupt and inadequate educational system that no longer teaches the art and science of critical thinking. More than this, it lacks the multidisciplinary and holistic skills needed to properly address emergent challenges. Indeed, our so-called graduate students have no idea how to use the *Science Citation Index* and the *Social Science Citation Index*, among many other tools for finding exactly the right people with exactly the right knowledge and information. Compounding the paucity of processing tools is the paucity of integrated analytic tools.

- We need to completely reconstruct the educational system, the intelligence system, and the research system (Table 10.6). While this idea is strategic, its importance can only be appreciated at the tactical level. We have embedded self-interest and complacency within our youth, even those from the prestigious universities. No amount of technology will substitute for the loss of entire generations of "all-source" analysts able to think.

Table 10.6: Integrated local to global education, intelligence, and research.

Education, intelligence, and research blended at all levels across all topics			
Ephemeralism, human scale, panarchy, smart nation, world brain, global game			
Clarity	Diversity	Integrity	Sustainability
Whole systems thinking and understanding	Collective intelligence	Hybrid transparent governance	True cost economics

- We need to create a new meta-doctorate that integrates holistic analytics, true cost economics, and OSEE to the point that we can achieve the UN SDG within as little as ten years at a fraction of the cost of the existing dysfunctional paradigm.
- We need computer-assisted tools for analysis such as were clearly defined in 1985–1989 (Webb et al., 1989) and still do not exist today, $1.2 trillion dollars having been spent by the U.S. IC alone, never mind vastly more by IBM and everyone else pretending to do machine analytics (Figure 10.6).

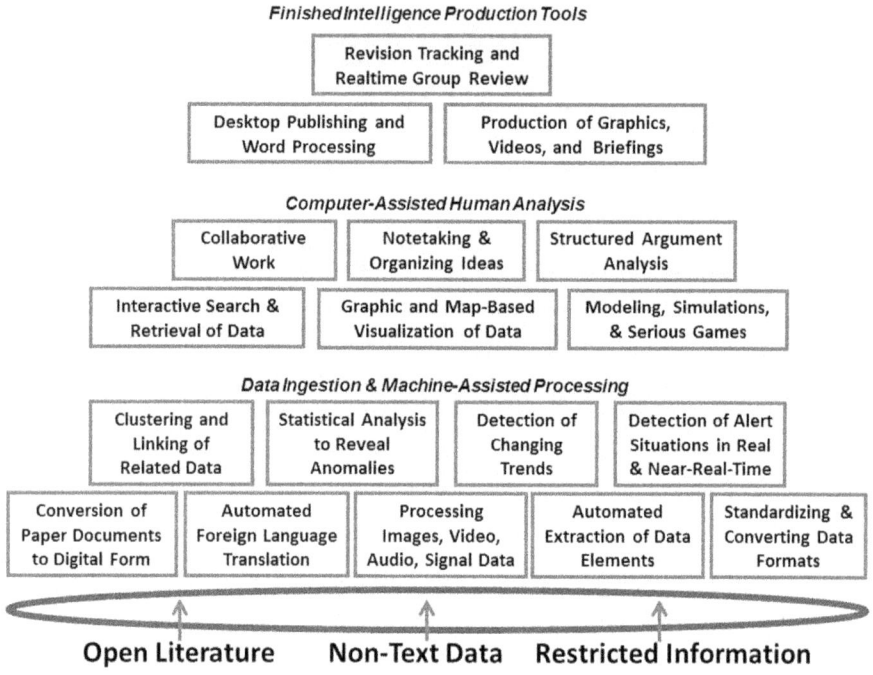

Figure 10.6: Computer-assisted tools for human intelligence. Defined in the 1980s, still not available in one open package today.

Dissemination

Across many democratic societies, the public now has a fraction of the attention span needed in order to contribute as citizens and stakeholders. A single graphic and a 3-minute video appear to be the means by which we communicate knowledge and information. Most of what we teach and how we teach is dependent on antiquated textbooks that are grotesquely overpriced. To be sure, classrooms where bright young people are held prisoner for 18–26 years (required to sit still and squelch their creativity) all need to be "flipped."

- We need to completely displace the Elsevier and Thomson Reuters approach to the dissemination of knowledge, while moving Sci-Hub to the mainstream and deepening it to the point that *all* publications are subject to both peer review at the paragraph level, *and* citation linkage at the paragraph level. We need a sparse matrix in the cloud capable of holding all information in all languages all the time, tagged across time and space and independent of language. Above all, we need to empower individuals so that they can move markets overnight by being informed at the hand-held level (Table 10.7), to the point that we might put the Koch Brothers, Monsanto, Coca Cola, and Nestle out of business within a few weeks (Liszkiewicz, 2011).

Table 10.7: True cost economics at point of sale—cotton T-shirt example.

Water	Energy	Emissions	Toxins	Child labor	Tax cheat	Regulatory cheat
570 gallons	8 kWh, 11–29 grams	NOx, SO_2, CO, CO_2, N_2O,++	1–3 gram pesticides, metal dyes	17 countries, 50 cents/day	Most companies	Most companies

Conclusion

While I respect what the many researchers, innovators and entrepreneurs are trying to do with IA and AI, it is my firm belief that as long as we ignore the fundamentals of human intelligence, all of this work will be marginal to the kind of augmented intelligence we desperately require. Tom Steyer, the West Coast left-leaning billionaire has been emblematic on this point. Steyer acknowledged in 2014 that his $75 million spent trying to influence U.S. politicians on climate change had been wasted. Reading the media story on that admission woke me up to the fact that no single issue and no single demographic is going to get an honest hearing from the USG or any other government, until we achieve Electoral Reform and restore integrity to our electoral process, our governance process, and thence to our economy and our society, a campaign now underway as #UNRIG.

As I have argued throughout this chapter, both IA and AI are severely limited for analogous reasons. The main issue is that the IT industry has become corrupt: good people trapped in bad systems—without question good people but also without question very bad systems. Until the IT industry reconnects with human intelligence and human integrity as "root," until the IT industry embraces holistic analytics, TCU, and OSEE as the trifecta for optimizing the Human Factor in the larger context of a sustainable Earth able to nurture five billion creative minds (now repressed by poverty, dictators, and predatory financial, legal, and information systems), humans will remain little more than chattel—expendable farm animals.

In fact, I made this case very early on in an invited séance for Paul Allen's INTERVAL Corporation in 1993 (Steele, 1993). In my humble opinion, the IT industry and the U.S. IC have betrayed the public trust for over a quarter century, precisely because they have disrespected the human as "root" and sought instead to focus on profits for the few rather than productivity for the many.

In fact, it's never too late to find God, embrace ethics, and be all you can be (Steele, 1992). In the context of augmenting human intelligence, this means a transformational focus on human–machine integrity.

References

Ackoff, R. (2014). Transforming the systems movement. *Proceedings of the Russell Ackoff Conference*, Philadelphia, PA: University of Pennsylvania.

Alexander, M. (2011, October 12). More black men are in prison today than were enslaved in 1850. *Huffington Post*.

Alexander, M. (2012). *The new Jim crow: Mass incarceration in the age of colorblindness*. New York, NY: The New Press.

Amato, T. (2009). *Grand illusion: The myth of voter choice in a two-party tyranny*. New York, NY: The New Press.

Annan, K. (2005, April 13). Billions of promises to keep. *New York Times*.

Arnold, S. E. (2014, August 1). 1% of science gets published—what cost to economics? *Phi Beta Iota Public Intelligence Blog*, hereafter *PBI*.

Bamford, J. (2002). *Anatomy of the ultra-secret National Security Agency*. New York, NY: Anchor Books.

Bilmes, L., & Stiglitz, J. (2008). *The three trillion dollar war: The true cost of the Iraq conflict*. New York, NY: W. W. Norton.

Danalylov, N., & Steele, R. (2016, February 5). Robert Steele on open source everything—ethics is an operating system. Singularity Weblog and YouTube (1:21:32).

Donovan, S. (2015). *An overview of the employment-population ratio*. Washington, DC: Congressional Research Service.

Dubose, L., & Bernstein, J. (2006). *VICE: Dick Cheney and the hijacking of the American presidency*. New York, NY: Random House.

Durden, T. (2015, October 23). How the U.S. government "Covers Up" 72% inflation before your very eyes. *ZeroHedge*.

Engelbart, D. (1994, December 28). Toward high-performance organizations: A strategic role for groupware. *PBI*.

Hedges, C. (2016). *Wages of rebellion: The moral imperative of revolt*. New York, NY: Nation Books.

Jacubowski, M. (2016). Global village construction set. *Open Source Ecology*.

Jordan, K. (2015, June 12). MOOC completion rates: The data. *KatyJordan.*
Kelly, K. (1995). *Out of control: The new biology of machines, social systems, & the economic world.* New York, NY: Basic Book.
Kelly, K. (1999). *New rules for the new economy.* New York, NY: Penguin Books.
Klavans, R. et al. (2008). Graphic: Web of Fragmented Knowledge. *PBI,* August 15.
Kolbert, E. (2014). *The sixth extinction: An unnatural history.* New York, NY: Henry Holt.
Lewis, C. (2014). *935 Lies: The future of truth and the decline of America's moral integrity.* New York, NY: Public Affairs.
Linden, E. (2006). *The winds of change: Climate, weather, and the destruction of civilizations.* New York, NY: Simon & Schuster.
Linebaugh, P. (2014). *STOP, THIEF!: The commons, enclosures, and resistance.* Oakland, CA: PM Press.
Liszkiewicz, J. (2011). Graphic: True Cost of a Cotton T-Shirt. *PBI.*
McKendrick, J. (2013, December 16). "Only four percent complete massive open online courses: Setback or growing pains? *ZDNet.*
Meeker, M. (2014, May 29). Mary Meeker's internet report 2014—explosion in hand-helds and data—less than 1% of data analyzed. *PBI.*
Ortel, C. (2016, June 27). Is Clinton foundation a $100 billion charity fraud—zero financial statements, millions of cases of wire fraud and solicitation fraud? *PBI.*
Palmer, M. (2005). *Breaking the real axis of evil: How to oust the world's last dictators by 2025.* New York, NY: Rowman & Littlefield.
Peer to Peer Foundation. (2015). Category: Open source everything. P2P Wiki. Retrieved from https://wiki.p2pfoundation.net/Category:Open_Source_Everything
Rampton, S., & Stauber, J. (2003). *Weapons of mass deception: The uses of propaganda in Bush's war on Iraq.* New York, NY: TarcherPerigee.
Rheingold, H. (2000). *Tools for thought: The history and future of mind-expanding technology.* Cambridge, MA: MIT Press.
Risen, J. (2014). *Pay any price: Greed, power, and endless war.* New York, NY: Houghton Mifflin.
Sifry, M. (2014). *The big disconnect: Why the internet hasn't transformed politics (Yet).* Sebastopol, CA: O/R Books.
Slemrod, A. (2015, February 20). Only five percent of pledged aid reaches Gaza. *Middle Eastern Eye.*
Spinney, F. (1985). *Defense facts of life: The plans/reality mismatch.* Boulder, CO: Westview Press.
Spinney, F. (2014, November 14). Chuck spinney: Killing America—government specifications cost plus. *PBI.*
Steele, R. D. (1976, October 18). Graphic: Preconditions of revolution. *PBI.*
Steele, R. D. (1992). E3i: Ethics, ecology, evolution, & intelligence. *Whole Earth Review,* Fall, pp. 74–79.
Steele, R. D. (1993). God, man, & information—comments to INTERVAL In-House, PBI.
Steele, R. D. (2002a). Graphic predicting illegal immigration break-out. PBI.
Steele, R. D. (2002b). *The new craft of intelligence: Personal, public, & political–citizen's action handbook for fighting terrorism, genocide, disease, toxic bombs, & corruption.* Oakton, VA: Open Source Solutions, Inc., Figure 25, Page 98.

Steele, R. D. (2006). *Reinventing intelligence*. Oakton, VA: Open Source Solutions, Inc.
Steele, R. D. (2007) Open source intelligence. In L. Johnson (Ed.), *Strategic intelligence: The intelligence cycle* (pp. 96–122). Westport, CT: Praeger.
Steele, R. D. (2009). Intelligence for the president—AND everyone else. CounterPunch.
Steele, R. D. (2010). *Human intelligence: All humans, all minds, all the time*. Carlisle, PA: U.S. Army Strategy Studies Institute.
Steele, R. D. (2012a). *The open source everything manifesto: Transparency, truth, and trust*. Berkeley, CA: North Atlantic Books, Evolver Editions.
Steele, R. D. (2012b, December 26). Proposal for a world brain institute and development of a global game. *Humanity Plus*.
Steele, R. D. (2013a, June 25). $500 million to resettle 1 million on a moonscape with sun, dirt, & salt water. ... exploring the practical edge of intelligence with integrity—2.0 habitat cost sheet posted. *PBI*.
Steele, R. D. (2013b, March 2). Open power: Democracy lost & found essay, book review blurbs and links. *PBI* [Updated 3 March 2015].
Steele, R. D. (2013c, January 19). Reflections on the inability of Washington to think with integrity. *PBI*.
Steele, R. D. (2013d). The evolving craft of intelligence. In R. Dover, M. Goodman, & C. Hillebrand (Eds.), *Routledge companion to intelligence studies*. Oxford, UK: Routledge.
Steele, R. D. (2014a). Applied collective intelligence: Human-centric holistic analytics, true cost economics, and open source everything. *Spanda Journal, 2*, pp. 127–137.
Steele, R. D. (2014b). *Beyond data monitoring—achieving the sustainability development goals through intelligence (decision-support) integrating holistic analytics, true cost economics, and open source everything*. Oakton, VA: Earth Intelligence Network.
Steele, R. D. (2015a, October 17). Applied collective intelligence 2.0. *PBI*.
Steele, R. D. (2015b). *Supporting the president's interest in 2015 defense, diplomacy, and development innovation—the open source (technologies) agency, digital deserts, & global stabilization*. Oakton, VA: Earth Intelligence Network.
Steele, R. D. (2015c). Foreword. In S. E. Arnold (Eds.), *CyberOSINT: Next generation information access*. Harrod's Creek, KY: Xenky Press.
Steele, R. D. (2016a, April 1). Can Thomson Reuters [or Bloomberg] be a $20B+ per year world brain? *PBI*.
Steele, R. D. (2016b, February 16). Open source everything engineering (OSEE)—achieving the SDG goals in a fraction of the time at a fraction of the price. *PBI*.
Steele, R. D. (2017a). *Eradicating fake news and false intelligence with an open source agency that also supports defense, diplomacy, development, & commerce (D3C) innovation to stabilize world*. Oakton, VA: Earth Intelligence Network.
Steele, R. D. (2017b). How The Deep State Controls Social Media and Digitally Assassinates Critics: #GoogleGestapo—Censorship & Crowd-Stalking Made Easy," *American Herald Tribune*, November 7, 2017.
Steele, R. D. (2018). #GoogleGestapo: Censorship & Surveillance (Including Amazon, Facebook, Google, MeetUp, Twitter, YouTube), *PBI*.

Strassmann, P. (1992). *Remarks of the director of defense information*. McLean, VA: Conference on National Security & National Competitiveness: Open Source Solutions.

Suleman, K. (2014, May 1). The human cost of a smartphone. *ITPro*.

Taibbi, M. (2014). *The divide: American injustice in the age of the wealth gap*. Berlin, DE: Spiegel & Grau.

Thorton, J. (2001). *Pandora's poison: Chlorine, health, and a new environmental strategy*. Cambridge, MA: MIT Press.

United Nations. (2016). *Sustainable development goals: 17 goals to transform our world*. New York, NY: United Nations.

United Nations High-Level Panel on Threats, Challenges, and Change. (2004). *A more secure world: Our shared responsibility*. New York, NY: United Nations.

Webb, D., McCormick, D., & Oehler, G. (1989). *CATALYST: Computer aided tools for the analysis of science & technology*. Washington, DC: Central Intelligence Agency.

Williams, J. (2017). *ShadowStats.com*.

CHAPTER ELEVEN

For Pleasure or Productivity

Divergent Paths in Intelligence Augmentation

JAMES D. MILLER

Introduction

Improved nutrition, superior training, and better drugs have made today's top athletes the best in recorded history. At the same time, tastier food, abundant sedentary entertainment, and labor-saving devices have contributed to morbid obesity. Just as technology has increased the variance of physical ability, and I predict that Intelligence Augmentation (IA) will soon do likewise.

As a mere economist, I am unqualified to predict exactly which types of IA we will become predominant. Instead, I'm going to consider two broad classes of IA by assuming that IA will impact *productivity* and/or *happiness*. It would seem obvious that productivity improvements will increase wages earned in a market economy perhaps by boosting intelligence, increasing motivation to work, reducing the need for sleep, and/or through improving emotional control. IA might be expensive, moderately priced, or even free. IA that boosts productivity could increase or decrease happiness. This chapter explores various scenarios, taking care to mark those in which IA increases the variance of human productivity.

One can best predict the future by extrapolating from the past, so whenever possible I will try to justify an IA prediction by pointing to how people use current analogous technologies. For example, widespread use of productivity-destroying but happiness-inducing drugs like crack and heroin show that many people voluntarily eviscerate their market wage in return for a happiness boost. Similarly, the use of performance-enhancing drugs such as steroids, Adderall, and Modafinil demonstrate that people are willing to accept some health risks in return for boosting their performance at work.

Today, governments mandate (primary school), subsidize (college), ignore (caffeine), regulate (Adderall), and ban (cocaine) various performance-enhancing measures. Governments tolerate some pleasure-inducing drugs (alcohol), criminalize others (marijuana), and have declared war against still others (cocaine). We should, therefore, expect states to adopt a wide variety of approaches to future technologies that boost productivity and pleasure.

Today, elite colleges admit students with bright futures, and then raise these students' expected future incomes, thereby greatly increasing inequality. We can think of elite colleges as a type of wage-enhancing IA, and extrapolate from the effects of elite colleges onto how IA will impact society. The possibility that colleges boost wages primarily through signaling complicates such an approach, although future IA might also bestow signaling benefits on users (see Spence, 1973).

This chapter will build from a simple scenario in which cheap and effective productivity-enhancers are for sale, then consider the implications of the enhancers being expensive, then the consequences of different quality enhancers being for sale, and next, what happens if the enhancers directly increase or decrease happiness. Then, the chapter will assume that people can also buy brain chips that greatly raise happiness. Finally, the chapter will explore very long-run forecasts under the assumption that evolutionary selection pressures shape human preferences for IA.

Productivity Enhancers

Let us start by assuming that the only IA available in the near future is a cheap and safe productivity enhancer that nearly everyone uses. This enhancer will probably increase income inequality. If, say, the enhancer increases users' capacity to concentrate on boring work, then it will help both lawyers and waiters. But because lawyers have much higher average wages, it will likely raise their incomes by a greater dollar amount. Similarly, a productivity enhancer that reduces the need for sleep will most likely increase the incomes of those who previously had the highest wages.

I can imagine a productivity enhancer that reduces inequality by, say, boosting an individual's intelligence, the less intelligent that person is. But it seems likely that most productivity enhancers would, on average, do far more for those who already have high market value in a manner similar to the way elite college education today increases intellectual differences because smart people are better able to take advantage of it. If enhancers reduce productivity inequality, it will likely be through eliminating conditions, such as severe depression and anxiety, that prevent otherwise productive people from finding high paying jobs. For the rest of this chapter, however, I'm going to assume that productivity enhancers increase your income more the greater your income would have been in a world without IA.

Let's complicate our analysis by assuming that the productivity enhancer is expensive enough that many people in the United States, let alone those in poor nations, can't buy it even though they would eagerly use it if it were free. The enhancer might be expensive because of material costs, patent holders demanding large payments, the need to customize the enhancer to individuals, or because of the surgical expense of implanting it in a body. Only people with high incomes would find it profitable to buy an expensive productivity enhancer. For example, (ignoring discounting, interest rates, and risk) if the enhancer would raise your lifetime income by 50% and costs $2 million, you would only profit from buying the enhancer if your lifetime income without the enhancer would exceed $1 million. Expensive enhancers, consequently, would greatly increase inequality similar to the way elite college education does today.

When predicting who will buy this and other types of IAs, we should consider potential buyers' wealth and expected future incomes. Someone, say, an 18-year-old Harvard student from a poor family can have little wealth but still have a high expected future income. Just as such a person today can borrow funds to pay for an elite college education, we can expect a similarly situated future person to borrow enough to acquire productivity enhancing IA. People with low expected future incomes would likely have neither the ability nor the desire to borrow to purchase expensive productivity enhancers. Expensive productivity enhancers, consequently, will likely increase the variance of future productivity in part because only the relatively highly productive would acquire them.

Let's now deepen our scenario by assuming that different quality productivity enhancers will be for sale, with the relatively more expensive enhancers being more effective. People with already high productivity will purchase much better enhancers than those with moderate or low productivity, which of course will further increase the variance of human productivity.

Might governments combat future inequality by subsidizing expensive enhancers for low productivity people? Governments in rich countries spend enormous sums educating low ability students. But brighter students and students from richer families tend to get a much better than average education. Governments today seem to put more care into improving the productivity of bright students and the children of the affluent and so it's reasonable to predict they would continue to do so in a world with IA.

If a professional field requires an expensive enhancer, market wages will adjust accordingly so that people going into that field find it profitable to get the enhancer. For example, let's say that to succeed in Field X you need to have a naturally high IQ and a $5 million productivity enhancer. If the wages of people in Field X are determined by the supply and demand for qualified laborers in this field, then the fewer workers in Field X, the higher the wage. If the market wage in Field X becomes low enough that it's not worth paying the $5 million to get the enhancer, then no new people will enter the field, which because of retirements will eventually drive up wages to the point that it again becomes profitable for some people to get the enhancer so they can enter the field.

Rich Countries Will Have More Enhancers

Professionals of equal skill tend to earn much higher salaries in rich countries than in poor ones, and consequently the economic value of having an enhancer will likely be greater for those who live in already rich countries, and so, all else being equal, people in rich countries will buy more enhancers. Spillover effects will intensify this tendency.

Consider an expensive enhancer that reduces your need for sleep. If I am working with other people than the more hours they work, the greater the value of the enhancer to me. Consequently, the more people who get this enhancer, then the greater the value of having it will be, and the more people will buy it. As a result, there might be multiple equilibria, one where lots of people in a profession have the enhancer and another where almost none do, with the first equilibrium being more prevalent in rich nations than in poor ones.

Economist Garrett Jones has shown that there are positive IQ spillover effects in countries, meaning that if you have a high IQ you make other people in your country more productive (Jones, 2011). If IA that increases intelligence is also subject to national spillover effects, then the value to you of having an IA IQ-booster will increase in the number of other people in your country that already have one, and in the number of already smart people in your country. As a result, countries with the highest average IQs will (holding all else constant) receive a greater IQ boost from IA.

You can borrow money only if you can find willing lenders. Today, in many developing nations, lenders are often unwilling to give money to poor people because they don't trust the legal system to foreclose on the property of the poor (which is often undocumented) (De Soto, 2001). As a result, an extremely smart and hardworking 18-year-old in a poor country might not be able to borrow money to go to college, whereas her counterpart in the United States easily could. In countries where the poor cannot borrow money even for investments that, over time, will more than pay for themselves, only those who have a high expected income *and* significant current wealth would be able to purchase expensive productivity enhancers.

Productivity Enhancers and Signaling

Expensive productivity enhancers would likely bestow a signaling benefit on users similar to that created today by colleges. To understand the signaling theory of education, consider what you would surmise from knowing that someone is either (A) a U.S. Marine, or (B) a member of an elite modeling agency. You probably think the marine is strong, disciplined, and deadly whereas the model is beautiful, poised, and photogenic. The Marine Corps undoubtedly has high entry standards, but the primary reason you don't want to get into a fight with a Marine is because of the training he or she received. In contrast, although modeling agencies likely provide useful beauty tips to their employees, the primary reason that their employees are so attractive is that elite modeling agencies tend to hire only people who are already gorgeous.

College graduates earn much higher salaries on average than nongraduates do. But are colleges closer to the Marine Corp in that they teach the skills that help their graduates succeed, or a modeling agency in that they select for people who already have traits that will let them go on to have successful careers? The signaling theory of education holds that colleges, especially elite ones, are more similar to modeling agencies than the Marine Corp.

But if colleges select mainly for talented people rather than imparting useful training themselves, why do so many people pay so much for college? Let's reasonably suppose that the highest paying jobs young adults can get are jobs in which employers look for applicants who are (1) smart, (2) hardworking, and (3) willing to do what they are told. Getting into and succeeding at an elite college is strongly correlated with having these three traits. If most people who have these three traits go to college, employers looking for people with these traits would rationally not bother interviewing noncollege graduates. In such a signaling equilibrium it's very hard for you to prove that you have these traits if you didn't go to college. Even if, say, you could point to high standardized tests scores as evidence of your intelligence, a potential employer might think you skipped college because you knew you wouldn't be able to handle getting up early for class. In general, if X is a desirable trait, then to credibly signal that you have X you must do something that people without X either can't do or would find relatively costly to do.

It would be (on net) very costly for you to buy an expensive productivity enhancer if you knew that you were not a highly productive person, because the boost in future wages that the enhancer would give you wouldn't cover the expense of purchasing the enhancer. Consequently, having an expensive enhancer would be a credible signal that the user had a high opinion of his or her productivity. This signal would raise the value of the enhancer, making it even easier for its users to get top entry-level jobs, and so, further increase the difference between the lifetime salaries of people with and without these enhancers.

If Productivity Enhancers Affect Happiness

Let's deepen our scenario by assuming that productivity-enhancers also affect happiness. If we assume that happiness is what economists call a "normal good" then as someone gets richer they will want to buy more of it. In this scenario you can acquire happiness two ways: directly from the enhancer (although perhaps with a negative sign) and through (often costly) goods and experiences that your brain translates into happiness. It's therefore possible that an enhancer that directly lowers happiness might overall increase your happiness by raising your income, allowing you to buy additional goods and experiences that give you more in happiness than you directly lose from the enhancer.

Assume first that productivity enhancers increase happiness. This will increase the amount people are willing to pay for the enhancers, and so even further boost productivity inequality by widening the gap between how much the rich and non-rich spend on enhancers.

Now assume that productivity enhancers lower happiness, in direct proportion to their capacity to boost productivity. People with higher productivity, and therefore higher lifetime incomes, will be less willing to use powerful enhancers. Someone born with low abilities might rationally choose to use a powerful enhancer to raise his or her lifetime income.

Superstar effects characterize fields in which the top people earn vastly higher salaries than average members of those fields do. Think of how much a heart surgeon who is 1% better than anyone else could charge billionaires. To be a superstar in a competitive field, you likely have to take every advantage meaning you would have to use the best productivity chip even if it decimated your happiness. (Analogously, if performance-enhancing drugs significantly improve athletic outcomes in a sport in which the top athletes win wealth, fame, and sex, then it becomes a safe bet that the top performers are going to use the drugs whether or not the drugs are dangerous and illegal.) In such an economy, the economic superstars will be people with a high tolerance for direct unhappiness, and who receive a relatively high amount of happiness from having a high income, especially since they would probably have enough natural talent to earn a decent living if they didn't use enhancers.

Productivity enhancers that greatly lowered happiness might give dictatorships an economic advantage as they could force their most productive citizens to use enhancers to be even more productive. Of course, forcing highly productive people to be significantly unhappy, might lead to political instability.

Happiness Boosters

Let's now explore what would happen if pure happiness boosters were for sale. Internet porn offers us a good base for extrapolation.

The Internet is one of the greatest technological achievements in human history, and yet one of its prime uses is to "transport moving pictures of lesbian sex by pretending they are made out of numbers" (Yudkowsky September, 2007). Evolution shaped our preferences in an era without pornography, and so until extremely recently, it was never even "considered" possible for human beings to prefer interacting with virtual partners to having sex with an actual human being. Pornography arises from the application of human intelligence to triggering the pleasure centers of the brain—centers that were supposed to be activated by reproductive sex. Human intelligence, in this and other situations, actually works against evolutionary success. IA could take this *much* further.

Imagine a brain "bliss" chip that lets you experience having sex with anyone you wanted, whenever you wanted, and the only way that you could tell that the experience wasn't real was because your "partners" were impossibly good looking (see Nozick's pleasure machine; Nozick, 1974). Or, if you got bored of sex, the brain chip would let you imagine ruling a country, hunting a lion, playing professional football, or making great scientific discoveries. And if this wasn't good enough for you, the chip would maximize your pleasure by giving you more joy than a drug addict received from his first hit of heroin or crystal meth.

Such a chip would make you very happy but would also almost certainly destroy your desire and ability to do anything productive. I suppose it's possible that this happiness chip could turn you into a blissed-out zombie, and maximize your pleasure while taking control of your arms and legs to perform useful tasks.

But I strongly suspect that software smart enough to do this could more efficiently manage the relevant using robots.

Widespread use of bliss chips would destroy an economy unless robots were advanced enough to take over for humans. But if the chips were sufficiently inexpensive governments could use them to save resources by substituting them for welfare and old age pensions. Most governments today tolerate unproductive people getting most of their happiness from alcohol, and so might allow use of the chip.

Aging populations are saddling most rich countries with an increasing percentage of citizens considered too old to work. Compounding this problem, technology seems to be increasing the number of "zero marginal product workers;" adults who can't be profitably employed by companies at any positive wage (Cowen, 2010). The rise of unproductive citizens poses an enormous threat to the future economic welfare of many rich countries. Governments, however, might turn to selective use of bliss chips to cheaply keep their unproductive citizens happy: they give the old and poor bliss chips and just enough money to survive. Interestingly from the viewpoint of inequality, this welfare strategy would cause those with the least resources to be the happiest.

Bliss chips might also make for weapons of occupation for conquering countries too ethical to use genocide. When one nation takes over another it could pacify the enemy population by putting them all on the chips.

If people had a choice of whether to take a productivity enhancer or a bliss chip, they would probably be more willing to take the enhancer the greater the income they could earn with the enhancer. This type of choice would vastly increase the variance of productivity, at least in the short run.

Darwin Wins

Over the long run, humankind might thwart evolution by destroying itself or by ceding control to a single entity that determines who can breed. But if neither of these happens, evolution will have just as much influence on human IA as it does on the size and shape of finches' beaks.

Evolution only cares about spreading genes. Imagine that a small set of humans pick the IA that helps them maximize the spread of their genes. Unless there was some organized conspiracy against them, they would do a better job spreading their genes than other humans would. If using the right IA significantly helped you spread your genes, then part of the gene combinations that evolution would most favor would be those that caused you to want to use IA to help you spread your genes.

No life form has ever made spreading its genes its sole goal, mostly because, until very recently, no life form knew what a gene was (Yudkowsky November, 2007). But since humans can understand genetics, a man could, theoretically, have his only goal in life be the spreading of his genes. Philosopher Nick Bostrom calls these kinds of people "non-eudemonic agents" (Bostrom, 2004); I'll refer to them as Super-Darwins because they not only understand Darwinian evolution, but make it the totality of their existence. A Super-Darwin could come about through IA that controlled its hosts' preferences.

A Super-Darwin would eat only foods that contributed to his reproductive success. He would happily work 100 hours a week at boring, repetitive tasks, if this maximized the number of his surviving offspring. He would take no pleasure from nonreproductive sex; pornography would bring him no utility. If his environment changed, a Super-Darwin would reoptimize his behavior to fit his new circumstances. Most important of all, to maximize the number of descendants he will have, a Super-Darwin would want all of his children to be Super-Darwins.

A Super-Darwin hoping to copulate with an ordinary person would learn about topics such as sports, art and culture to attract a mate. But in a Super-Darwin's eyes, an ideal mate would be another Super-Darwin, with whom he could work to maximize the number of children they spawn. Once Super-Darwins started dating only each other, they would effectively lose their souls in the single-minded pursuit of reproductive success.

I confidently predict that almost no parent alive today would want his or her children to be Super-Darwins, as they would lack all the values most of us hold dear. I'm also confident, however, that among the billions of humans alive today, at least a few would enjoy founding a genetic empire, and would sire Super-Darwins if the opportunity arose.

Even if no one deliberately made Super-Darwins, Super-Darwins would arise by degree given enough time. People who chose IA to more marginally align their goals to evolution's desires would gain a Darwinian advantage, and the subset of their children who became somewhat more Super-Darwinish would gain a further advantage.

It would take only a few first-generation Super-Darwins for such a group to quickly become a major demographic bloc. In 1800, a woman in the United States had an average of seven children, indicating that some must have had over ten (Klein, 2012). A healthy woman in a rich country who had a child each year from age 14 to 45 would have 32 children. Realistically, in some years she would likely fail to conceive, but with the help of fertility technology she could give birth to multiple offspring in other years, making it feasible for a Super-Darwin woman to have fifty children. Super-Darwins could add to their total by renting the wombs of surrogate mothers.

Rich countries today provide poor parents with enough resources to keep all their children alive, regardless of how many children they have. Politicians, however, would almost certainly change these rules after even a few parents started having twenty or more offspring. But an American Super-Darwin couple with average abilities could support dozens of kids by themselves. The family would save a lot of money because they had no interest in luxuries and would be, literally, happy to eat cheap but healthy foods. The parents would willingly spend every waking hour earning income and taking care of their kids. The children would be much better behaved than ordinary children. But there would be some conflict between parents and children as a parent would roughly care for all of his or her children the same whereas each child would care more about itself than its sibling.

Super-Darwins who lived in rich countries would maximize the number of children they could support if they paid people in poor countries to raise their kids, since many impoverished families in underdeveloped nations would undoubtedly raise a child in return for $500 year. At this rate, a successful Super-Darwin lawyer could easily support 1,000 children.

Once Super-Darwins arose, only coercion could stop their demographic tsunami (Bostrom, 2004). When I first started to think about Super-Darwins, I assumed that politicians would quickly outlaw them. Now I'm not sure because I suspect that Super-Darwins would initially make fantastic citizens.

As money would pose the most significant constraint on Super-Darwins' reproductive capacity, they might seek to earn high incomes and consequently pay lots of taxes. Super-Darwins would have no sense of morality, and would rape, murder and plunder for even a slight long-term net gain. In a hunter-gatherer world, you wouldn't want them as your neighbors. But in a well-run market economy, Adam Smith's invisible hand would often make socially productive use of a Super-Darwin's amorality.

The great 18th-century economist Adam Smith wrote that "It is not from the benevolence of the butcher, the brewer, or the baker, that we can expect our dinner, but from their regard to their own interest," and "by directing that industry in such a manner as its produce may be of greatest value, he intends only his own gain, and he is in this, as in many other cases, led by an invisible hand to promote an end which was no part of his intention" (Smith, 1991). Wealth in modern industrialized nations mostly arises from individuals and businesses acting in their own self-interest, in ways that just happen to make society better off. A Super-Darwin would be willing to acquire income in a manner that harmed the common good.

But in reality, many present-day businesses are already willing to take this path if and when it leads to profits.

A Super-Darwin would likely turn to crime if it offered them the best career choice. But in most rich nations, crime doesn't pay. To be sure, the majority of socially destructive crimes are committed by people who lack workplace skills, who have impulse-control issues, who get a thrill from danger, or who don't worry about long-term concerns—all characteristics that Super-Darwins would lack.

In some ways, Super-Darwins would be more trustworthy than ordinary people are because of the economic benefits of a positive reputation. They could be trusted to work hard as they would gain nothing by slacking off and, say, watching pornography when they are getting paid for supposedly working.

When you cheat someone you usually gain a short-term advantage but suffer a risk of long-term reputational loss. Because they would think in terms of generations, Super-Darwins would be extremely future-oriented compared to ordinary people. They would cheat for a large enough payoff, but as they would be concerned with not just their reputation but those of their descendants, only an enormous gain would push them off the path of honesty.

The gains of specialization would stop Super-Darwins from being all alike, especially as their numbers grew. Changing environmental circumstances and improvements in genetic technology would also cause each generation of Super-Darwins to be different from those of the past, as parents sought to make their children better adapted to the world.

Super-Darwins would be enthusiastic consumers of IA, since being smarter would undoubtedly help them achieve their evolutionary aims. Unlike most ordinary people, a Super-Darwin would use risky enhancement technologies as long as the expected reproductive gain exceeded the costs. If some experimental brain/machine implant would either double a Super-Darwin's reproductive success or immediately kill him, the Super-Darwin would take the implant if it had a sufficiently high chance of working.

Super-Darwins' large numbers of children would burden society, but the children's near perfect behavior would mitigate this cost. Providing for the elderly who don't work but who have significant health care needs is the greatest fiscal challenge of governments in rich nations. But the Super-Darwins would (while of able mind and body) never stop working, and once they became too frail to help their descendants they would happily accept death. Many health care dollars are spent to give extremely sick people a few more months of life—expenditures that Super-Darwin's wouldn't want.

Eventually, if Super-Darwins raised the population of Earth by a large enough amount, we would start to run short of fixed resources such as land, raw materials and fresh water. However, technology would almost certainly mitigate this problem as it has in the past. Super-Darwins' lack of interest in having more than the bare minimum amount of living space, their desire to eat cheap but nutritious foods, and their total disinterest in nonutilitarian travel would likely cause each of them to have a much smaller environmental footprint than ordinary people do.

Super-Darwins would eagerly seek to colonize space, dreaming of having trillions of descendants scattered throughout the universe. If ordinary people started worrying about the population explosion, the Super-Darwins would likely explain that their tireless work to perfect space travel would mean that most of them would soon leave Earth.

Unfortunately, this desire to colonize space would probably give Super-Darwins control of the universe, as no other group could hope to match their reproductive success. At some point, when they were strong enough, an army of Super-Darwins would likely come back to conquer Earth to use its resources to breed further.

During their long years of space colonization, Super-Darwins would utterly annihilate themselves because even a slight deviation from evolutionary maximization would eventually doom a Super-Darwin strain to extinction. For example, imagine that total devotion to evolutionary success causes one group of Super-Darwins to double its population every ten years, whereas having a bit of interest in culture causes another group to double in size only every ten years and fifteen days. After eight hundred years the first group would be around 25% bigger than the second, a number likely large enough to cause the first to steal resources from the second. As Super-Darwins would seek to maximize the spread of their genes, powerful genetically related groups would probably ally to take resources from weaker groups.

I know that the idea of Super-Darwins seems bizarre, but it's actually our current situation that's strange. Imagine a species of insect that recently acquired the ability to fly because of a new inheritable genetic mutation that gave it wings. This species, let's postulate, flies away from danger, but crawls when pursuing prey, even though flying would make it a more successful predator. Many would wonder at the insect's "stupidity" even though we could tell a plausible story about how the insect's predatory instincts haven't yet had time to coevolve with its wings. We would surely guess that evolution would soon "correct" the insect's behavior by selecting for those that did fly after prey. Human intelligence and understanding of evolution are analogous to the insect's power of flight—both have a colossal untapped evolutionary advantage, and in both cases we should suspect that (given enough time) evolutionary selection could give each species the capacity and will to exploit the advantage.

Conclusion

You have goals; intelligence is what helps you figure out how to achieve these goals. Most humans have a terminal goal of happiness. Future IA, I predict, will help people achieve this goal by either (A) boosting their income to allow them to buy better goods and experiences that bring happiness, or (B) by directly raising their happiness by stimulating the pleasure centers of their brains. Unfortunately, people who take route (B) will likely so impair their reward structure that they will destroy their own productivity. If (B) can be done cheaply, governments might permit unproductive citizens to use IA to bliss out, while their productive workers follow path (A). In the long run, however, we are likely just evolution's playthings and so we will work toward evolution's goal of maximizing our ability to spread our genes, and most of our descendants will probably use IA solely for this purpose.

References

Bostrom, N. (2004). The future of human evolution. In *Death and anti-death: Two hundred years after Kant, fifty years after Turing* (pp. 339–371). Palo Alto, CA: Ria University Press.

Cowen, T. (2010). Zero marginal product workers—Marginal REVOLUTION. Retrieved July 30, 2016 from http://marginalrevolution.com/marginalrevolution/2010/07/zero-marginal-product-workers.html

Jones, G. (2011). National IQ and national productivity: The hive mind across Asia. *Asian Development Review, 28*(1), 51–71.

Klein, H. S. (2012). *A population history of the United States*. Cambridge: Cambridge University Press.

Nozick, R. (1974). *Anarchy, state, and utopia*. New York, NY: Basic Books.

Smith, A. (1991). *The wealth of nations*. (A. S. Skinner, Ed., Vol. 3). New York, NY: Prometheus Books.

Soto, H. D. (2001). Dead capital and the poor. *SAIS Review, 21*(1), 13–43.

Spence, M. (1973). Job market signaling. *The Quarterly Journal of Economics, 87*(3), 355–374.

Yudkowsky, E. (2007, November 11). Adaptation-executers, not fitness-maximizers. Retrieved July 30, 2016 from http://lesswrong.com/lw/l0/adaptationexecuters_not_fitnessmaximizers/

Yudkowsky, E. (2007, September 1). Stranger than history. Retrieved July 30, 2016 from http://lesswrong.com/lw/j1/stranger_than_history/

CHAPTER TWELVE

Building Human Character in a World of Augmented Intelligence

DARLENE DAMM

Can we imagine a world in which human beings have sensors directly attached to their brains, perhaps deeply embedded in their neocortex? What would it mean to *think* in this world? What would it mean to be an individual? And what would happen to human character? While a world in which technology connects human brains directly to one another or to the Internet and to artificial intelligence (AI) may seem like science fiction, the truth is we are much closer to that reality than many might think. This chapter explores the implications of augmented intelligence for the future development of human character and recommends strategies that leaders and educators might implement as augmented intelligence enters into our lives.

Understanding Augmented Intelligence

In 2015, researchers at Duke University (Pais-Vieira, Chiuffa, Lebedev, Yadav, & Nicolelis, 2015) used digital sensors to link the brains of four rats. They found that if they stimulated the brain of one rat, the others rats sensed the same stimulation in real time. Amazingly, the rats felt in their own bodies what was happening to the bodies of other rats. In addition, the scientists linked together the brains of rhesus monkeys and taught them to jointly control images on a screen (Ramakrishnan et al., 2015). While it took some practice, they eventually began working together to jointly move an image on a screen in a coordinated fashion. While we don't actually know what these animals were experiencing in these experiments, it would appear that their brains were seemingly merged—at least temporarily—so that they felt together, thought together, and behaved as one.

Beyond experiments on animals, scientists have performed similar experiments with humans. In August of 2013, the University of Washington (Armstrong & Ma, 2013) enabled one person to control the movements of another person through a special set of headsets that interacted with brainwaves. More recently, in 2015, humans were enabled to guess what another person was thinking using only a brain-to-brain interface (Koebler, 2015). Other experiments (Gorman, 2015) have also been successful in technologically linking the brains of paralyzed individuals with different machines that move various muscles and limbs restoring movement.

As we begin connecting human beings to one another, we are also developing the very basics of a technology that will accelerate the augmentation of human intelligence through AI. In fact, a number of companies including Google, Facebook, Microsoft, IBM, Amazon, and others have been actively building advanced AI software over the last decade and incorporating this technology into their products and services.

While recent experiments in augmented intelligence might seem startling, they are in fact quite inevitable when we consider the accelerating advance of technology over the past few decades. In a relatively short time, human beings have evolved from using giant computers in the workplace, to personal computers on our desks, to smartphones in our pockets and purses, and most recently, to various wearables, implantable chips, earpieces, goggles and other devices augmenting and connecting our senses and our lived realities.

Notwithstanding the fact that the initial cost of inventing technology can be prohibitively expensive, many of the components required to produce new technologies (i.e., software, sensors, and computers) continue to decline in cost. Much as we have seen a steep decline in the cost of cell phones, the same will be true for technologies supporting augmented intelligence. Indeed, we have already seen a rapid drop in the cost of virtual reality goggles—with Google Cardboard now available for about $10. Even major companies are starting to open source software and computing. Google, for example, has open sourced machine learning through TensorFlow; IBM has created a freemium version of their Watson Analytics; Microsoft has invited the public to use LIQUi|—their quantum computer simulator; and OpenAI, a nonprofit foundation introduced by Elon Musk, Reid Hoffman, Sam Altman, Jessica Livingston, Peter Thiel, and others is developing open source AI. In addition to this, companies like Facebook and Amazon are also incorporating AI into many of the services that billions of humans are using every day.

All of these developments suggest we are quickly heading into a world where any human will have access to another's experiences as well as endless amounts of information and the intelligence to process and use that information at extraordinary speeds.

In this world, people will be connected to one another in immersive ways at levels we have never seen before. Initially, these deeper connections will require that human beings develop increasingly higher levels of empathy, ethics and character as any one person's actions may well impact millions of other people. To be sure, over the long term these connections will also challenge our notions of self. Identity will become more fluid and malleable rather than permanent and given, as will a person's sense of reality, truth, space and time.

The Coming World of Accelerating Technological Change

As we human beings have increasingly begun using computers and the Internet over the past several decades, we have seen that we can more easily and quickly share knowledge with one another, as well as collaborate together. This has resulted in our world changing at an accelerating rate.

Access to low cost computers and the Internet is increasingly giving more and more people the power to use technology. This is not only accelerating the rate of change but also adding more voices, ideas and opinions into the mix, and most importantly it is creating a world where more and more people are empowered to leverage technology to their own ends. In the industrial era, only a few hierarchical companies, institutions or governments held the power, making most of the decisions that shaped human history. But we are now moving into an era in which any individual or small group of networked individuals can be significantly empowered, creating changes that impact millions or even billions of people.

In truth, this transformation has happened gradually. Thomas Friedman, for example, began to document many of these changes in his 2005 book, *The World is Flat*. Since that time, we have begun to see nations around the world transition toward flatter, more entrepreneurial societies. Business schools, universities, and even high schools have begun teaching innovation and entrepreneurship as core skills and countries have begun trying to create their own versions of Silicon Valley. Young adults, in particular, have become particularly focused on building start-ups and nonprofits right after college or in some cases even earlier.

At the same time, the Internet has evolved. More than a place to consume information, it has become a place where more and more people can post their own views, content, media. These changes, along with the social media platforms that have leveraged this shift, have disrupted mainstream media and created ways for individuals to connect to millions (and soon billions of people) to share their voices and coordinate their actions in real time.

As social media has grown, we have witnessed its impact on events, including the election of Barack Obama in 2008, the launch of the Arab Spring in 2010, and the global following and philanthropic response to natural disasters such as the 2011 Tohoku earthquake and tsunami in Japan.

Consider that in 2014, both ISIS and the Ice Bucket Challenge emerged on social media without warning. ISIS used social media to recruit 20,000 soldiers and launch a global terror campaign on the Internet and the Ice Bucket Challenge emerged using social media to engage millions of people through play, connection, and generosity to raise $200 million to cure ALS (Amyotrophic lateral sclerosis), a progressive neurodegenerative disease. These two concurrent events illustrate just how much easier it has become to enable small communities of people using the Internet to translate their own values onto history, potentially impacting millions of other human beings on the planet, within just a few months. This has been a dramatic shift. It is a shift from a world in which it would take—at minimum—a few years or more often a few decades for an individual or small group of people to bring about change in the world, to a world of real-time communication and collaboration at a distance. In many ways, the Internet's activity at the beginning of the millennium illustrates a turning point when it became possible for any person with an Internet connection to quickly, easily, and cheaply impact the lives of billions of others, and thus also a turning point in history when each person has became exponentially more powerful and thus ethically responsibly for their own behavior in a new way.

Furthermore, while the Internet and social media is powerful, it is just one of many technologies that are coming—each of those even more powerful than the last. As we add technologies like virtual reality, augmented reality and brain-to-brain interface, we will connect people even more deeply to one another and increase their ability to help or harm others.

In a fascinating example, Amnesty International, one of the first nonprofits to incorporate virtual reality into their work, reported that when they invited random people on the street to view a virtual reality experience of bombings in Syria, their fundraising increased by 16% (Steains, 2015). In 2015, the United Nations showed *Clouds over Sidra*, a virtual reality experience exploring a girl's life in a refugee camp in Jordan and raised $3.8 billion rather than a projected $2.3 billion

(Harris, 2015). Similarly, when UNICEF has offered virtual reality experience at fundraisers they have seen their donations double (Harris, 2015).

In this case, technology is amplifying our empathy for one another and facilitating collaboration and problem solving. Unfortunately there are also incidents where people are using these tools to act out violence toward others. A recent example includes the case of a Louisiana high school student who used an augmented reality app to simulate shooting classmates (Edghill, 2013). Other examples include sexual harassment in virtual spaces such as AltSpace (Lorenz, 2016). With the arrival of low-cost, affordable commercial virtual reality and augmented reality technologies in 2016, we will see both the benefits of connection and the challenges broadly scale. While still a few years away, technologies like brain-to-brain interface will be even more powerful as they will interface instantly with a person's brain and being, rather than a virtual online representation of a person.

While all of this is happening, we are not only deepening our connection to one another. The Internet is also connected to the emerging Internet of Things, an infrastructure that will soon enable human beings to instantly control powerful applications that manage robots, drones, sensors, and more. As we add AI to the equation, the Internet of Things will also become "smart" and self-evolving.

If that is not enough to boggle the mind, we are simultaneously also starting to transform our physical bodies through biotechnology. In 2014 and 2015 we began to see people transform some of the most basic parts of their identity in high profile ways. While many people have been cosmetically and surgically changing their gender over the last few decades, in 2014 Caitlin Jenner made headlines for his high profile gender change. At the same time, Rachel Doleza made headlines for cosmetically passing as an African American. In 2015, Liz Parish became the first human being to take gene therapy to reverse aging with her initial results suggesting she has already reversed the aging of her telomeres by 20 years (Roy, 2016). In the meantime, other surgeries such as facial reconstructive surgery and bariatric surgery are rapidly on the rise and biohacking and genetic engineering is becoming more and more imaginable with the arrival of CRISPR technologies. As this is happening, we are also seeing more and more people incorporate artificial limbs, chips and other devices into their bodies. Some of these people are formerly paralyzed individuals or veterans returning from battle (Biofabris, 2015) while others are simply interested in enhancing their bodies with technologies. As costs continue to go down and technology continues to grow in sophistication, more and more people will begin changing what we think of as basic components of personal identity, such as their age, gender, weight, facial features, or ethnicity, perhaps multiple times throughout their lives.

Finally, as our minds and bodies are becoming more fluid, so is our reality. As we spend more time online, it is becoming harder and harder to know what is true and what is false on the Internet. In a world where editors are fading away and anyone can report the news or write blogs, it is difficult to fact check what is true or what is false. This will become even more challenging when we start combing reality with augmented reality and virtual reality.

Many websites and virtual sites do not specify dates when content was created. This will increasingly transform our sense of space, time and history. Susan Sontag once wrote, "Time exists in order that everything doesn't happen all at once … and space exists so that it doesn't all happen to you" (Dilonardo, 2007). Yet in a world where one can simultaneously connect one's mind to thousands of other minds around the world through a brain-to-brain interface, we may indeed live in a world where everything might all happen at once, to me, you and everyone else, in one and all locations. Our understanding of history and geography may fundamentally change as we begin to increasingly augment reality.

While such a world does not yet exist, if one observes the technological changes in the pipeline and looks to historical trends as guideposts, all the components necessary for such a world to exist are on track and in development. Given this, what are the skills that we as humans need to be developing to be ready for this new era?

New Skills for Humans

Given the impending arrival of these new technologies and their potential impact on humanity, it is essential that we help both children and adults increase their capacity for two related social skills—empathy and individual character development.

As technology increasingly links individuals to one another through the Internet, virtual reality and the Internet of Things, any one person increasingly has the power to impact millions of other human beings through their words or actions. We can see this on a small scale through incidents such as online bullying with youth on social media and on a large scale through groups like ISIS. As noted, these actions will only be further amplified through virtual reality and AI. Given that "regulators," whether that be a nation's law enforcement trying to control the use of drones or a parent trying to manage the social interactions of a teenager but just can't keep up with the pace of technological change, one solution is to help every human being develop the personal skills to navigate this world. It is essential that every person develops a strong sense of empathy, as well as the strength to navigate harmful words and actions.

As we bring brain-to-brain interface into the equation, it is also possible that skills like empathy and social emotional intelligence will dramatically increase on their own, as we will literally be merging our minds and beings with others. This new perspective may generate more empathy and care for others as illustrated by the virtual reality experiments with Amnesty International, or perhaps we will actually consider ourselves a part of the other person or people and our definition of self-interest will dramatically expand.

As our empathy for others increases, it is just as important that we hold on to our own sense of character. Anyone who has connected themselves to the Internet and social media over the last few decades will have experienced a countless number of increasing messages created by the public, media or advertising units. It is very easy to take on all of these thoughts as our own, without thinking much, especially given that we are bombarded all hours of the day.

In addition to being bombarded by so many other people's ideas, opinions, products and services, we are increasingly depending on computers and AI to do our decision making for us. Our default is to use calculators to do our math, translators to translate, decipher and speak foreign languages, GPS to map our driving directions, algorithms to find our significant others. AI will only increasingly assist us in making our decisions. In this it is essential that both children and adults find ways to continue to think for themselves and continue to make their own decisions. Our decision-making roles as humans is not simply something that is a task that needs to be done—rather it is essential to the core of our character and our happiness.

In her TED Talk, "How to make hard choices" the philosopher Ruth Chang (2014) points out that our character is actually shaped by the illogical decisions we make. She points out that we assume humans make decisions based on a simple straightforward objective process. But this is not true—if it were, every human would be making the same objective decisions. For example we might all eat the same food or wear the same clothes or live in the same type of house. Instead, humans choose very different things that reflect their preferences and values. This becomes especially clear when we have to make hard decisions where two choices might be equally good or equally bad—such as choosing between two job offers, two potential spouses or what city we might like to live in. In easy decisions one decision is clearly better than the other, but in hard decisions, neither decision is better or worse. During those times, she argues, we make decisions based on who we want to become in the future. In the process, we take a stand and through choosing, declare our true preferences and values. We take responsibility for our decisions and their outcomes. This is how we build character. In a world where AI is making our decisions for us—potentially taking the responsibility and thinking out of our own hands—it is also taking away our opportunities to build our character, our personality and our own ethical value systems.

Research by Peter Gray (2010) also suggests that decision making is a key element to human happiness. Through his work studying children he found that not allowing children to make their own decisions leads to depression and anxiety. While his initial work explored overparenting and oversupervision of children by parents, it could also apply to a society that depends too much on AI to make our hard decisions and navigate the world for us:

> ... free play and exploration are, historically, the means by which children learn to solve their own problems, control their own lives, develop their own interests, and become competent in pursuit of their own interests ... By depriving children of opportunities to play on their own, away from direct adult supervision and control, we are depriving them of opportunities to learn how to take control of their own lives. We may think we are protecting them, but in fact we are diminishing their joy, diminishing their sense of self-control, preventing them from discovering and exploring the endeavors they would most love, and increasing the odds that they will suffer from anxiety, depression, and other disorders. ... Given freedom and opportunity, without coercion, young people educate *themselves*. They do so joyfully, and in the process develop intrinsic values, personal self-control, and emotional wellbeing.

Given all of this, it may encourage some of us to want to skip the next wave of coming technologies. However it is not so simple. We will likely need to be "connected" to participate in society and there is a danger of some humans connecting and accessing super intelligence while others are left behind.

Instead, as a society we need to rapidly begin investing in ensuring that we teach humans the human skills they will need to survive in this world.

A Curriculum for the Future

For thousands of years humans have informally been teaching topics such as empathy, ethics, philosophy, values and character development through religious teachings, story-telling, and the family setting. Some countries and cultures have also emphasized formal education of these topics through the study of the liberal arts.

Given our changing world, we need to start mainstreaming these skills into our global education system as soon as possible. In some ways, as we start to ask, "what will be the purpose of education if robots and AI are performing so much of human's work in the future?" One response might be that the purpose of education is to teach humans the human skills.

There are a number of schools and organizations that are already pioneering the way and leading this transformation. Montessori schools have been incorporating empathy and social emotional intelligence into the classroom for decades and in the mid-1990s the idea of Social Emotional Learning (SEL) became well-known, led by organizations such as CASEL (Collaborative for Academic and Social Learning) and Six Seconds, which help leaders and educators understand the importance of SEL and incorporate them into schools.

Others have crafted curriculums, activities and toolkits for fostering social emotional skills. Mary Gordon, a Canadian educator and social entrepreneur, developed Roots of Empathy, a highly successful evidence based program for teaching empathy that has scaled to ten countries and measures long-term and likely permanent increased levels of empathy in children. Dovetail Learning, a nonprofit in the United States, has created a toolkit that teaches kindergarten through sixth grade students empathy and social skills in conjunction with how they relate to one another, their teachers, parents, and communities. More recently, Alt Schools has built technology to create personalized curriculums and manage administrative tasks, allowing teachers to spend their time on Montessori like interactions with students rather than on other tasks. Given that these technologies are scalable, these new opportunities for teachers to focus on human development are also scalable. Ashoka, the world's largest organization of social entrepreneurs, launched a global initiative to help all schools incorporate empathy into primary education. The program engages hundreds of thousands of teachers, parents and students in over 30 countries in sharing best practices for cultivating empathy in schools and classrooms. Finally, many design schools and business schools now teach empathy and social emotional intelligence as a critical skill in design, product development and entrepreneurship.

In addition to schools, it is important that governments and policy makers develop a deeper awareness of the coming technologies and how they will impact society. In 2016 the White House recently hosted a series of town hall meetings on "AI" to open up such discussions. Each country will need to engage in similar activities and develop their national strategy for AI and work with Ministers of Education to map and offer the social emotional and character development skills their citizens will need in the future. International and multilateral organizations like the United Nations and World Bank can also incorporate new measurements around empathy and character development into their already existing human capital and education programs.

On the one hand, it can be daunting to think about how much technological and social change is now coming our way—and what we need to do to prepare. On the other hand, these very technologies are also forcing us to think more proactively than ever about what it means to be human and how we want to shape our humanity in the coming years. While our governments, companies and education systems will all have a significant say in this, each of us also has the opportunity to envision for ourselves what kind of human we want to be in this new future. The key question now is "Whom do you want to become?"

References

Admin. (2015). 3D printing more than a helping hand for a wounded war veteran. *Biofabris*. Retrieved from http://biofabris.com.br/en/3d-printing-more-than-a-helping-hand-for-a-wounded-war-veteran/

Armstrong, D., & Ma, M. (2013). Researcher controls colleague's motions in 1st human brain-to-brain interface. *UW Today*. Retrieved from http://www.washington.edu/news/2013/08/27/researcher-controls-colleagues-motions-in-1st-human-brain-to-brain-interface/

Chang, R. (2014). How to make hard choices. [Video file] Retrieved from http://www.ted.com/talks/ruth_chang_how_to_make_hard_choices#t-868117

Dilonardo, P., & Jump, A. (Eds). & Sontag, S. (2007). *At the same time: Essays and speeches*. New York, NY: Farrar Straus Giroux.

Edghill, L. (2013). Virtual reality violence too real to ignore. *World*. Retrieved from http://www.worldmag.com/2013/09/virtual_reality_violence_too_real_to_ignore

Gorman, S. (2015). Brain-computer link enables paralyzed California man to walk. *Reuters*. Retrieved from http://www.reuters.com/article/usa-health-paraplegic-idUSL1N11T2LM20150924

Gray, P. (2010). The decline of play and rise in children's mental disorders. *Psychology Today*. Retrieved from https://www.psychologytoday.com/blog/freedom-learn/201001/the-decline-play-and-rise-in-childrens-mental-disorders

Harris, B. J. (2015). How the United Nations is using virtual reality to tackle real-world problems. *Fast Company*. Retrieved from http://www.fastcompany.com/3051672/tech-forecast/how-the-united-nations-is-using-virtual-reality-to-tackle-real-world-problems

Koebler, J. (2015). The most advanced human brain-to-brain interface ever made. *Motherboard*. Retrieved from http://motherboard.vice.com/read/the-most-advanced-human-brain-to-brain-interface-ever-made

Lorenz, T. (2016). Virtual reality is full of assholes who sexually harass me. Here's why I keep going back. Tech.Mic. Retrieved from https://mic.com/articles/144470/sexual-harassment-in-virtual-reality#.0aUTCYjhl

Pais-Vieira, M., Chiuffa, G., Lebedev, M., Yadav, A., & Nicolelis, M. A. L. (2015). Building an organic computing device with multiple interconnected brains. *Nature*. Retrieved from http://www.nature.com/articles/srep11869

Ramakrishnan, A., Ifft, P. J., Pais-Vieira, M., Byun, Y. W., Zhuang, K. Z., Lebedev, M., & Nicolelis, M. A. L. (2015). Computing arm movements with a monkey brainnet. *SciRep*. Retrieved from http://www.nature.com/articles/srep10767

Roy, A. (2016). First gene therapy successful against human aging. Bioviva USA, Inc. Retrieved from http://bioviva-science.com/2016/04/21/first-gene-therapy-successful-against-human-aging/

Steains, R. (2015). Amnesty international UK's virtual reality in street fundraising. *Sofii*. Retrieved from http://sofii.org/case-study/virtual-reality-in-street-fundraising

About the Contributors

Daniel Araya (Volume Editor) is a researcher and advisor to government with a special interest in technology, public policy, and learning. He is a regular contributor to various media outlets including The Brookings Institution, Singularity Hub, and Medium. He has spoken at universities and research centers around the world including the U.S. Naval Postgraduate School, Harvard University, the American Enterprise Institute, the Center for Global Policy Solutions, Stanford University, and Microsoft Research. His newest books include: *The Evolution of Liberal Arts in the Global Age* (2017) and *Smart Cities as Democratic Ecologies* (2015). He has a doctorate from the University of Illinois at Urbana-Champaign and is an alumnus of Singularity University's graduate program in Silicon Valley.

John Seely Brown (JSB) was Chief Scientist of Xerox Corp and Director of its famous/infamous Palo Alto Research Center (PARC). Currently he is a visiting scholar and advisor to the Provost at the University of Southern California where he facilitates collaboration between the Schools for Communication and Media and the Institute for Creative Technologies (ICT). JSB is also currently Independent Co-Chairman for Deloitte's Center for the Edge where he pursues research on radical innovation, institutional innovation and a reimagined work environment built on digital culture, ubiquitous computing, and the need for constant learning and adaptability. His newest book (with Ann Pendleton-Jullian) is *Design Unbound—Designing for Emergence in a White Water World* (2018).

Darlene Damm is Vice Chair and Faculty for Global Grand Challenges with Singularity University. She is a social entrepreneur and previously served with Ashoka, where she was critical to building their fundraising infrastructure and leading efforts in the Silicon Valley. Darlene was an early co-founder of Matternet, one of the world's first commercial drone companies. She is also the founder of the space company DIYROCKETS, which crowdsources and democratizes space technology. She received her bachelor's degree in History from Stanford University and her master's degree in International Affairs from Johns Hopkins SAIS. She is the holder of one patent, writes for a number of media outlets, and speaks around the world.

Yana B. Feygin is a doctoral student in bio-statistics at the University of Louisville. She holds a Bachelor of Science degree in Economics from the University of Rochester.

Colin Harrison retired from IBM in January 2013 as an IBM Distinguished Engineer. He was IBM's technical pioneer in Smarter Cities and in the application of Systems Theory to the sustainable management and disaster resilience of cities. He remains active globally with scientific communities working on a Science of Cities and on solutions for regional and urban resilience. He was the inventor of IBM's Smarter Cities technical architecture, which grew out of 2007 work on Energy & Environment offerings and a technology assessment on the Instrumented Planet. From 2007–13 he was Director and later Distinguished Engineer in IBM's corporate strategy group, leading business strategy development for Smarter Cities. He is also an IBM Master Inventor. He was previously Director of Strategic Innovation in IBM's Integrated Technology Delivery in Europe and Director of Global Services Research in IBM's Research Division, where he held many leadership positions.

Rita Kop is Research Manager and teaches online at the Faculty of Education at Yorkville University and the online Ed.D. Program of the University of Liverpool. After a career spanning many years of teaching and research and development related to education and technology in Canada, the United Kingdom, and the Netherlands, she currently investigates how emerging technologies might support "the human" in learning through the design and development of advanced learning technologies. She is used to leading complicated educational and technological research and development projects and programs, and implementing change in institutions of higher education. As an advocate for open and networked learning, she has worked actively with community groups, universities and governments for more than 15 years, contributing to educational policy and community-based and online services for adults living in areas of economic and social deprivation.

Susan Liepert Dr. is currently a special advisor in the Dean's office at the College of Fine and Applied Arts at the University of Illinois. She earned her PhD in eighteenth-century English literature, specializing in body theory from the perspective of the change from midwives to doctors. In particular, she focused on how that transition was negotiated in fiction and medical literature. Susan's previous work included a role with the Regional Economy initiative of Metropolis Strategies in Chicago, supporting its program team's work on policy issues related to strategy for regional economic growth. In addition to a range of design-related projects, she developed a unique database of regional economic development organizations and initiatives.

James D. Miller is Professor of Economics at Smith College, with a Ph.D. in Economics from the University of Chicago and a J. D. from Stanford Law School. He is the author of Singularity Rising (2012), a non-fiction book exploring the future economic implications of enhanced human and machine intelligences.

Kelly Morris has a BA in psychology from Bellarmine University and is currently enrolled in the University of Louisville's Speed School of Engineering's undergraduate program, studying Computer Science and Computer Engineering. She is interested in pursuing research in the field of Artificial Intelligence, specifically where systems attempt to mimic or replicate human intelligence.

Rodrigo Nieto-Gómez is a strategist and futurist focused on the consequences of the accelerating pace of change in homeland security and policing environments. He is a research professor at the National Security Affairs Department and at the Center for Homeland Defense and Security at the Naval Postgraduate School, and he is also a certified facilitator for the California Commission on Peace Officer Standards and Training (POST). For a decade, Dr. Nieto has taught hundreds of high-ranking law enforcement, military, and homeland security leaders how to create and execute strategies to transform their agencies to meet the requirements of rapidly changing environments. As an innovation expert and an academically trained geostrategist, he has built a reputation as an expert on future threats to national security and policing and how to confront them.

Ann Pendleton-Jullian is an architect, writer, and educator of international standing whose work explores the interchange between architecture, landscape, culture, science, and technology within complex contexts. She is currently Full Professor and former Director of the Knowlton School of Architecture at

Ohio State University, distinguished Visiting Professor out of the President's Office at Georgetown University, and periodically co-teaches world building studios at USC's School of Cinema. From 1993–2007, she was a tenured professor of architecture at MIT and Associate Head of the Department for three of those years. She is a fellow at the Center of Advanced Studies in Behavioral Sciences. Her newest book (with John Seely Brown) is *Design Unbound—Designing for Emergence in a White Water World* (2018).

Jovan D. Rebolledo-Mendez is a researcher in Artificial Intelligence at the University of Tokyo, Jovan Rebolledo-Mendez is CTO & Co-founder of Tactile Analogics and AffectSense, working toward the visions of a multi-dimensional intelligent skin and making hardware more intuitive to human emotions. He is also Strategic Director of Exponential Japan (ExJ), an organization that is bridging exponential thinking and exponential technologies between Japan and the rest of the world. He has written international, peer-reviewed publications in Adaptive Systems, Artificial Intelligence (AI), Bioinformatics, and Micro-fabrication. He is directing or advising several startups in the United States, Japan, Mexico, and the Democratic Republic of Congo, including projects with drones, AI, robotics, and other exponential technologies. He has received a variety of competitive scholarships, including from MEXT and Google, among others.

Alix Rübsaam is a PhD candidate at the Humanities faculty of the University of Amsterdam, with a BA in English Literature and MA in Cultural Analysis. She is currently affiliated with the Amsterdam School for Cultural Analysis and is pursuing research in Posthumanism and Posthuman theory. Her investigation focuses on the intersection between humans and technology, where the latter augments the first. Specifically, she identifies a retention of Humanist thinking in Posthumanist environments. For her PhD research she is writing on the urgency of reevaluating the fluidity and porosity of the human (academic) subject in the face of technology that allows human agency and cognition to take place in environments that are traditionally considered non-human.

Stan Ruecker is Anthony J. Petullo Professor in Design at the University of Illinois at Urbana-Champaign, where he is also a member of the Design Research Initiative. For the past twenty years, Dr. Ruecker's research has focused on the future of reading, where his research teams have developed more than two dozen prototypes for use in algorithmic criticism. He is currently exploring physical interfaces for complex conceptual work, such as text analysis, modeling time, and designing experience. Along with Jennifer Roberts-Smith and Milena Radzikowska, he is co-editor of a collection due out in

2019 entitled *Prototyping Across the Disciplines: Proposals for Better Futures*. He is also part of an international group developing new theories of key concepts for use by designers. Their current topic is "What is an opinion?" More about the research group and their projects can be found at publish.illinois.edu/designconceptslab.

Jim Spohrer directs IBM's open source Artificial Intelligence (AI) efforts. Previously at IBM, he led Global University Programs, co-founded Almaden Service Research, and was CTO Venture Capital Group. After receiving a BS in Physics from MIT, he developed speech recognition systems at Verbex, an Exxon company, before receiving his PhD in Computer Science/Artificial Intelligence from Yale University. In the 1990s, he attained Apple Computers' Distinguished Engineer Scientist and Technology title for next generation learning platforms. With over ninety publications and nine patents, Jim has won the Gummesson Service Research Award, the Vargo and Lusch Service-Dominant Logic Award, and a PICMET Fellowship for advancing service science.

Robert David Steele has been a Marine Corps infantry officer, a Central Intelligence clandestine service operations officer, and the second ranking civilian in Marine Corps intelligence, responsible for creating the Marine Corps Intelligence Activity (MCIA). He was a founding member of the national Advanced Information Processing and Analysis Steering Group (AIPASG), and served on the Information Handling Committee (IHC), and the Foreign Intelligence Requirements and Capabilities Plan Committee (FIRCAP). Since 1993 he has been a Chief Enabling Officer (CeO) teaching Open Source Intelligence (OSINT) and more recently Open Source Everything Engineering (OSEE). He is the author of many books including *Intelligence for Earth: Clarity, Diversity, Integrity, and Sustainability* (2010) and *The Open Source Everything Manifesto: Transparency, Truth, & Trust* (2012). His education includes an AB (Muhlenberg College), MA (Lehigh University), MPA (University of Oklahoma), and Graduate Diploma (Naval War College). He was recommended for the Nobel Peace Prize in 2017. Learn more at http://robertdavidsteele.com.

Md. Abul Kalam Siddike has been a visiting scholar at IBM Research, Almaden, San Jose, USA, and is currently a PhD candidate at the School of Knowledge Science at Japan Advanced Institute of Science and Technology (JAIST). Recently, he completed his Master's in knowledge science from JAIST, Japan. His areas of research interest combine rebuilding evolution, service science, resource integration, cognitive mediators, and wise service systems.

Kevin Stolarick, dubbed the "Official Statistician of the Creative Class," combines expertise on cities, urbanization, statistics, design, and economic development with an appreciation of the importance of finding and sharing the knowledge or "pearls of wisdom" gained from leveraging his research, writing, management and organizational skills. The author of over 100 peer-reviewed articles and commissioned reports, he has presented over 75 invited keynote speeches and presentations and over 100 print, radio, television, and online media interviews and appearances. He holds a PhD in Business Administration and an MBA from Carnegie Mellon, a Masters in Higher Education Leadership, and a BS in Honors in Applied Computer Science. Kevin provided quantitative research and analytical support for Richard Florida's books including *The Rise of the Creative Class* and *Rise Revisited*. He continues in collaboration with other researchers in the development of measures, indicators, and approaches for Creative Economy theory.

Roman V. Yampolskiy is a tenured associate professor in the Department of Computer Engineering and Computer Science at the Speed School of Engineering, University of Louisville. He is the founding and current Director of the Cyber Security Lab and an author of many books, including *Artificial Superintelligence: a Futuristic Approach*. During his tenure at the University of Louisville, Dr. Yampolskiy has been recognized as: Distinguished Teaching Professor, Professor of the Year, Faculty Favorite, Top 4 Faculty, Leader in Engineering Education, Top 10 of Online College Professor of the Year, and Outstanding Early Career in Education award winner, among many other honors and distinctions. Yampolskiy is a senior member of IEEE and AGI, a member of the Kentucky Academy of Science, a research advisor for MIRI, and an associate of GCRI.

Index

#UNRIG, 207
18th century, 31, 150
19th century, 31, 35, 54
19th-century humanism, 159
20th century, 35, 41, 151, 157, 178
20th-century body, the 152
21st Century, 42, 54, 62, 178
3D analog world, 156
3D digital information, 156
3D image, 165
3D printers, 56
3D Printing, 27, 130–131
9/11 attacks, the, 20

A

Abu Dhabi, 35
accelerating technological innovation, 1
adapting our existing senses, 156
Adderall, 213
advanced bionics, 105
advanced cognitive systems, 54
advanced robotics, 27
Aeolian Harp, the, 150
Afghanistan, 193
African-Americans, 193
Age of Information, 5, 15, 19, 29, 31, 33, 35
age of machine intelligence, the, 92
agent is a superintelligent system, the, 162
Agricultural Revolution, 1
AI, 3, 7, 41–42, 45, 47–49, 52, 54–55, 131, 135, 140–141, 165
AI research, 52, 126
AI safety, 126
AI systems, 50
AI technologies, 47, 54, 57
AI technology and capabilities, 49
AI-core disciplines, 47
AIPoly, 135
AI-powered chatbots, 49
AI-powered cognitive systems, 47
Airbnb, 36
Aireal (AIREAL), 135

algorithm technologies, 173
algorithm, the, 2, 6, 14, 22–23, 33, 50–51, 130–131, 167, 173, 175–183
algorithm-based platform developers, 181
algorithmic ideology, 177
Alibaba, 22–23
AlphaGo beat Lee Sedol, xvii
Alt Schools, 233
Altman, Sam, 226
Amazon, 22–23, 204, 226
Amazon's Echo, 43
Amazon's Mechanical Turk process, 30
Amazon's Mechanical Turk, 10
American economy, 52
American law enforcement, 100
American Navy Seal, 100
American Revolution, the, 31
Amnesty International, 231
amyotrophic lateral sclerosis, 228
Apple's Siri, 43
Application Program Interfaces, 204
Applied (Collective) Intelligence, 189
Applied Collective (Human) Intelligence, 7, 187
Arab Spring, 228
Araya, Daniel, 1–9
architecture of cyberspace, the, 178
architecture of the Web, the, 175
artificial cochlea, 105
artificial intelligence, xiii, 2, 27, 107, 130, 158–169, 171–172, 182, 186–188, 197, 207, 225–227, 229–230, 232–233
artificial sensorial organs, 103
Artificial Stupidity, 188
Ashoka, 233
Auger, Michael, 100
augmentation technologies, 106
intelligence augmentation, 106
augmentation technologies, 109
augmentation technology, 100, 107
augmentation, 107
augmented human cognition, 167
augmented intelligence systems, 14
augmented intelligence, 6, 12, 14, 36, 48, 155, 175, 180, 225
augmented reality technologies, 129
augmented reality, 107
augmented smelling capabilities, 141
augmenting technologies, 142
Australia, 188, 195
automated learning, 181
automation, 92
autonomous transport, 27

B

Bacon, Francis, Sir, 24
bankers, 195
Bartlett, Jamie, 107
Bauwens, Michel, 193
BeMyEyes, 135
Bergland, Robert, 11
Berkeley, 51
Big Data, 26–27, 29, 177–179, 189
Big Data analysis, 13
Biocca, Frank, 97
bioconservatist versus transhumanist perspectives, xii
biocrime, 109
bioidentity conflict, 105
bioidentity, 109
biological humans, 126
biomechatronics, xiv
bionic technology, 104
biosensors, 135
biotech, 140
biotechno design, xiv
biotechnology, 27, 108
bliss chips, 218–219
Bloomberg, Michael, 20
blue-collar jobs, 30
bodily existence and computer simulation, 164
body, the, 155
Bostrom, Nick, 112, 161–167, 220–221
Bostrom, Nick, *Superintelligence*, 161, 165

INDEX | 245

bounded rationality, 40
Boyd, Danah, 178
Boyd, Danah, and Crawford, Kate, 178–179
Braille readers, 135
brain emulation, 113
brain in a vat, 152
Brain Simulation Platform, 112
brain uploading, 126
brain–computer interface, 102
brain–computer interfaces, 103, 105
brain–computer technology, 102
brain-controlled interaction controlled devices, 154
brain-controlled interaction research, 154
brain-controlled interaction, 154
brain-neurosciences curriculum, 52
brain-neurosciences, 51
brains of rhesus monkeys, the, 225
brain-to-brain interface, 226, 229–231
Brown, Phillip, Lauder, Hugh, & Ashton, David, 91
Brynjolfsson, Erik & McAfee, 63
Brynjolfsson, Erik & McAfee, Andrew, *The Second Machine Age*, 3

C

calm technologies, 153
capabilities, 141
capacity to boost productivity, 217
Carbon Disclosure Project, the, 33
carbon-based brain/computer, 102
case of Blade Runner, the, 106
cashiers and retail salespersons, 75
Catania, Kenneth, 133
Central America, 16
cerebrospinal fluid, 101
Chang, Ruth, 231
changing phenomenological status of the human, 155
chemoreceptors, 156
Chief Executive Officers on The Future of Jobs (a survey), 26

China, 16, 187
Chomsky, Noam, 178
Civil War, the, 54
Clark, Andy, 169–171
Clark, Andy, *Natural Born Cyborgs*, 169
climate change, 37
Cloud technology, 26
Cloud, the, 176
Coca Cola, 207
cochlear augmentation, 105
cochlear implant technologies, 104
cochlear implant, 102, 104–107, 109
codification of creativity, 92
cognitive assistants, 43–44, 50, 54, 56
cognitive hybridization, 169
cognitive labor, 63
cognitive machinery, 170
cognitive mediators, 42–43, 50, 55–56
Coleridge, Samuel-Taylor, 151
Collaborative for Academic and Social Learning, 233
collective future, 113
collective intelligence, 15–16
commercial intelligence, 27
commoditized labor, 91
comparative studies, 195
compound annual growth rates, 30
computational knowledge economy, 63
Computational Revolution, 1, 63
computer & mathematical occupations, 77
computer and network systems, 141
computer science/AI researchers, 51
computer systems engineers/architects, 74
computer-based approximation, 114
concept of intelligence, the, 174–175
creation of new senses, the, 156
creative thinking, 87
creative workers, 91
credit analysts, 65–66, 76–77, 82, 87
CRISPR technologies, 229
CRISPR/Cas9 technique, the 131
critical posthumanism, 159
critical posthumanism, 161
crowdsourcing, 27

cyber hacking, 142
cybercrime, 109
cybernetic mechanism and biological organism, 164
cyberwarfare, 49
cyborg initiatives, 140
Cyborg Manifesto, 159
cyborg status, 98
cyborg, 159

D

Dan Harmon's, *Rick and Morty*, 163
Danaher, John, 178
DARPA, 154
Darwinian advantage, 220
Darwinian evolution, 220
data and IT industries, 193
data and publicity-wars, 180
data, 187
database administrators, 74
database architects, 74
DataBridge, the (MODA 2), 2
data-driven technologies, 181, 183
data-workers, 179
deaf culture, 103–106
deaf people, 104
Deakin University, 44
Declaration of Helsinki, 120, 123
DefCon conference (2015), 100
degree of automation, 72, 78
dematerialization, 132
democracy, 31, 163, 188, 198
Descartes, Rene, 129
Diakopoulos, Nicholas, 178
Dick, Philip, K., *Minority Report*, xv
Digital Biology, 130–131, 140–141
digital networking system (ARPANET), xvii
digital Taylorism, 91
Disney Research, 135
disruptive technologies, 4
DNA donation, 116

DNA, 119, 131
Doleza, Rachel, 229
Dorsen, Norman, 116
Dovetail Learning, 233
drone capabilities, 49
drug cartels, 99
Duke University, 225

E

Eagleman, David, 101, 134, 156
Earth Intelligence Network, 191
eBay, 36
echolocation, 133
education, 31, 91–92
eight information tribes, the, 203
electronic noses, 141
Elsevier, 203, 207
embodied augmentation technology, 104
embodied intelligence augmentation technologies, 108
embodied intelligence augmentation, 109
Embodiment, 146, 155, 169
Emerge, (a startup from Singularity University), 135
emulated brain, 116
Engelbart, Douglas, C., 1, 8, 40, 97, 201
Engelbartian augmentation, 98
engineering, 19
engineers & designers, 77
England, 17
Enlightenment, the, 152, 159
entrepreneurial innovation, 92
eSkills, 41
Ethiopia, 187
Europe, 188, 195
European refugee crisis, 12
exascale computing, 1
Excel, 97
expensive productivity enhancer, 217
expensive productivity enhancers, 214
exponential technologies, 130, 139
extruding operators, 75

F

Facebook, 204, 226
Fascism, 188
Fast food workers, 75
FDA, 120
federalist papers, 48
feminist historians and philosophers of science, 179
Fenwick, Tara, 176, 179
Feygin, Yana, B., 6
fiber-optic cables, 171
financial professionals, 77
financial services & investors, 30
First Machine Age, the, 3
first principal-agent problem, the, 162
Flowers, Michael, 20
force multipliers, 107
Free/Libre/Open Source Software, 193
Freedom Scientific, 134
French Revolution, the, 150
Friedman, Thomas, *The World is Flat*, 227
frontal lobe, the, 133
full-spectrum human intelligence, 196
future artificial superintelligence, 113
future workforce, the, 32
future-oriented hybrid man/machine governance, xii

G

Gardner, Howard, 123, 145, 174
genocide, 104
Genomics, 27
Georgia Institute of Technology, 45
Gesundheit, 149
Gillespie, Tarleton, 177
global computing industry, 197
global financial network, the, 37
Global Game supportive of holistic analytics, 201
global information-sharing concept, 203
Global Systems Science and Policy program in Europe, 24
Global Village Construction Set (GVCS), 187, 194
Global Village Construction Set, 187
God, 149, 208
Google Patents, 136
Google Scholar, 136, 138
Google, 23, 97, 204, 226
Google's Now, 43
Gordon, Mary, 233
GPS navigation Systems, 11
GPS navigation, 33
GPS, 231
graphic designers, 65, 73, 76–77, 80, 82, 87
Gray, Peter, 232
Greek empire, 16
Grey's Anatomy, 147
Guzman, Chapo, 100

H

HA, 194
Halberstam, Judith, 159
half-life-of-facts, 40
Hamlet's father, 149
Haraway, Donna, 159–160
Harrison, Colin, G., 5, 10–39
Hayles, Katherine, N., 166–167, 170, *How We Became Posthuman*, 164–165
health, 151
Hedges, Chris, 198
Heffernan, Theresa, 160
Heidegger, Martin, 173
Henshaw, John, M., 102
higher lifetime incomes, 217
Hoffman, Reid, 226
holistic analytics, 191, 194
HoloSens, 129
homo economicus, 13
Homo sapiens, 2, 15, 27, 36, 96, 160, 165
Howard Gardner's, Theory of Multiple Intelligences, 122

HTC Vive, 129
human assistive technologies, 45
human bioidentity, 106
human brain, the, 56, 100, 112, 125–126, 130, 165, 169, 171, 187, 225
human capital, 4, 62, 91, 187, 233
human cognition, 2–3, 25, 33, 37, 161, 165–170
human communication, 179
human conflict, 5, 96
human consciousness, 108, 129, 164–166, 171,
human factor, the, 189, 195–196, 207
Human Genome Project, the, 118–120, 125
human intelligence, xii, 1–2, 4, 6–8, 23, 114, 158, 160, 164–165, 168–169, 171, 176, 186–188, 196–197, 207–208, 218, 223
human interaction, 182
human subjects, 120
human umwelt, 103, 105, 109
human/machine being, 107
human/nonhuman divide, xii
human-centric World Brain conceptualization, a, 187
human-computer interaction, 2
human-computer interfaces, 97
humanities, the, 19
human–machine integration, 200
human–machine integrity, 208
human-machine symbiosis, xi, xvi, 2–3
human-subjectbased research projects, 119
human-technology symbionts, 169
hyperspectral images, 135

I

IA design, 6
IA IQ-booster, 215
IA, 3–7, 41, 47, 54–55
IBM piloted a Cognitive Build initiative, 52
IBM Watson Health team, 25
IBM Watson, 30, 43, 49
IBM, 53, 206, 226
IBM's Watson Engagement Advisor, 45
ice bucket challenge, 228
impoverished families in underdeveloped nations, 221
incremental innovation, 99
Industrial Age, the, 31
Industrial Revolution, the, 1, 5, 32, 35, 63
industrial Taylorism, 91
industrial-era scientific reductionism, 201
Industry 4.0 proposals, 49
infallible memory, 114
information technology (IT), 11, 19, 27, 30, 35–36, 47, 49, 187, 197
information tribes, 190
intellectual property (IP), 136–138
intelligence agencies, 21
intelligence augmentation (IA), xii, 2, 100, 105, 107–108, 173, 186–188, 190, 194, 197, 207, 212–215, 218–219, 222, 224
Intelligence services, 20
intelligent electronic eyes, 141
interacting with computers, 72–75, 81
interactive learning ecosystems, 182
International Space Station, the, 105
Internet of Things, the, 12, 19, 27, 30, 33, 153, 229–230
Internet porn, 218
Internet, 2, 40, 53, 114, 132, 152, 156, 187, 204, 218, 225, 227–231
Internet, the growth of, 132
interoception, 154
interoceptive systems, 154
IQ, 108, 174, 215
IQ, scores 107
Iran, 191
Iraq, 193
I-shaped graduates, 41
I-shaped professionals, 41–42
ISIS, 228, 230
IT industry and government agency reassurances, 49
IT systems, 34
Italy's economy, 54

J

Jacubowski, Marcin, 193
James Bamford, *Body of Secrets*, 187
Jenner, Caitlin, 229
Jobs, Steve, 5, 95
Jones, Garrett, 215
Jordan, 228
Juarez cartel, 100

K

Kalam Siddike, Abul, 5
Kelly, Kevin, 197
Kenya, 187
King Canute, 11
Kirschenbaum, Matthew, 152
Kitchin, Rob, 178
knowledge burden, 40
knowledge-based economies, 92
knowledge-worker jobs, 52
Koch Brothers, 207
Kop, Rita, 6
Kotler, Steven, 135
Kurtzweil, Ray, *The Singularity Is Near*, xi, 130
Kurzweil Educational Systems, 134

L

large-scale DNA sequencing, 119
law of accelerating returns, the, 130
learning environments, 181
learning systems, 181
Leonardo da Vinci, 149
Liberal arts, 41
Liepert, Susan, 6
Lieutenant General Dr. Brent Scowcroft, 191
life-long monitoring, 121
Linear B, 19
LinkedIn, 33

LIQUil, 226
Livingston, Ira, 159
Livingston, Jessica, 226
Lucini, Fernando, 175

M

Machine Age, the, 62, 92
machine intelligence, 2, 7, 62, 92, 186–187, 197, 200
machine learning algorithms, 51
machine learning technologies, 6, 173
machine learning, 1, 27, 46, 57, 176, 226
machine processing, 188
machine tools, 188
machine translation, 188
machine-based abstractions, 37
Mager, Astrid, 177, 180
magnetic fields, 156
management information systems, 35
marine corps, the, 216
Maslow's hierarchy of human needs, 28–30, 37
Massachusetts Institute of Technology (MIT), 3, 51
massive open online courses (MOOCs), 188
Matrix, 98
Mayor's Office of Data Analytics, the (MODA), 20
McDowell, Alex, xv
media, entertainment, and information, 30
medical theory, 150
medieval body, the, 149
MeetUp, 204
mental circuitry, 170
mental donor, 118
Mercury, Gemini, and Apollo programs, 117
microblogging, 176, 181
Microsoft, 226
Middle East, 16
militarization of the U.S. economy, the, 197
military forces, 99
military intelligence, 27

military-police intelligence industrial complex, 188
Miller, James, 7
mind donor, 122
mining and analysis of big data, the, 179
ministers of education, 233
miscellaneous textile workers, 75
MIT Media Lab, 22
mobile and wireless technologies, 176
mobile internet, 26
Modafinil, 213
modern neurophysiologists, 145
Monsanto, 207
Montessori, 233
Monzon, Juan, 143
Moore's Law, 130
Moravec's paradox, 3, 63
Morris, Kelly, 6
MRI, 154–155
multiple intelligences, 181
Musk, Elon, 226

N

Naida CI Q70, 105
Nanotech, 141
Nanotechnology, 135, 130–131, 140
NASA, 117–118
National Security Agency (NSA), 186–187
natural capital, 187
natural telepresence communication, 141
Nauga Needles, 131
Nestle, 207
networks and computer systems, 130, 132, 140
net-zero city of Masdar, the, 35
Neuro-FAST, 154
Neuroplasticity, 134
Newton's Laws of Motion, 24–25
Nick Bostrom, 162–166, 171, 220
Nieto-Gomez, Rodrigo, 5, 95–111
Nobel Prize, 40
nonbiological circuitry, 169
nonhuman active algorithms, 181

nontraditional senses, 136
nuclear fission, xvi

O

Oculus Rift, 103, 129
OIST's recent Ukidama, 131
Olfaction, 133
on call sensors, 201
on call thinkers, 201
one-to-one structural replica of our brain, 127
Open Access, 201
Open Data, 33, 53
Open Document, 201
Open Hypertextdocument System, 201
Open Science movement, the, 33
Open Source (Technologies) Agency, 201
Open Source Ecology, 193
Open Source Everything Engineering, 188, 194, 197, 201, 206
Open Source Hardware, 193
Open Source Intelligence, 193, 196
Open Spectrum, 193
OpenAI, 226
OpenBTS (Base Transceiver Station), 193
open-ended Wild Cards, 191
organic Matrix, 101
Organization for Economic Cooperation and Development (OECD), 4, 64, 91
original brain, the, 165
original personality, the, 113
Oscar Pistorius, 106
outward behaviour, 113
Owen, Taylor, 180
Oxford Martin School, 3, 63

P

Palo Alto scientists, 153
Pandemics, 37
Parish, Liz, 229
Parkinson symptoms, 141

patenting, 136
patents, 138
patents, the growth of patent applications, 138
Patterson, Scott, *Dark Pools*, 22
Paul Allen's INTERVAL Corporation, 208
PayPal, 204
Peer-to-Peer (P2P) Foundation, the, 193
peer-to-peer platforms, 27
Pendleton-Julian, Ann and Seely Brown, John, *Foreward*, xi-xvii
Pepperell, Robert, 161, 167–169, 171
Pepperell, Robert, *The Posthuman Condition*, 166
performance-enhancing drugs, 212
person mind emulation interactions, 122
personality traits, 113
phase transition, 4
PhD engineers, 35
philosophers, 145
pilots of high-performance aircraft, 117
platform business models, 36
political intelligence, 27
political science, 195
politically contested technologies, 104
pornography, 218
Portable Document Format, 204
posthuman view, 164
posthumanism, 159–161, 167, 172
postindustrial economies, 87
Potential for Improved Performance (PIP), 48
precarious labor or precariat, 91
President Barack Obama, 228
President Donald Trump, 201
President Jimmy Carter, 11
Priest, Dana, 20
prioritized general skills, 32
productivity-enhancers, 7
progress, xii, 13, 15, 25, 27, 29–30, 33, 41, 44, 53, 126, 158, 182
progressive embodiment, 96–99, 102, 104–105, 107–109
Project Mercury, 117

prosthetic blades, 107
prosthetic legs, 106
prosthetic technology, 106
Python and R (technical Tools), 41

Q

Qualcomm, 53
quantified-self devices, 135
quants, the, 21

R

radio waves, 171
radioactive materials, 156
Ramachandran, Vilayanur, S., 153
Rebolledo-Mendez, Jovan, D., 6
Rebolledo-Mendez, Jovan, D., 6
Renaissance, the, 149–150
research involving, 120
retinal implants, 109
Rheingold, Howard, 197
Ricardo's Law, 41
RINGO, 22
RITA KOP, 172–185
robot soldiers, 49
robot teleology and human goals, 164
robotics, 27, 30, 46, 51, 130–131, 141
Rolling Stones, 28
Roman empire, 16
Roots of Empathy, 233
Rübsaam, Alix, 6
Ruecker, Stan, 6

S

Sagiv, Lilach, 115
Sandberg, Anders & Bostrom, Nick, 'Whole Brain Emulation: A Roadmap', 112
Sandvik, Runa, 100

Schwartz, Shalom, H., & Bardi, Anat, 'Value Hierarchies Across Cultures: Taking a Similarities Perspective', 115
science 19
Science Citation Index, 205
science fiction, 163
Scientific American, 95
scientific reductionism, 192
Sci-Hub, 207
SDG, 206
Searle's Chinese Room, 10
self and other, 152, 159
self-actualization, 28, 37, 50
sensorial embodied augmentation, 102
sharing economy, the, 27
Shaviro, Steven, 174
Sifry, Micah, *The Big Disconnect: Why the Internet Hasn't Transformed Politics (Yet)*, 198
Silicon Valley capitalist principles, 177
Silicon Valley, 96, 227
silicon-based chips, 130
Simon, Herbert, 40, 48
simulation tools, 50
Singularity University, 135
Singularity, the, xi, 26, 188
Singularity/AI domain, 186
Six Seconds, 233
Slack, 97
smart cities, xii
smart technologies, 2
Smith, Adam, 41, 221
social emotional learning, 233
Social Science Citation Index, 205
sociotechnical systems, 50
Socratic questions, 181
Somalia, 187
somatosensory nervous system, 132
Sontag, Susan, 230
space ready, 118
spacecraft, 117
specialized (stove-pipe) learning, 192
Spielberg, Steven, xiv, xv
Spinney, Franklin (Chuck), 197

Spohrer, Jim, 5
standard management techniques, 162
Stanford, 51
statisticians, 66, 76–77, 82, 87
Steele, Robert, 7
Steele, Robert, *The Open Source Everything Manifesto: Transparency, Truth, and Trust*, 193
STEM skills, 64
Steyer, Tom, 207
Stolarick, Kevin, 5
stove-pipe organizational approach, the, 201
subjective well-being, 115
super-Darwins, 220–223
superintelligence, 163
superintelligent being, 114
Supreme Court justices, 116
Surround Haptics, 135
sustainable development goals, 194
synesthesia, 141
synthetic technology, 109
Syria, the virtual reality experience of bombings, 228

T

Tactile Analogics, 130, 135
Tactus Technology, 134
taste-changing silverware and cutlery, 141
Taylorism, 91
TCE, 193–194
TCU, 207
technological determinism, 167
technological displacement, 64
technological singularity, 3
technological unemployment, 63
technologists, 195
TED Talk, 231
telepresence tactile, 141
TensorFlow, 226
terrorism, 191
terrorist and criminals hacking into systems, 49

Thacker, Eugene, 160
the sociotechnical system design loop, the, 53
Theory of Mind, 15
Thiel, Peter, 226
Thinking Creatively, 72–73, 81–88
Third Wave, xiv
Thomson Reuters, 203, 207
Toffler, Alvin and Heidi, xiv
Tohoku earthquake and tsunami in Japan, 228
Tower of Babel, the, 190
TrackingPoint, 98, 101, 107, 109
traditional intelligence cycle, 200
traditional senses, 136
transhumanist advantage, 107
transhumanists, 107
T-shaped graduates, 56
T-shaped professionals, 55, 41–42
Turkey, 191
Twitter, 176, 181, 204
tyranny of the possible, xvi

U

U.S. Bureau of Labor Statistics, 3, 64
U.S. Congress, 21
U.S. Department of Labor, the, 52
U.S. Government, 191–193
U.S. Occupational Information Network (O*Net), 5, 52, 62, 64, 70–71, 74, 78, 80–81
U.S. secret intelligence community, 191–192
U.S. Supplemental Nutrition Assistance Program, 34
Uber, 36
Uganda, 187
Umwelt, the (German for environment), 101
UN sustainable development goals, 195
UNDP, the, 53
unenhanced human body, the, 109
UNICEF, 229
United Nations (UN), 116, 187, 194, 206, 233

United Nations High-Level Panel on Threats, Challenges, and Change, 191
United Nations Open-Source Decision-Support Information Network, 201
United Nations secretary general, 116
United Nations, *Clouds over Sidra*, 228
United States Government (USG), 191–193, 207
United States Intelligence Community (U.S. IC), 192, 196–197, 206, 208
United States, 31, 45, 48, 62–63, 116, 186, 188, 195, 216, 220, 233
United States' economy, 54
universal language, 178
University of Austin, 49
University of Washington, 226
use of drones, the, 230

V

vendor-specific data processing barriers, 201
Venezuela, 191
vestibular labyrinthine, the, 102
Vice President Joe Biden, 201
Victorian body, the, 151
Vinge, Vernor, xi
virtual reality (VR) headset, 103
virtual reality (VR) environment, 103
virtual reality (VR), 101, 135, 226, 228–231
virtual reality/AR, 135
visual cortex, 101
Von Neumann, xi, xvi

W

Walmart, 22–23
Warwick, Kevin, 140
Washington DC, xv
Watson Teacher Advisor, 45
Watson, 25
Waze, 97
weak cloning, 44

weak telepathy, 43
Web Administrators, 74
Web, the, 176–177, 179, 181
Western governance paradigm, the, 197
White House Office of Science and
    Technology Policy, 47
White House, the, 233
whole brain emulation, 125–126, 165
wide ideas of intelligence, 175
wired bioreceptors, 101
Wolfe, Cary, 160
wombs of surrogate mothers, the, 221
World Bank, the, 233
World brain concept, 201
World Brain Institute, 201
World brain, 7
World Brain, a, 188
world building, xv
World Economic Forum, 45
World Economic Report, 46
World Federation of the Deaf, the, 103
World Medical Association, the, 120
World War II, 20
Worldwide Web, the, xvii, 24, 27

X

xenotransplantation,
xenotransplantation, 120–121

Y

Yampolskiy, Roman, V., 6
YouTube, 204
zero marginal product workers, 219

Z

Ziman, John, 25

Colin Lankshear & Michele Knobel
General Editors

New literacies emerge and evolve apace as people from all walks of life engage with new technologies, shifting values and institutional change, and increasingly assume 'postmodern' orientations toward their everyday worlds. Despite many efforts to take account of such changes, educational institutions largely remain out of touch with the range of new ways of making and sharing meanings that increasingly mediate and shape the lives of the young people they teach and the futures they face. This series aims to explore some key dimensions of the changes occurring within social practices of literacy and the educational challenges they present, with a view to informing educational practice in helpful ways. It asks what are new literacies, how do they impact on life in schools, homes, communities, workplaces, sites of leisure, and other key settings of human cultural engagement, and what significance do new literacies have for how people learn and how they understand and construct knowledge. It aims to challenge established and 'official' ways of framing literacy, and to ask what it means for literacies to be powerful, effective, and enabling under current and foreseeable conditions. Collectively, the works in this series will help to reorient literacy debates and literacy education agendas.

For further information about the series and submitting manuscripts, please contact:

> Michele Knobel & Colin Lankshear
> Montclair State University
> Dept. of Education and Human Services
> 3173 University Hall
> Montclair, NJ 07043
> michele@coatepec.net

To order other books in this series, please contact our Customer Service Department at:
> (800) 770-LANG (within the U.S.)
> (212) 647-7706 (outside the U.S.)
> (212) 647-7707 FAX

Or browse online by series at:
> www.peterlang.com

www.ingramcontent.com/pod-product-compliance
Ingram Content Group UK Ltd.
Pitfield, Milton Keynes, MK11 3LW, UK
UKHW021844140426
5217IPUK00022B/1583